EMPIRE WITHOUT END

WITH A FOREWORD BY MARIO PEI

TRANSLATED BY JOAN MCCONNELL AND MARIO PEI

EMPIRE WITHOUT END

LIDIA STORONI MAZZOLANI

A HELEN AND KURT WOLFF BOOK

HARCOURT BRACE JOVANOVICH

NEW YORK AND LONDON

Some of the translations from the Latin historians
are based on Loeb Classics Editions of Sallust, Livy, and Tacitus.

Library of Congress Cataloging in Publication Data

Storoni Mazzolani, Lidia.
Empire without end.

"A Helen and Kurt Wolff book."
Translation of L'impero senza fine.
Bibliography: p.
Includes index.
1. Sallustius Crispus, C.   2. Livius, Titus.
3. Tacitus, Cornelius.   4. Rome—Historiography.
I. Title.
DG206.S3S7613   937'.007'2022   76–20672
ISBN 0–15–128780–5

First edition

BCDE

Contents

For these I set neither limits of time nor of achieve-
ments.
Empire without end have I given them.
— Vergil *Aeneid* 1. 278–279

There is no man that hath power over the spirit to
retain the spirit.
— Ecclesiastes 8 : 8

FOREWORD

Those who will not learn from others' experiences must themselves undergo those same experiences. Nations that will not learn from past history have to live through historical vicissitudes similar to those they overlook.

Both in theory and in practice, Americans are among the foremost peoples of the world in the physical and mathematical sciences. It is this quality that has put them in the forefront of modern civilization. Their achievements in chemistry, biology, physics, engineering, computer technology, aviation, space travel are little short of earth-shaking. Their type of mind responds spontaneously to everything mechanical, from gadgets to space vehicles, from inert rocks to molecular structures. They, more than any other people, are the world's builders, inventors, discoverers of ways and means to utilize natural phenomena.

For this they pay a price. Despite all their vaunted psychology and pursuit of so-called social sciences, they are among the world's worst psychologists and students of human nature, and how human nature affects historical processes that in turn affect the future of mankind. In addition to being naïvely idealistic where human relations are concerned, they are reluctant to study human beings in their documented, historical progression. Not only will they set up for themselves a human and social ideal in direct conflict with factual reality; they will also resent anyone who undertakes to enlighten them concerning that factual reality, and who suggests that their ideal of man and mankind should perhaps undergo some revision in the light of historical experience.

Side by side with this characteristic, which partakes of both ignorance and indifference, there is another, which pertains not to time, but to space. Supremely self-centered, Americans refuse to believe that others are not like themselves. In consequence, they take little interest in geography and all that goes with it, particularly geography outside of the United States. The average American can, in vague fashion, name and locate most of the American states. How many Canadian provinces can he name and locate? How many states of the neighboring Republic of Mexico?

Linking geography and history, what are the present names of the former Belgian Congo, the former Northern Rhodesia, the former German East Africa? What are the modern names of the ancient Euxine Sea, the Pillars of Hercules, the Roman province of Armorica? By what other names has the present Turkish capital of Istanbul been known?

With geography, the problem is primarily one of factual information, which can be acquired by rote, if there is a will or a need to do so. With history, the acquisition of names, dates, events is only the preliminary part of the study. The true historical sense lies in the interpretation of past events and its application to present-day problems. Viewed in this light, history becomes one of the most relevant and immediate of our studies. How and why did certain past events occur?

Given suitable premises, can they occur again, in our present or future? What parallels can be established between the events described by ancient historians and those that are happening today? Can we learn from the past how to conduct ourselves in the present? Which solutions of our current problems should be favored, which avoided? What standards of conduct, individual and collective, what forms of political belief and action have proved successful, which have failed? In brief, can we use the past as a guide for the present?

If the answer is affirmative, Dr. Lidia Storoni Mazzolani's book is one of the very best for the purpose. Written on the basis of consummate scholarship and with the sureness of touch that can be conferred only by thorough familiarity with the topic, it brings to the reader a historical picture that spreads over more than three centuries and sheds light on the growth and initial decline of the world's most enduring empire. The story is told in the words of three Roman historians, who described both the past and the present as it unfolded itself before their own eyes in the last century B.C. and the first two centuries of the Christian era. For good measure, there is an account of happenings and impressions of the second century B.C., when Rome achieved the status of world power, supplied by a non-Roman historian, Polybius; along with abundant considerations offered by other contemporary observers.

Dr. Storoni Mazzolani displays rare insight into individual and public motives and a keen understanding of the period with which she deals. Nowhere does she attempt to moralize, pronounce judgment, or link the events of the four centuries of her choice with later history, least of all that of our own times. Her intent is to seek for and put in evidence the awareness and anguish of the three historians, who sensed and feared the coming decline, each giving his own interpretation from his particular point of view. Without stating it as her purpose, she proves conclusively that the events that happened subsequently, in the third, fourth, and fifth centuries A.D., did not come unannounced and unforeseen; Sallust, Livy, and Tacitus are shown as the alerting sentries of the future.

My purpose in writing this extended foreword is somewhat different. It is to establish comparisons with present-day attitudes and events, not for the purpose of sounding a knell of inevitable doom for our own civilization, but to make readers aware of points of similarity and difference in the two situations.

To the natural and obvious query "Are we of modern America destined to undergo a fate similar to that which befell the Roman Empire?" my answer is: "Not necessarily. Not if we take heed and warning from earlier experiences. It's later than most of us think, or have thought until very recently. But it is not yet too late to learn from history what can happen to the materialistically inclined, the devotees of the 'good' life, the self-satisfied, the overconfident, those who think there can be no end to a situation that seems to favor them, and that fortune will never cease to smile upon them."

Above all, this foreword is directed to those who think that all we have to do is to go on as we have been going, without self-examination, without constant revision of our points of view to adapt to changed historical conditions, and without consideration for the viewpoints and feelings of others whom in the past we could afford to overlook as unimportant, but who are even now knocking at our gates with growing insistence, as those misnamed "barbarians" knocked at the *limites* of the Empire without an end at the beginning of the third century of our era.

Dr. Storoni Mazzolani's main sources are three: Sallust (87-36 B.C.), Livy (59 B.C.-A.D. 17), and Tacitus (A.D. 60-120), strategically spaced to cover the first century B.C., the first century A.D., and the beginning of the second century A.D. Her minor sources are numerous. Chief among them is Polybius (204-122 B.C.), a Greek hostage brought to Rome in his early adulthood, who views Roman civilization as one who is foreign-born and foreign-trained, and therefore endowed with a more dispassionate viewpoint and a better basis of comparison than the others. But many additional observers enter into the picture she presents: Vergil, Horace, Cicero, Seneca, Lucan, Plutarch, to mention a few.

In her introduction, the author describes briefly the massive, rough-hewn character of the Roman Founding Fathers, their simple ways of life, their preoccupation with security against foreign aggression, which led them to seek allies and friends rather than subjects. But in the course of the struggles against Epirus, Macedonia, and Carthage, it became obvious to the Romans that their destiny was to become a world power, and that they had to show themselves worthy of inheriting the earth, through their ancestral virtues: frugality, valor, endurance of hardships, discipline, generosity toward the conquered. Livy cites Titus Quintius Flamininus, conqueror of Greece, according to whom the Romans wanted neither slaves nor tribute, but only that the Greeks acknowledge the existence of a nation which, at its own expense, risk, and labor, undertakes wars in order to bring freedom to other nations. This was a lofty statement of purpose, not altogether in accord with the facts, but it compares well with many similar statements made in modern times by numerous American leaders in their dealings, not only with Europe, but also with Africa, Korea, Cuba, Vietnam. (We are particularly reminded of Woodrow Wilson's "making the world safe for democracy," and of John F. Kennedy's public statement that it is America's mission to defend liberty everywhere throughout the world.)

Since Roman theory and Roman practice did not always coincide, it was perhaps natural that some of the nations regaled with the blessings of Roman rule and Roman liberty occasionally rebelled; where this was not possible, they at least prophesied that their own messiahs would emerge, not so much to "liberate" them, as to place them under their own native rulers, however tyrannical. This spirit, too, is something with which recent history has made us familiar.

The conquest of Greece opened up to the Romans a new dimension: that of culture, philosophy, art, and the leisure to enjoy them. But the new cult of leisure and refinement was at odds with the traditional Roman philosophy of action in the nation's service. Pronounced individualism and disciplined, concerted mass action are difficult to reconcile. The fact that the Romans were at a crossroad in their psychological outlook was first sensed by Polybius the Greek, who had come to Rome in 168 B.C., after the second Punic War, when Rome's hegemony was already manifest. He was the first to observe and describe the initial stages in the decay of the traditional Roman democratic process, which he cautiously placed in a framework of world history. Nations, he says, pass naturally from a state of autocratic monarchy to the rule of an aristocratic class; then, when the aristocrats abuse their privileges and neglect their duties, to full democracy. But the younger generations, born to freedom, fail to realize the obligations that liberty and equality entail; they turn to violence and excesses, and stir up the masses to follow their violent leadership. Chaos ensues, until a new despot emerges, seizes control, and restores order. The final step had not yet been achieved in Polybius's time. But he was a true prophet, prophesying in the light of the past history of his own native Greece, whose democratic city-states had succumbed to Philip of Macedon and later to the Romans.

For what concerned the immediate present of which he was

a part, he pointed out that the Romans had retained their traditional integrity until they had embarked on overseas wars and departed from the laws and customs of their ancestors. The Greek example, so enthusiastically embraced by so many Romans, was of ill omen. Greek-style luxury, music, banquets that turned into orgies, illicit, often disgraceful love affairs marked by sexual deviation, could not, in the long run, fail to break down the rough Roman fiber. "Two are the forces whereby a nation is exposed to perish, one internal, the other external." Of the two, the internal is by far the more dangerous. The Romans, says Polybius, possess the qualities that lead to success; but can those qualities endure when new social classes, new ethnic strains enter the state's composition? Can they survive the indifference of the citizenry, the carping criticism of the intellectuals, the hedonism of the newly rich, the breakdown of military discipline? A tightly woven net had held together the smaller Roman Republic of the past; now, with more people crowding into it, the net was being stretched and loosened; in spots, it was beginning to break.

Polybius does not offer too many examples to bolster his contentions; but a later historian, Livy, informs us of slave revolts that broke out at this period, fostered by Carthaginian War prisoners and hostages held on Italian soil; of Roman deserters joining Hannibal's army in Carthage; of Roman allies switching to Hannibal after Roman defeats. Plutarch tells the story of the patrician Gracchi, Caius and Tiberius, who spread the gospel of economic egalitarianism to the detriment of their own social class, which did not hesitate to have recourse to assassination in order to get rid of them. For all these events, it would be easy to cite analogies in our age.

Sallust, first of the three native historians presented in this work, turned to history rather late in life, having first enjoyed a military, political, and administrative career. His account of the Jugurthine War deals with events that occurred not too long before his time, but his Catilinian War speaks of things that he saw with his own eyes.

He paints a picture of a Roman society in the throes of change. The older, simple division into patricians and plebeians, with an equestrian middle class and large numbers of small, independent landholders, had given way to something more complex, with the expansion of the middle class into separate groups: businessmen, financiers, manufacturers, tax-gatherers, builders, merchants, whose interests coincided only in part with those of the patricians and holders of vast landed estates. The army had become a permanent professional body, composed of people of little or no wealth (earlier, Tiberius Gracchus had complained that these soldiers who had conquered the world did not own an ell of land), prone to support political dictators. There were hordes of unemployed, the victims of expanding slave labor; many sub-poor, living on free grain distributions and handouts from the rich who had political ambitions, and inclined to restlessness, violence, and crime.

The patrician oligarchy had lost the art of ruling, while the new leaders of the left, despite their humanitarian slogans and ambitious programs of social reform, were inspired mainly by a desire to occupy posts of political prominence and to feather their own nests.

A disheartening picture, and one that has parallels in our own times: the inability of America's traditional leading classes to lead in the days of the Great Depression; mass flight from the farms to the cities; the fragmentation of the old middle class into a more variegated assortment of middle classes (skilled labor, white collar, managerial, small business men, government employees, bureaucrats), with conflicting interests; unemployment fostered by vastly increased automation, the modern replacement of ancient slave labor; the rise of a permanent class of people on relief and welfare, ready to follow demagogues; a succession of elected executives, who,

while ostensibly remaining within the bounds of constitutionality, showed a disposition to make arbitrary and autocratic
decisions; political leaders promising the masses, under the
names New Deal, New Frontier, Great Society, a utopian
prosperity, or the illusion of a Generation of Peace. Coupled
with this, unpopular colonial wars, against Jugurtha in North
Africa then, in Korea and Vietnam recently, no longer enjoyed the broad base of popular support that had attended the
wars against Macedonia and Carthage, or those against imperial and Nazi Germany and aggressive Japan. In Sallust's
time, the fall of the enemies that had menaced Rome's existence led to a Roman pre-eminence that coupled prosperity
and the feeling of security with pride and greed for material
things, phenomena that became manifest in America's recent
past after the overwhelming triumphs of World War II.

Were he writing today, Sallust would qualify as a writer of
the liberal, democratic, moderate left. He opposed the concentration of both political power and wealth, and particularly the use of the second to gain the first. He offered a
solution for the problem of the urban poor and the welfare
recipients which was worthy of serious consideration then, as
now. Instead of letting them accumulate and fester in city
slums, why not encourage them to move back to rural areas,
with government aid to enable them to set up small farms and
restore to them the pride of ownership and labor? As a matter
of fact, Dr. Storoni Mazzolani points out, some of Sallust's
suggestions were in part followed by Julius Caesar when he
gained power, along with others originally advanced by the
Gracchi, limiting the use of slave labor on large landed estates.
(From a present-day standpoint, it is still a moot question
whether the wholesale extension of automation to industry
contributes more to unemployment by abolishing jobs, or to
full employment by creating new ones.)

The Jugurthine War in North Africa had revealed the conflict of interest between the new, enlarged middle classes and the old patricians and intellectuals. The former favored the conflict, which expanded their activities and investments; the latter preferred more conservatism at home and less expansionism abroad. There is a far from perfect parallel with the course of the Vietnam war, favored by industries and labor organizations that profited from planes, tanks, and napalm, opposed by college students, liberals, and other intellectuals who advocated a concentration of resources on domestic problems. The ancient clash ultimately resulted in the first great civil war, when Marius was the exponent of the interventionists, Sulla of the isolationists. The United States, fortunately, managed to avoid a final clash, despite the many demonstrations and disorders.

A later civil war, between Octavian and Mark Antony, is described in apocalyptic terms by Horace, who calls the conflict a fratricidal one: "This city, which neither Etruscans nor Gauls nor Teutons nor Hannibal nor Spartacus could overthrow, is now driven to the abyss by an unholy war. Its land will again be roamed over by wild beasts. The triumphant barbarian will trample its ruins with his horse's hoofs; he will insolently scatter the bones of Romulus to the sun and the winds." This prophecy was not to be realized for four centuries; but was a true prophecy nevertheless.

Meanwhile, Mithridates of Pontus and the restless Parthians heralded the downfall of Rome and the return of the center of power to the East. Sallust quotes from a spurious letter of Mithridates: "Asia is waiting for us and cries out for help: the Romans have succeeded in making themselves hated because of the greed of their Proconsuls, the extortions of their tax collectors, the injustices of their magistrates." Not only Sallust, but Horace, Propertius, Lucan, and others point to the two great unresolved problems that in their day were barely beginning to confront the massive Roman commonwealth:

the vulnerable border of the Rhine and that of the East. These are paralleled in our day by two great areas of doubt and conflict: the Middle East and the Far East.

In a letter to his friend and patron Julius Caesar (also possibly spurious), Sallust speaks of the rewards and punishments that inevitably attend good and evil deeds; even if their impact is delayed, our own conscience, individual and collective, warns us to expect them. Cities and nations prosper and rule insofar as they follow the laws of wisdom; where privilege, fear, and the love of pleasure prevail, their strength declines, their empire falls, and they are impressed into slavery. When love of country and love of work are replaced by sloth, morality by dissoluteness, justice by arrogance, fortune departs, and power is transferred from the worthy to the unworthy.

The Jugurthine War had been based on the pretext that Rome had a moral and juridical obligation to intervene in the internal affairs of an allied state. Sallust, rather illogically, supported this thesis; not so much because of intellectual conviction, but because it offered an opportunity to humble the power and authority of the aristocrats who opposed it. In this respect, he allowed his emotions to overrule his judgment. Marius, the plebeian leader from Arpinum, was neither a patrician nor even a native Roman. His ascent to power was a forerunner of a new state of Roman affairs, wherein the posts of highest command, hitherto reserved to the old Roman aristocracy, became accessible to new social classes and new ethnic strains. In the long run, this changed point of view opened the gates of power to some of the abler emperors, such as Trajan and the African Septimius Severus. But in Sallust's immediate present it also opened the way to Catiline and his conspiracy. This Sallust properly deplores, along with the mounting illegalities committed by the conspirators and by those who repressed them.

Cato the Younger, archconservative and archopponent of

Caesar, had ignored the onward march of both democracy and events, extolling the iron discipline of older days, inexorably applied. But today, he says in public Senate debate with Caesar, acquiescence goes by the name of understanding, the waste of public funds by that of generosity. Ambiguity in the use of words derives from muddled thinking, uncertain principles, failure to apply the laws. "We make no distinction between scoundrels and honest men . . . we have long since lost the true names of things."

Sallust records these utterances, perhaps among the very last samples of free parliamentary debate in a free republican society. Today free debate still exists in the halls of Congress. But we also witness the unnerving spectacle of qualified, scheduled speakers in our free colleges and universities prevented from speaking by audiences that demand that points of view they oppose be banned.

Livy, foremost among Roman historians, and probably our best source of information on ancient Rome, was more of a historical romantic than Sallust. A *laudator temporis acti* (praiser of the past), he was deeply committed to *Roma ab urbe condita* (Rome since the City's founding). The portion of his work that has come down to us is in part a fairly reliable historical account, in part a hodgepodge of legends. Almost to the same extent as Vergil, who has Jupiter say that he has placed no limit of time or achievements on the Romans, but has given them "empire without end," Livy has firm faith in his nation's divinely appointed mission to rule the world, not by violence and terror, but by prestige and authority.

Yet the memory of recent bloody events leads him to indulge in nostalgic reminiscences of those simple, pure virtues by which Rome had become great. He deplores, though in minor key, the civil wars, the disorders, the economic unrest of his own times, the servile materialism that inspires too many of his contemporaries, their inferiority complex in the face of the Greek culture they had adopted. He delights in the tale of Mucius Scaevola, stronger than the fire into which he plunged his hand to prove Roman fortitude, of Regulus, who voluntarily subjected himself to Carthaginian tortures rather than go back on his word, of Fabius Maximus Cunctator, whose delaying tactics defeated Hannibal, at the same time that he deplores Grecian luxury and vices, the greed and duplicity he sees around him, the fact that the young have no respect for their elders, and children spurn their parents' authority. He even quotes in their entirety the ancient formulas whereby the vanquished sued for the privilege of unconditional surrender to the Roman victors, and Scipio's address to his Numidian ally Masinissa to the effect that the real danger lies not in the arms of the enemy, but in the arms of pleasure.

Livy's civic concept is simple: the individual does not count, save as a member of the community. It is not fortune that leads to a nation's success, but courage and intelligence. The Carthaginians are described as cruel and perfidious, the Greeks as cunning and untrustworthy; but the Romans, endowed with civic consciousness, are destined to rule the world, so long as they retain their ancestral virtues and refrain from fratricidal conflicts.

Livy's antipathy for the Greek culture that was seeping into Rome is transferred in his writings to the historical characters he admires: Cato, Marius, Augustus, Tiberius refused to speak Greek, even though they were familiar with the language. He accuses the Greeks of conducting war only with words and writings, in which they excel. Certain Greek writers maintained that Alexander could have beaten the Romans had he turned westward instead of eastward, and that the Roman empire was founded on *fortuna* rather than *virtus* (luck rather than innate qualities). He goes to great lengths to refute this claim. The Romans have overcome far stronger armies than the Macedonian, and they will do it again and again, provided concord prevails at home. Is this proviso inspired by anxiety, by fear that internal peace may not last?

Livy's main political concern is with the concept of *libertas:* not so much freedom in the modern sense, but, rather, the harmonious working out of the democratic process under just laws, strictly and uniformly enforced, and the interaction of the various established social classes. The combination of "constitutionality" and "law and order" perhaps best summarizes this concept, whose opposite is *regnum*, the rule of an autocrat, often backed by a mob. Since the autocrat might seek access to power through measures designed to improve the condition of the lower classes, the concept of *libertas* is essentially an aristocratic one, not too unlike that of our Founding Fathers. Equality for all, particularly of the economic variety, is not contemplated, or viewed as desirable. The social and economic reforms sought by left-wing politicians and demagogues, in Livy's concept, are really designed to saddle the state with a tyrant, who will rule autocratically in the name of the "people" (what people?); and this marks the end of "liberty."

Order within the framework of the law is what distinguishes *libertas* from *regnum*. The laws may be harsh, and rigidly applied. No matter, provided they are equally and severely enforced. The power of the consuls was equal to that of the early kings of Rome; but the consuls were restricted by law to a limited term of office.

How, then, did Livy reconcile his principles with the existence of the two emperors under whom he lived, Augustus and Tiberius? He is at pains to inform his readers that Augustus never exceeded his constitutional powers and prerogatives. He turned down both dictatorship and life consulship, accepting the *tribunicia potestas perpetua* (the power of a tribune for life)—but *per legem*, through a duly enacted law. This brings to mind the ascent to power of Mussolini in Italy and Hitler in Germany, both of which took place within existing democratic laws and constitutions. It is merely an accident of history that Augustus never clashed with his Senate, as Mussolini did with his Parliament, or Nixon with his Congress. Livy's formula was safe, at least during his lifetime: *Sine lege nulla libertas* ("There is no freedom without law"). Cicero had previously enunciated a somewhat similar principle: *Legum servi sumus ut liberi esse possimus* ("We are the servants of the laws in order that we may be free"). Yet laws can be changed by a parliamentary majority, or even by an arbitrary Supreme Court decision.

"Liberty," in Livy's concept, is independence from foreign rule, from the dominion of a despot, or of a faction, from the supremacy of a social class, from mob rule, coupled with the exercise of both rights and duties in an atmosphere of strict legality. Liberty is extended to other nations after they are conquered and assimilated to the Roman superstate. Anyone who tries to remove himself from the rule of law is *ipso facto* a foe of "liberty"; so is anyone who stirs up the populace to break the law. One of the individual's most sacred obligations is that of appearing in court before a tribunal if accused of a crime. No one, however lofty his position, can be exempted from this obligation. The rule of law is supreme. He who cannot govern himself has no right to govern others. It is *libertas* that leads to *virtus*, and to orderly progress.

Can all these insistent statements of lofty principle be a symptom of a deeply buried fear that existing rulers, however benign, might one day destroy the liberty Livy loved? His Stoic philosophy, urging men to rely on their own inner resources, but ever in conformity with divine law, was at variance with the supernaturally inspired religions streaming in from the East, based in part on faith in survival after death, in part on superstition and astrology, and often predicting Rome's downfall. Long after Livy's time, when Christianity had overspread the Empire, there were still those who insisted that Rome's woes were due to the anger of the deserted ancient gods. Augustine of Hippo, with his *City of God*, rejects the Roman state that wanted to rule the world by force, and opposes the concept of divine grace to the old tradition of rule by merit. Man is justified by faith alone, not by works, said Augustine. Yet the Roman concept endures in part to this day, in the type of freedom established by the founders of the United States, in the "work ethic" still advocated by many among us.

But the problem remains: how to reconcile the "rule of law" with arbitrary one-man decisions and executive privilege.

Tacitus, writing approximately one century after Livy, finds himself facing a world different from that of his predecessors. The Roman Empire has consolidated, both as a territorial entity and as a regime. The democratic trappings of the late Republic have fallen into desuetude. Several autocrats have succeeded each other, some good, some bad, but all strengthening the authoritarian grip in which they hold the once free Roman people. Tacitus views the scene with pessimism, though his expression of that pessimism is necessarily guarded. There is ever-widening corruption, immorality, vice in Roman society. There is neglect of the law, which to Livy had been paramount. *Non mos, non jus* (Neither morals nor laws) best summarizes the situation at the beginning of the second century A.D. The spirit of liberty sung by Livy is no longer, and Tacitus, who cannot safely criticize living emperors, can at least point the finger of blame at the first of the series, Augustus, who re-established peace at the borders and order at home, but at the price of Rome's free institutions.

Peace and a leader is what the Romans now had; Lucan had previously confirmed it with his statement *Cum domino pax ista venit* (This peace comes with a master).

Was Augustus altogether to blame? A hundred years earlier, Seneca had stated that it is absurd to try to bring liberty back to life when the moral climate that makes possible the exercise of that liberty is dead. Yet the early dictators could justify their actions in the name of liberty from mob rule. Julius Caesar had stated that he wished *vindicare libertatem a factione paucorum* (to rescue liberty from the factionalism of the few), and Augustus had used almost identical words: *rem publicam a dominatione factionis oppressam in libertatem vindicare* (to restore to liberty the state, oppressed by the rule of a faction).

There were many contemporaries of Tacitus who viewed liberty as retirement from the battlefield of politics and from society and its obligations, to live in a sheltered, self-imposed cloister in order to develop their own talents and individuality. Tacitus opposes the concept of liberty to that of power: a regime of true liberty is one that does not force three successive stages of subjection upon the individual: *patientia, adulatio, servitium* (patience, flattery, servitude). "Patience" means endurance of the evil aspects of autocracy in order to attain peace and order. "Flattery" is exemplified by Pliny's address to Trajan: "If you order us to be free, we shall be free!" "Servitude" means that, in an autocracy, it is safer to speak and write of past glories than of present events. "Let me find out," says Juvenal, "what I am allowed to say about those who lie along the Flaminian and Latin ways."

Tacitus acquiesces. But he does name his four ideal guidelines for civic conduct: *virtus, senatus, patria, libertas* ("virtue" in the sense of those qualities by which Rome had achieved greatness; "the senate," which still existed and legislated, though more and more as a rubber stamp for the ruling despot; "the fatherland," always a safe concept, whether in a democracy or under an autocratic regime; "freedom," which also can be stretched, as shown by the fact that the praises of "liberty" were sung in both the Italian Fascist and the German Nazi anthems, and that those among us who most favor government intervention in the affairs of the individual have somehow pre-empted the name "liberals"). But Tacitus, using universally safe words, probably knew what he meant in the use of each of them.

When it comes to prophesying the future from the omens of the present, Tacitus displays anxiety, not only over Rome and her empire, but over the fate of men in general. How will it be possible, he wonders, to reconcile Rome's contradictory ideals, tradition and universality; to extend to the many a culture and a moral code devised by the few for a few? Is it possible to accommodate the structure of what was originally a single city to cover a vast, multiform, restless society in which there is economic, social, and ethnic discontent? Can the past be inserted into the present without doing violence to both? These are questions that might well be asked concerning present-day American society, with economic and social problems that the Founding Fathers never even dreamed of, with ethnic and racial groups that in recent times have been more and more firmly rejecting the old melting-pot concept on the ground that all it is designed to accomplish is the assimilation of minorities to a dominant majority, and to stifle minority cultures.

Not only is the society pictured by Tacitus seething with unrest. It is also beleaguered by the growing disregard of its laws, discredited by violence, intrigue, bribery, and corruption. There is a decline of all moral values, and the two universal standards that emerge in their place are power and gold.

A good deal of this criticism is subdued and disguised,

though Tacitus implies that an emperor's autocratic power could be restrained if it met with firm moral resistance on the part of the citizenry; that the legions would not saddle the state with a leader of their own choice if the individual legionaries did not expect to profit from that leader once he was in power; that the man illegally chosen would, after all, have the right to reject the nomination by legionary acclamation if he had the civic conscience to turn it down on the ground that it had not been sanctioned by the Senate. But all this is necessarily expressed in a minor key.

Where Tacitus abandons restraint is in his description of the new provincial and barbarian element that constituted the majority of the nation's armed forces. Far from deploring the presence of the barbarians, he admires them, and paints them in glowing colors, perhaps more than they deserve. They, if anyone, will be the salvation of the Roman state, which can no longer rely on its native sons.

Yet Tacitus opposes Roman colonialism on the ground that what the Romans bring to the nations they conquer is not their ancient *virtus*, but their current vices. He points to Britain, recently pacified by Agricola, one of the most enlightened of Roman generals, as an example. The once free and proud Britons have finally succumbed, not so much to Roman arms as to Roman luxury and pleasures. They have taken on Roman ways and customs, discarding their own, in much the same fashion that the Japanese and Italians took on American ways after World War II. To their advantage or to their detriment? This question still awaits an answer.

The Britons, fully Romanized after the defeat of Queen Boadicea, who had resisted the invaders to the last, showed then a prime example of what Tacitus calls *patientia*, endurance, even cheerful acceptance of foreign and autocratic rule, in return for the economic advantages and military protection the Romans brought.

But the Germanic barbarians on the Rhine-Danube frontier are horses of another color. They know no private property, nor do they dwell in well-ordered cities. Their gods have no temples, but are worshiped under the lowering northern skies. They obey a chieftain to whom they are bound by a personal bond of loyalty, and who is equally bound to his followers and consults them before making important decisions. There is among them neither usury nor corruption, no immorality, infidelity, abortion, or infanticide, no taking on of vices in order to get ahead, no social or economic discrimination. Forty years earlier, Seneca had compared them to the Romans of an earlier period. Tacitus confirms this description, and adds that pristine *virtus* still exists among them.

But he goes further. Large numbers of Germans have joined the Roman armies, filling the ranks deserted by plea-sure-loving, soft-living Roman youth. Can the newcomers be trusted? Or will they eventually make common cause with the rebels of Gaul, Spain, and Britain? These mercenaries, whose task it is to defend Rome from Rome's own degen-eracy, will they not one day inherit Rome's empire? Spanish-born Lucan goes even further, cheering for the Galatians, Sy-rians, Gauls, and Iberians, who, since the great civil wars, have constituted the bulk of Rome's legions and the Empire's population; but Rome rewards them with taxes and oppres-sion, for Rome's greed knows no bounds. In Rome itself, nothing remains of the old civic conscience, the old equality. All are sycophants, awaiting the ruler's nod.

For this situation, Tacitus is unable to suggest a remedy. The great men of the past are gone. Rome, once a city of heroes, is now filled with the world's dregs. The younger generations have gone over to idleness, vices, and corruption, while many of the older generation succumb to *taedium vitae*, weariness of life, and in ever-increasing numbers commit sui-cide or seek obscurity in retirement.

Some of this pessimism rubs off on Tacitus, who stares death in the face without flinching, though he does not seek it out. The untimely death of his friend Agricola, perhaps brought about by a tyrant's poison, affects him deeply, and colors his accounts with melancholy.

The gods are indifferent to the affairs of the individual, says Tacitus, exemplifying with accounts of the success of scoundrels and the misfortunes of worthy men. But the gods do punish states and nations that fail in their appointed mission, and this bodes ill for Rome.

Tacitus makes no mention of Christianity, the new spiritual movement welling up from below that might have saved the Empire and, in a sense, did so, though not materially. It is probable that like many of his pagan contemporaries he lumped the Christians with the Jews, whom he condemns for their hardheaded obstinacy and rebelliousness to Rome. Yet it was precisely from the Christians and the Jews that the Romans might have learned how to restore those moral values whose loss Tacitus deplores.

From the composite four-century picture painted by Polybius, Sallust, Livy, and Tacitus, one can obtain a comprehensive view of the Roman state at the peak of its power. One can also point to a striking sequence of similarities between that greatest and most powerful of ancient states and our own commonwealth. The Romans and the Americans, throughout their historical evolution, have had many things in common: the illusion of hegemony without an end; the sense of a historical mission to further and defend their chosen form of government and way of life throughout the world; a pristine belief in the rule of laws, not of men, that is gradually supplanted by a desire for peace abroad, social order at home, to the point where many are willing to give up liberty to attain them; a civic conscience based on a sense of duty, and individual responsibility that gradually gives way to love of ease, wealth, and luxury, then to vice and corruption, selfishness, materialism, lastly to widespread crime and violence, both against individuals and against the state.

Many of the manifestations and episodes in the history of the two commonwealths have strong points of resemblance: democracy turning into demagogy; a lack of leadership on the part of those who should lead; a tendency to disorder, mob rule, infringement of free speech and the rights of the individual; political assassinations; class cleavages that may lead to civil wars; the creation of a monstrously voracious bureaucracy; the creation of a welfare state that drains the nation's finances; executives who arrogate dictatorial powers; a citizen army that turns into an army of hired mercenaries inspired not by patriotism, but by personal advantage; ethnic unrest and clashes; colonial wars of a controversial nature that extend the power and influence of the nation abroad, but fail to solve the international problems they create, and create vast new problems at home.

The sum total of these similarities would lead us to think of a similarity of outcomes. But before we reach this conclusion, it may be well to examine the differences in the two situations, which are far-reaching. Some seem to be in our favor, others against us.

One striking difference is that while Roman hegemony after the Punic Wars was absolute, ours after World War II was not. Rome's major rival was obliterated. We not only did not obliterate our opponents; we contributed to the emergence of a new and fearsome rival, the Soviet Union, and countenanced that of another, Mao's Red China, both inspired by an ideology that is, at least on the surface, the opposite of ours.

The existence of one, potentially two, formidable contenders for world supremacy marks a decided difference between the status of the Roman Empire and that of the American

commonwealth. It is idle to speculate on what might have
been had the United States pushed its advantage to the full
immediately after World War II, when it was the sole posses-
sor of atomic weapons. No one in America echoed, with the
appropriate change of name and language, the slogan of Cato
the Elder in the Roman senate: *"Carthaginem esse delendam!"*
("Carthage must be destroyed!") We must place the credit
for this to the difference between the ruthless realism of the
Romans and the visionary idealism of the Americans.

Another essential difference lies in the nature of the labor
force at the disposal of the ancient and of the modern world.
The Roman economy (indeed, Roman society as a whole)
was based on the institution of slavery, something so repulsive
to the American conscience that a civil war was fought to
eliminate it. Let us remember, however, that slavery was prac-
tically universal in the ancient world, though it differed in
extent and degree from nation to nation. It was the norm in
ancient China, India, Babylonia and Assyria, Egypt, Greece,
Carthage. It was practiced even by those noble barbarians
whom Tacitus praises. Prisoners taken in war were either put
to death or spared to serve their captors. The Hebrews, who
seemingly practiced slavery only in a very restricted sense,
were often the victims of it. The slave of antiquity, like his
counterpart in early American history, was legally a chattel,
enjoying no civil or human rights. Yet many Roman slaves
were people of culture and refinement, having enjoyed high
status in their own communities prior to their capture. The
bulk were used for hard labor, particularly on large estates.
The Roman historians deplore this use, but only on the
ground that it causes unemployment among the free poor and
turns them into welfare recipients. It was only with Christianity, with its basic tenet of the equality of all human beings,
that the institution of slavery began to be questioned.

Slave revolts occurred with some frequency in the ancient
world, and Rome knew one serious slave war, led by Sparta-

cus, which actually endangered the structure of the Roman state. Yet, while paganism prevailed, it did not occur to anyone to view this time-honored institution as anything but normal and natural. Free workers in the Roman state were unorganized, and contracted for their services on an individual basis.

The labor picture today is vastly different. In the United States free workers are largely organized into powerful labor unions that know how to assert their wants. Labor is now not merely an economic, but also a political and social factor. Skilled labor, and a good deal of the unskilled, regards itself as a branch of the middle, not of the lower class, and has acquired a typically middle-class mentality and attitude. It is as much a factor of stability in the American social structure as slave labor was a factor of instability and weakness in the Roman.

But modern society in general and American society in particular have another advantage over the ancients. The Roman Empire, for all its longevity and enduring greatness in many fields, did not produce a single major invention or innovation, though it made considerable improvements in the production and use of things of a mechanical nature that were already in existence. Transportation and travel when Rome's empire ended were still based on the sail and the horse, as they had been when Rome began, and indeed as they were until the early nineteenth century. The steamer, the motorboat, the railroad, the automobile, the airplane are all acquirements of the nineteenth and twentieth centuries. Rome had the early mechanical devices, such as the pulley, the lever, the wheel. She had the traditional sources of power not supplied by man himself—the winds and the waters. The utilization of steam, coal, oil, electricity, atomic fission as sources of heat, energy, and power to do man's work is a recent development.

More perhaps than any other modern people, the American

has demonstrated his ability to explore and control the forces of nature, to apply them to technological advancement, and this is said with full recognition of the fact that many other nations have contributed and continue to contribute to our technical civilization. This fortunate circumstance endows the United States with an enormous advantage, which could easily outweigh all the disadvantages previously enumerated. Though not from a position of hegemony in the Roman sense, it wields far greater effective power than the Roman Empire could envisage.

MARIO PEI

Introduction

If you want this city to be immortal, its empire to be eternal, and its glory to last forever, then we have to beware of our greed.[1]
—Cicero *Pro Rabirio Perduellonis Reo* 12. 33

The Roman state rests on its ancient customs and on its men.[2]
—Ennius *Annales* 1. 390

The Roman Empire, both in appearance and in actuality, had something of the miraculous. To understand this prodigy we must go to some isolated corner of Latium where to this day the faces and attitudes of the people recall those of the ancients. The rules of good husbandry laid down in Cato's handbook of agriculture, *De Re Rustica*, still regulate the measured movements of the tillers of fields, and traces of archaic Latin still echo in their speech.

The oak and the ilex, trees venerated by the ancients in their cults and prized for their fruits, continue to flourish along with more recently developed and remunerative crops. Before Saturn refined this rough, unhewn race of men—*gens virum truncis et duro robore nata*[3]—they looked to the oak, not to humankind for their origins. Once the branches of this sacred tree crowned Jupiter, kings, and victors. In its shade, flocks of sheep and herds of pigs continue to graze. At dusk

1. Notes are on pages 209 to 220.

the shepherd still moves the animal enclosure made from pointed stakes lashed together with a leather strap, in exactly the same way as did his forefathers. He uses the same harsh-sounding, pithy words as his ancestors did to express his basic needs: *focus* (fire), *quercus* (oak), *porcus* (pig), *pecus* (cattle). He boils his simple vegetable-and-lard soup, seasoned with mint and garlic, over a twig fire. This modest fare has always been the peasant's meal. In the words of the poet Vergil, this is how the Latins and Etruscans, Romulus and Remus lived. Yet Rome was built on this very foundation.[4]

These men from Latium have rugged but regular features and the large hands of their ancestors, who, laying down their spades, took up spears to conquer the Sabines, the Aequii, the Volscians, the Etruscans, and the Samnites. To defend themselves against inroads from Epirus, they invaded Campania and Apulia. They occupied Sicily, Spain, and Sardinia in order to create a buffer against Carthage, on the African coast. To escape encirclement from the east, they built a bridgehead in Illyricum, and finally moved against Macedonia, Syria, and Asia Minor. By the middle of the second century B.C., they were already masters of the Aegean Sea and the coast of North Africa. Yet they still prayed to the humble gods of their solitary, rocky countryside, the very same gods they had invoked at twilight when they gathered their herds and led them to the trough, a hollowed trunk into which fresh water trickled from the spring. Diana guarded their woods, Faunus protected their sheep from the wolves, Pales made their women fertile and their pastures green, Mars Silvanus, before becoming the god of war, watched over their crops.

These men, intolerant of any threat to their borders, were moved more by a desire for hegemony than by an appetite for expansion. They preferred to transform conquered nations into allies, satellites, or protectorates, rather than into provinces. Reluctant to assume the direct responsibilities of government, they exacted tributes from the vanquished and support in their wars. The attitude they assumed depended on whether they were dealing with barbarians or civilized populations; they flaunted the former in their triumphal marches, and they used the latter as living examples of Roman clemency.

In their wars with Macedonia (215–168 B.C.), Syria, Pergamum, and the Achaean and Aetolian leagues, the Romans came in contact with a mosaic of city-states and kingdoms founded by the successors of Alexander that remained proud of their heritage in spite of their declining fortunes. This world cherished the remembrances of Alexander's passage, the echo of his great deeds and of those of the free Greek cities. It valued an ancient tradition of thought and poetry, of political and religious experience. And here among these peoples art flourished, myths sprang from their glens, springs, and mountains. In the heat of battle, in the grim celebration of victories, the Roman legionaries found themselves drawn into a world where marvels were the norm. In addition to the exquisitely chiseled jewels and transparent gowns they brought home to their women, they were carriers of legends, evocative poems, and somber prophecies. They described the marble sanctuaries in which solemn rites were performed. They told of having seen within the recesses of temples fair goddesses with serene and thoughtful brows, deities who tormented their spirits with desires to answer to a penetrating but distant voice, an undecipherable call. They had conquered, but their elation was tinged with anxiety.

The spirit of Rome was changing, too. Wars, famine, and plagues had made the Romans turn to new gods.[5] Orphic and Pythagorean cults, preaching the astral origin of the soul, re-emerged from Magna Graecia. Astrology, from Mesopotamian sources, opened dazzling glimpses into the future, in contrast to the ambiguous ones of Etruscan soothsayers. The destiny of each man was seen linked to the position of the stars, and the scanty meteorological notions of simple tillers of the soil were enriched with hidden meanings. These intimations, however, barely rose to the surface of their consciousness.

On their return home, the veterans found confining, low horizons, rude, vindictive gods, and crude images in tufa sanctuaries. Remembering the lands and the peoples they had seen, they were overcome by a vague sense of unease, of inadequacy, and of the precariousness of existence. Far away from home, the past had spoken to them in a mighty, distant voice. They had met warriors fighting with curved bows; there had been fierce melees, battlefields strewn with corpses; they had seen sumptuous royal palaces, strange peoples, houses appointed with golden tableware, handsome haughty women of whom the poets still sang. Troy had fallen. All that remained of Mycenae were gray stones and the deserted gate with its twin heraldic lions, guarding wind-swept ruins. At Argos and Tiryns, only the walls were still standing. In Crete, they had heard tales about King Minos; in Sparta, stories about a queen who had caused a long war. But nothing remained of those dazzling halls, those arms damascened with gold. Time, insistent and incessant, like the waves of the sea, had erased everything.

They began to question the caprice of fortune. Did history obey its own hidden laws? Were events determined by fate or by the will of the gods? Was there an inscrutable power behind the working of history, or was that disconnected chain of events, that waste of human lives, that headlong race of every sovereign state toward its own end, merely the result of chance?

Recent conquests raised further questions that needed to be answered. Was it right to extend and exercise sovereignty? Did that empire which had spread from the Atlantic to Asia in fifty short years depend on the Romans' *virtus* or on their *fortuna*? Slow disintegration or sudden catastrophe had weakened every power: would Rome alone be spared?

Thus myths and reassuring prophecies, which have come down to us in later versions, were elaborated to confute the baneful predictions that the enemy nations used as a psychological weapon against their conquerors. Romulus, who had vanished in a whirl of mist on the Field of Mars, reappeared to urge the Romans to cultivate the arts of war, since it was the will of the gods to make Rome the capital of the world. While founding the Temple of Jupiter on the summit of one of Rome's seven hills, Tarquinius found the skull of a man called Olius from Vulci, in Etruria, when the hill was named Caput Oli (Italian, Campidoglio; English, Capitoline Hill). Etruscan augurs immediately interpreted this omen to mean that Rome was to become the Caput Mundi (head of the world).[6] In the first phase of Rome's expansion toward the east, the Oracle of Delphi, predicting the future, warned the Romans to guard against worldly pleasures.[7]

Prophecies that had been impressed on the Roman consciousness confirmed the certainty of their future as a great power (". . . the origin of such a great city was, I think, the working of Fate . . ."[8]). Concurrently, however, there was also the disquieting feeling that this very greatness was precarious because of its disproportionate size, that the rampant internal disintegration was far more insidious than enemy forces from without. To endure, Rome must preserve or resurrect her ancient virtues.

The Romans found any comparison with their Eastern adversaries, who flaunted their divine lineage while luxuriating in opulence, both humiliating and stimulating. The contrast made them aware of their own unique qualities and loyal to their peasant ancestry. Between conducting wars and looking after the affairs of the state, Scipio withdrew to his fields at Liternum,* and Cato took up his spade. Yet these rugged, frugal men turned the world's kings into Rome's vassals.

Given these attitudes, the first inclinations toward luxurious living, the slightest concessions to pleasure, caused a shudder, the uneasy feeling of having transgressed supernatural injunctions or broken covenants—no less binding for being un-formulated—with watchful, jealous gods. Forewarnings of the decline to come were seen in the adoption of the simplest comforts of living.

Insidious doctrines, prophecies, and visions began to spread. The Magians, a Persian sect established somewhere between Mesopotamia and the Aegean, had adopted the astrological theology of the Chaldeans and predicted the end of the world. According to a very ancient myth, the universe was a chariot drawn by four horses who charged across the heavens. The horses represented the elements. As the solar horse raced around his circular track, he would set the earth on fire with his burning breath. After everything had gone up in flames, the cycle of life would begin anew.[9] In their cosmological theories, the Pythagoreans and the Stoics taught that time flows at a rhythm as regular as breathing, divided into cycles of equal duration; ten epochs, each lasting a hundred years, would follow one another, and at their completion everything would revert to chaos. The end would come about by either fire or flood; the elements would separate, then re-form in new combinations, until finally creation was to be restored. The divine seed would return to earth by way of a virgin, the first link in the chain that was to disseminate the divine race throughout the world. Vergil would later give

---

* On the coast of Campania; the modern Patria.

these myths poetic expression. Heaven would send a beneficent mediator, an emanation of the sun, a saviour, a providential monarch to restore a reign of peace and justice: "A
new progeny will descend from above."[10]

All these theories, linked by remote associations, infiltrated
Rome from faraway countries or reached her through the
lower strata of society. But they gave rise to unrest and spiritual longing among intellectuals also.

According to other speculations, once a nation had reached
its apex of grandeur, it could not remain at that height forever. The body politic would grow, mature, age, and eventually die, as is the common fate governing everything that is
born—of states and individuals alike.[11] In such moments of
expectant terror, prodigies multiplied. Statues sweated blood,
monstrous animals and children were born, the earth shook,
stones rained from the sky, fires broke out spontaneously.
Livy meticulously relates all the instances he had culled from
the annals. He was aware of the important role that religious
experience played in the period about which he wrote, and
he was sympathetic to it. He does not label the celestial
omens that affected the community as *prava superstitio* (de-
praved superstition), but as individual cases of mystic ecstasy.
An ox is supposed to have told a consul, "Rome, beware!"[12]
Exceptionally solemn rites were performed to placate divine
wrath and to protect the Republic from misfortune.

During the long periods of hostility, nuclei of anti-Roman
propaganda sprang up in the enemy countries—from Carthage to Pergamum and from Alexandria to Epirus. Rumors
were spread about the imminent downfall of a nation that
continued its relentless expansion. Mysterious connections
were established between political events and natural cataclysms. The earthquake during which the island of Thera
(modern Santorini) rose up from the Aegean Sea occurred in
the same year that the Romans defeated the Greeks at Cynos-

cephalae (197 B.C.). The sibyls immediately linked the two events: "Among the thunderclaps and the fiery jets that rise from the waves and hurl rocks, a nameless island will emerge; then the least brave will triumph over the valiant in a bitter struggle. . . ."[13]

The anathemas of impotent wrath that the Jews had hurled against Alexander and the kings of Syria, who first introduced the seeds of Western iniquity into their closed society, were again activated. Israel would repeat these same imprecations against the Romans—Pompey, Titus, Hadrian—the desecrators of her temples and her holy city. Later on, the Christians would mock their persecutors with the same inspired, scorching taunts.

When the Romans set foot as victors in the East, they felt themselves to be desecrators. Venerable deities dwelled in sanctuaries and grottoes, on the white summits of mountains that rose high above groves of olives and cypresses. And other divinities watched from the endless sparkling waves.

Macedonia did not constitute as great a threat as Carthage, but she was "more imposing because of the glory of her past kings, the ancient fame of her people, the number of the nations she had once conquered. . . ."[14] This comment indicates the psychological tension between Rome and the East, the Roman sense of uneasiness and inferiority that existed prior to open conflict. Faith in the right to rule other peoples is difficult to maintain when they continually boast of their cultural superiority. Philip of Macedonia, like Pyrrhus, was amazed by the order that reigned in the Roman camps, because he did not expect those "barbarians"[15] to be capable of such discipline.

The Romans lacked the psychological defenses to ward off this attack bred of derision and scorn. Just as omnipresent threats and continual misfortunes caused Israel to believe in her role as the "chosen people," so the influx of foreign influences forced the Romans to set themselves apart. They considered frugality, peasant solidity, the patriarchal tradition, and rough, severe manners not only as admirable but also as essential to the fulfillment of Rome's universal mission. Cato the Censor was among the first to claim that Roman ethical standards were unique and must be preserved intact. Under Augustus, this same thesis assumed a tenor of hagiographic solemnity: others, writes Vergil, may be able to sculpt or to scan the heavens, but the Romans alone bear the task of conquering the world and governing it by the laws of reason. Latin literati answered the sarcastic quips, the defamations, the baneful predictions by celebrating the virtues of the togaed race. They silenced the Greeks' braggadocio by comparing the prodigious Roman conquests with those of Alexander the Great.

In the course of the Macedonian wars, as the Romans marched along the routes that Alexander had followed, they learned about his deeds. The figure of Alexander, his curly, disheveled head tilted toward the sound of divine voices, towered luminously against the horizon. Alexander, the perennial object of hostility and admiration, was loathed by the Stoics because of his ambition, but emulated by the emperors because of the alluring message of universal harmony that he was alleged to have been the first to proclaim. In the light of this concept of a unifying theocracy, the Empire assumed a providential role, perhaps even compatible with the Greek philosophers' doctrines. Guided by that mirage, the Romans began to glimpse the wellspring of their dominion, to hope and devoutly wish that theirs would not be as short-lived as Alexander's.

Although its spheres of influence were extensive, the Republic did not yet admit to the designation of empire, but the surnames taken by its generals—Scipio Africanus and Scipio

Asiaticus—implied ambitions for world domination. And yet, when war was declared on Macedonia (215 B.C.), the populace revolted. Perhaps they were weary of fighting, or were prey to undefinable fears. At all the rallies, the centuries (early Roman units of one hundred voters, organized along military lines) voted against the war, while the tribune protested against the senseless urge to ask once again for the gods' support in extending Rome's boundaries. However, the consul explained that there was no alternative. Since aggression by Macedonia was imminent, a strike to block the threat was imperative. But when, in 191 B.C., Rome was preparing to move against Syria, its aim to expand into fabled lands was no longer rationalized. The goal was made explicit and the spirit, the mentality, necessary for world mastery was in the making. All the nations from Spain to the Red Sea were about to fall under the Roman yoke. All the world would pay homage to the nation that would exercise power "second only to the gods." Therefore the consul urged the Romans, "Prepare your souls to be worthy of this."[16]

It was a long war of fluctuating fortunes, alliances that were forged and then broken, betrayals, battles, setbacks—in short, all the characteristics of war. But this time, Rome coveted a prey that would neither figure among her war trophies nor be valued by its weight in gold. Titus Quintius Flamininus granted liberty to the conquered Greeks and refrained from imposing tributes, demanding recruits, or installing garrisons. He did not want gold. He only wanted the Greeks to admit that "therefore there does exist in this world a nation which, at its own expense, risk, and travail is willing to wage war in order to bring the gift of liberty to other peoples."[17]

The Romans, aware that they were dealing with nations that had centuries of history behind them and conscious also that they would be measured against those nations, drew on their own spiritual resources and established standards of virtue that were to remain uniquely theirs: frugality, valor in war, magnanimity toward the vanquished, endurance of hardship and discipline. Lost among so many and varied myths, dreams, and visions, Rome continued to refute the theory that all power is ephemeral and that only a god can bring equality and justice into the world. Rome instead pointed to the achievements of her ordinary citizens, endowed with mere human powers. She assimilated from the Greeks a cosmic vision and, at the same time, appropriated the civic virtues the Greeks had demonstrated when they stemmed the Persian threat from the East.

Rome willingly accepted the flattering myths that came from varied and remote sources. She took the story about the flight of the Trojan refugees to Italy and wove a legend around it to idealize her origins and to give her conquests the sanction of divine decree. Aeneas, the Trojan hero, had escaped the flames of Troy and had fled to Latium to become the founder of a stern, vigorous race. By choosing Italy as the site for a new, exemplary race, he was obeying divine orders and transferring the spirit of his city to Latium. Trojan blood therefore ran in the veins of the Roman conquerors. The gods who presided over the founding of Rome had a premonition of her future grandeur. The desertion of Dido foreshadowed the Carthaginian Wars. From Cato, Naevius, Varro, and Dionysius of Halicarnassus, the legend was passed down to Vergil, and acquired the status of a national dogma that was to live on throughout the ages.

As they established light but solid ties between the Eastern provinces and their empire, the Romans acted neither barbarously nor brutally. They were guided by a supernatural will; they faced a lofty task—that of building a race, not marble monuments, to serve as a guide and model to other nations. During the years when Titus Quintius Flamininus granted liberty to the Greeks and posed as the patron of the democratic *pòleis* against enemy kings, a confused, obscure legend was converted into a clear and luminous policy.

Not all the voices and not all the legends were reassuring. Ambiguous and disquieting omens arose in the interim between the victory of Cynoscephalae and that of Magnesia (197–190 B.C.), won on the plain dotted with temples that had been built by Cyrus and Artaxerxes. A prophecy of Daniel's made its way into the Roman milieu and was then passed down by historians and philosophers to Saint Jerome. This was Nebuchadnezzar's dream. The sleeping king saw a great image, his head of gold, his breast and arms of silver, his stomach and thighs of brass, his legs of iron, and his feet of iron and clay. Daniel interpreted this vision. He told the king that after the fall of his kingdom, others would follow, corresponding to the various parts of the image's body; thus their value would continually diminish. Once all the earthly kingdoms had perished, a new kingdom would be created, it would never be destroyed, or left to other people, and it would stand forever.[18]

Was this simply a metaphysical vision, or an allusion to everlasting dominion? Various hypotheses were offered. The Medes, the Persians, the Macedonians, the Carthaginians had successively ruled the world, but each had been displaced. The crucial question was who would govern the final kingdom, destined to last forever. Rome aspired to this position, and many authors granted her this right. They created fantastic myths with scrupulous accuracy in their details. Rhythmically scanned measures and symmetrical verses were arranged according to a rigorous chronology that corresponded to the centuries lost in the dark mists when Rome had no history. Each city destined to rule the world had to be founded in the same year that its predecessor fell. Thus, Rome was born the same year that Babylon fell.

Imposing Roman law on the vanquished nations was a long, bloody undertaking. As Roman rule became more severe, the conquered populations used prolonged guerrilla warfare, and eventually monothematic prophecies, to resist their oppressors. Since the Romans protected the rich and the *aristòi* (best people), resistance, whether armed or oracular, operated at the lowest social levels, where there were neither rhetoricians nor historians, but only visionaries. Uncouth, ragged men labeled the Romans greedy, lustful, violent, men whose power would be annihilated by a catastrophe; this iniquitous yet frail empire would be succeeded by one based on justice—messianic theories that Augustus tried to focus on Rome, and which became very widespread through Christian preaching; they had, however, been current as early as the second century B.C.

The prophecies concerned with the fall of Rome synthesized the tenacious aspiration to reverse the existing ethnic and social order. Since it seemed impossible to achieve this goal through human means, it became necessary to augur the advent of a flaming messiah, armed with an avenging sword; or the coming of one or another former enemy of Rome, mythicized historical figures, such as Alexander, restored to life, or Aristonicus, presumed to be the illegitimate son of the King of Pergamum, or Mithridates, or Mark Antony, or the mysterious child whom Vergil prophesied in the *Fourth Eclogue* as the harbinger of an era of peace, or the son of Mark Antony and Cleopatra, who had the doubly symbolic name of Alexander Helios, or, later on, even Nero, who was never believed to be dead and who was expected to return from Persia, where he was supposed to have taken refuge and whence he would come at the head of Parthian forces.[19] Those suffering under a wicked regime found solace in theories about the impending end of the world, its rebirth, or even its cyclical renewal.

From the second century B.C. to A.D. 410, when the Visigoths sacked Rome, there were varied but recurring types of prophecies based on chronology and numerology. Seven was the prophetic number for the Biblical writers. The seventh day was the day of rest, and represented the peace granted to the good as an eternal reward. At the end of the seventh millennium, the world was supposed to end, just as on the seventh day God had rested.

For the Romans, however, the magic number was twelve. The twelve vultures that Romulus saw supported the prophecy that the Empire would last twelve centuries or twelve millennia. There were the Twelve Tables of the law, the twelve months of the year, the twelve priests of Mars, the twelve *Fratres Arvales* (Arval Brothers) charged with celebrating the rites to ensure the earth's fertility, the twelve lictors who walked before the king, the twelve *ancilia* (shields that had been used by the Salii, priests of Mars; one had fallen from the sky and had been preserved for the city's safety, while the other eleven were simply perfect copies).[20]

One could say that as early as Romulus plowed his furrow to mark the boundaries of his city, the idea of the end arose. Some of the theories that subdivided time into regular periods originated in Etruscan circles. Of particular interest was the theory of the Great Year, which would last either 365 or 440 years. When this period expired, everything would begin anew, and only then would brotherhood reign and the lion lie down with the lamb. Given the difficulty in accurately establishing the advent of this new century, it was believed that the gods would provide a sign. Strange phenomena would certainly accompany or precede the revolving of the cycles, the end of a century, and the beginning of the next.[21] These moments of renewal and of expiation were solemnized with purification rites. At the conclusion of each cycle, creation began again with a new year, and this sequence was celebrated to affirm the rhythmic continuity of time. The *Ludi Saeculares* were instituted as a festivity, repeated every hundred years in order to assure the safety of the community for the successive century. To mark the end of each year, it was the practice to hammer a nail into the Temple of Jupiter.[22]

Periodic renewal was reassuring and helped overcome the obsession with the end. Cicero writes, "It will happen at some future time that all this world will burn with fire. . . ." "We are in the last age that the Cumaean Sibyl prophesied in her song," wrote Vergil, "and now the reign of Saturn will be renewed, and a new progeny will descend from above."[23]

The Romans, athirst for stability, were ensnared in these contradictory versions of the future. Just as a new planet is immediately caught up in the rotating motion of the cosmos, so Rome, once she had entered the orbit of history, was forced to trace the entire parabola without ever being able to return to her point of departure.

The Romans clung tenaciously to a few fixed points of reference. The Palladium, which Dardanus had personally brought to Troy, had symbolized protection for that city. Consequently, when Troy went up in flames, Aeneas saved the Palladium and carried it away with him to Italy. On the banks of the Scamander, it had represented the city's spirit. Wherever it went, it brought along its inherent vitality, which outlived the destruction of buildings and walls. As Demosthenes wrote, "I have not fortified the city with stones and bricks"; its strength lay instead in its spiritual cohesion. This concept came down through the centuries to Plotinus and Saint Augustine. "What do I care if a city falls," said the Bishop of Hippo when he heard the news that Rome had fallen; and he repeated the thought twenty years later, on his deathbed, as the Vandals were besieging his city: "A city does not consist of stones and beams but of citizens."[24]

Once in Rome, as in Troy, the Palladium became the warrant of the city's safety. "If you can save that celestial image," wrote Ovid, "you will save the city." Cicero defined the Palladium as "a sign from heaven."[25] The fire of Vesta, which never goes out, is reminiscent of the light of the stars; it, too, is an emblem and a warranty of everlasting duration.[26] The Capitoline rock (*Capitoli immobile saxum*),[27] which rises over the City and defies the passing of centuries, likewise symbolizes the continuity of the *urbs*.

These, then, were the prophecies, the myths and legends to which the poets gave artistic form after fifty years of civil wars had spread the belief that the end was imminent. When Antony proposed officially recognizing Cleopatra's empire, a proposal that threatened the myth of Roman ethnic superiority, the ideological counterattack was efficacious and coherent; but at the time of the Macedonian Wars, there were no writers like the later ones of Maecenas's inner circle. The Romans continued to ask uneasy questions about the legitimacy of their conquests and the purpose of their mission, and they felt obliged to answer all these interrogatives. Their tiny republic dominated the entire Mediterranean; but on the basis of what premises, and for what future purposes?

The broad new horizons opening up before them inevitably forced the Romans to break with their past. A cultured society, clearly influenced by the Greeks, was spreading new customs, different values, a courtly mode of life, a *humanitas* that was incompatible with their plain, primitive way of living. Cultivated Romans, sensitive to beauty and inclined to be benevolent, began to wonder if their rule actually fulfilled the designs of Providence, if their dominion was indeed the universal society for which the Stoics so longed.

It was not always easy for such men to reconcile an amiable character, the softness of peace, and the lofty ideas acquired from their contact with Greek thought and Greek people with their own harsh warrior fiber and their ancient sternness.[28] Culture implied *otium* (leisure), learned conversation, solitary meditation, and unproductive quiet. For the Romans, the supreme value was, instead, service to the nation, risk and hardship for the welfare of that city over which those rustic, frugal gods still watched as thin puffs of smoke rose from its houses.

The Greek Polybius was the first author to offer a rational explanation for the past and thus point to a definite direction for the future. He was a political exile. Along with about a thousand fellow citizens, he had been taken to Rome as a hostage after the defeat of the Macedonians at Pydna in 168 B.C. He spent many years in Rome. Because of the intellectual and social class to which he belonged, he was a guest of the Scipio family and a member of the Scipionic Circle. He wanted to explain how, in only fifty years, Rome had succeeded in winning the second and third Punic wars, three wars against Macedonia, others against Illyricum, Syria, and the Achaean and Aetolian leagues, while at the same time subduing Gallic insurrections along the Po Valley, crushing uprisings in Spain, and building roads, which still run through the Italian peninsula from north to south: the Flaminian, the Cassian, the Aemilian, the Domitian.

Observing his conquerors at first hand, he concluded that the best thing for the Greeks to do was to resign themselves to Roman rule. His reasons were based not so much on the often repeated view of Roman ethnic and political superiority, which might justify the subjugation of other peoples, as on those particular aspects of Roman institutions and customs that had favored the rise of that nation of shepherds and would continue to sustain its authority. In his universal vision of the future, the city emerged as an agent for unity: Roman discipline, cohesion, and frugality (virtues that, he maintained, were declining even when he wrote) had been the determining factors in her growth and would likewise determine her duration.

A question that has long bothered scholars is whether Polybius was really convinced that Rome alone would be saved from the fatal process of decay that threatens all living organisms. Though this conviction appears in some of his statements, in others he points to symptoms that foreshadow the end. He analyzes the existing institutions in their most elementary forms: monarchy, aristocracy, and democracy. He finds that they are all governed by an unfailing process of genesis, development, and decadence—the same that a botanist finds in plants and a biologist in cells. The first rudiments of justice induce men to create a king, who, when he exceeds the legitimate limits of the authority granted to him, is removed and replaced by the very men who have ousted him—that is, the *optimates*, or aristocrats. Their heirs, who have grown up as privileged individuals, become haughty and forget the responsibilities of their position; they in turn are thrown out and are replaced by a democratic government. And once again it is the younger generation that ruins everything. Born in a free regime, its members cannot appreciate the preciousnesss of equality and freedom of speech. They yield to violence and other excesses. They incite the masses: people are condemned, the land is divided, and the nation sinks into chaos. And only a new despot can stamp out this disorder (6.7).

In this way, the rotation of various types of government follows a natural process: governments rise, decline, fall, but all return to the original model. "Considering these premises (*i.e.*, the evolutionary process), anyone who wants to pronounce judgment on the future of nations may miscalculate the duration, but very rarely the evolutionary process of each single model and the pattern of succession. On the basis of this criterion, we shall now turn to consider the origin, the development, and the flowering of the Roman state and therefore its inevitable decay. Just as every state follows the dictates of this life cycle, so too will Rome fall, once she has passed through the two earlier stages of genesis and development" (6.9).

In Rome, however, the three institutions do not exist in pure form. Unlike what happens in other countries, they coexist, and this particular characteristic constitutes Rome's originality. The consuls, the Senate, and the Tribunes represent, respectively, the king, the aristocrats, and the people, and thereby exercise mutual control and moderation (*loc. cit.*). Degeneration is inevitable for a kingdom that lets itself decay into tyranny, for an élite government that transforms itself into an oligarchy, for a democracy that sinks into anarchy, because all organisms are subject to this order; it presides over their development in much the same way that the molecular structure of crystal follows an unalterable pattern. But the Roman definition of government is perfect in every respect, since it contains the best of the three fundamental institutions, and, therefore, like a good ship that can weather a storm, it will survive longer because of this balance among its internal components.

Though far from certain, this is the conclusion reached by an acute political observer who, as a foreign guest, was probably unwilling to express his most secret thoughts. This is the conclusion that he reached after a lengthy comparison between Rome and her vanquished enemies—Athens, Sparta, Crete, Carthage. The powers that have fallen constitute a clear majority.

Decline and fall are the themes ever present in page after page of his coldly narrated facts, building up, fading out. Scholars have tried to explain his contradictory judgments regarding Rome—namely, Rome will endure, but she, too, will be subject to decline. They have tried to date this dual judgment to see if they can find traces of afterthoughts, due perhaps to the influence of the Stoic Panaetius (a member of the Scipionic Circle) or to the revolution of the Gracchi.

They have looked for ideas or facts that may have induced a conservative like Polybius to stray from the optimstic predictions that he had developed in the patrician milieu of the Scipios. In the detachment from the community preached by the Stoics, or in the protests of the Gracchi, which enlisted support from pressure groups within the system, an acute observer like Polybius could not help reading the internal signs of disintegration, which, though remote, was nevertheless inevitable.

This conviction was further strengthened by the disturbing crescendo of corruption as the Romans began to import from Greece works of art, precious furnishings, as well as a vast array of human merchandise—mimes, dancers, musicians, cooks, slaves, doctors, and, most dangerous of all, philosophers—who brought in their wake hitherto unknown forms of refinement and vice. "The Romans," Polybius observed, "maintained their integrity until they crossed the seas to do battle, until they forgot the laws and customs of their ancestors" (18.35). The example of Greece, bitterly decried by a Greek in exile, had been unlucky for the Romans: "Some abandoned themselves to shameful love affairs, others to harlots; by now almost everyone went wild for the music, the banquets, and the luxury they learned to enjoy from Greece . . ." (32.11).

In Polybius's vision there is a human constant: "A state can perish because of two forces—internal or external" (6.57). The relaxation of customs represented the internal destructive force. It was all the more dangerous because of the false security in which the Romans wallowed after the destruction of Carthage and their victories in the east. "With Macedonia annihilated, Rome sensed that she had ensured her domination of the world . . ." (32.11). As Scipio Nasica[29] (Corculum) had predicted when he opposed Cato and his determined *Carthaginem esse delendam* (Carthage must be destroyed), peace, coming in the wake of terror, had weakened the fiber of the Roman people and had made them lazy. This observation reached Sallust through Posidonius and then became a cliché.[30] It appeared in a different guise when Polybius compared the Athenians to a ship's crew: discipline and harmony lasted as long as the storm threatened, but as soon as fair weather returned, the crew argued about the routes to be followed and refused to obey orders (6.44).

Polybius's declared intent was to narrate the facts that had led the Romans to build an empire, to investigate the causes and pinpoint the factors behind her rapid growth. But beneath his documented, objective work runs an undercurrent of other purposes and interests, revealing the questions put to this authoritative foreign guest by the Roman élite. He conveys to us the proud certainty of the ruling class, but at the same time its need to be reassured and prodded on to action. Polybius pointed to the Romans' outstanding qualities as the decisive factors for their succcess, yet he doubted that these qualities could survive the rise of new classes and amalgamation with new races. He did not fear declared opponents or external dangers, but, rather, indifference on the part of the citizens, criticism by the intellectuals, hedonism among the newly rich, lack of discipline in the army. A close-meshed net had held the Republic together, but it had to be stretched to fit Rome's new empire. Its mesh had been pulled so taut that in many places it was already ripped apart.

Polybius's observations indicate a direction but they fail to offer that theoretical basis which could both morally justify sovereignty and prophesy its duration. It was, instead, Panaetius and, later on, his pupil Posidonius who supplied the Romans with the answers. During an imaginary dialogue in the house of Scipio Aemilianus, Cicero had Laelius expound these arguments, which are borrowed from Aristotle: "Authority and subordination are not only inevitable but also useful states of affairs . . . the soul governs the body with the authority of a master, reason brakes the appetites . . . and the same holds true for mankind." *Ipse dixit* (he said this himself). Ever since the world began, obedience to the élite, according to the upper classes, has been supremely useful (*summa utilitate*) for the lower classes. Government rightfully belongs to the best, and therefore it is proper to bend to their will.[31] But if the justification for sovereignty presupposes moral superiority, it naturally follows that the former will inevitably decline as soon as its basis is weakened.

The principle that power belongs to the best is aristocratic, and postulates aristocratic deportment by those who govern. The cultured class in Rome recognized the importance of such a behavior model for itself and its superiors. An ethical code has been established of which no decalogue exists; however, from funeral eulogies and literary texts we can deduce its principles. Its sources were threefold: the Greeks, who in their turn had formulated a code of ethics in their polemics against the Persians; the social and economic organizations to which the *gente* belonged; and, finally, Stoicism, which had placed the stamp of its doctrinal authority on the austere precepts of the Roman code.

Polybius, and, later on, Titus Livy, believed that the aristocrats exemplified the illustrious virtues of the race. Scipio Aemilianus, head of the Scipionic Circle, is the invisible protagonist in Polybius's histories. Quite probably this historian, who had lived in the intimacy of the Scipio family for so many years, absorbed his host's point of view more than he influenced the formation and judgment of this brilliant young man, the son of Aemilius Paullus, adopted by the son of Scipio Africanus. Throughout Roman history, there are various cases of historians from vanquished nations supporting their conquerors: in the Augustan era, the Greek Dionysius;

under Titus, the Jew Josephus Flavius; and in the fourth century, the Antiochian Ammianus Marcellinus, who, under the influence of Julian the Apostate, expressed the spirit of pagan Rome in his writings.

Polybius recognized in his young friend the highest qualities of the Roman race: moderation, integrity, and valor,[32] character traits already on the wane. During Polybius's era, the bourgeois of the *municipia*, along with Cato the Censor, decried the rampant moral laxity, and in the next century— the last century of the Roman Republic—Marius, Cicero, Cato the Younger, and Sallust stepped forward as the supporters of these traditional values. These humbly born men defended the virtues of the patricians, who had created Rome's greatness, because they, too, viewed these values as part of their heritage. "The City," thundered Cato in 184 B.C., sixteen years before Polybius arrived in Rome, "suffers from two vices: greed and love of luxury; these are the two scourges that have dragged all great empires down to ruin."[33]

This general uneasiness was heightened by social ferment. Carthaginian prisoners and hostages held in Setia and Norma instigated the slaves to a revolt that could have had far-reaching consequences. Despite severely repressive measures, which included five hundred executions, another uprising broke out in Etruria.[34] Symptoms of an alarming lack of concern with the government's purposes are recorded in the pages of the historians. Roman deserters strolled through Carthage undisturbed, and left Hannibal's army only to enlist in the Macedonian one.[35] At the beginning of the expedition to Macedonia, two city legions were recruited to crush any eventual Italic secessions or revolts, since many of Rome's allies had sided with Hannibal in the first two Punic Wars.[36] The view of a united nation poised to conquer the world was a myth that needed many qualifications.

After the Roman victories, the Greeks and Asians were not satisfied with the "moderate liberty" Titus Quintius Flamininus, the victor of Cynoscephalae, had urged them to accept. The imagination of these subject peoples was inflamed by political theorists whose utopian expectations and visions of universal brotherhood recalled those previously projected by Iambulus* and Alexander. After proclaiming himself the son of King Eumenes of Pergamum, a certain Aristonicus declared war on Rome. His army of slaves, social outcasts, and malcontents faithfully supported him because he had promised that their reward would be the City of the Sun. This revolt, in effect an insurrection against a concrete historical, economic, and political reality, took the shape of a flight toward unreality, both as a doctrinary hypothesis and as a form of belief in the millennium. Blossius of Cumae, a former adviser to Tiberius Gracchus, went to fight for Aristonicus. He even died for this cause because the two young patricians, mouthpieces of those equalitarian principles that undermined the foundations of their own class, had spread such fear among the conservative senators that they had had recourse to special illegal measures to suppress them.[37]

The century preceding that of the end of the Republic was tense with revolutionary and innovatory ferment. Profound upheavals were maturing in the social structure and in the Roman spirit. Even before Marius called for plebeian volunteers, the army had begun to be proletarian in its composition. "These soldiers," said Tiberius Gracchus, "who are called the masters of the world, do not own even one square inch of land."[38] Once demobilized, they had to be recompensed. Economic demands were accompanied by ethical and metaphysical ones; but Polybius did not perceive them. He hoped

* Greek author of the third century B.C. who wrote a fantastic record of his travels in which he described a kind of communist utopia that later influenced Sir Thomas More.

that Rome would restore her vanished former customs and that men of the stature of the Scipios, with their *gravitas* (authority) and, above all, their social background would again head the government. Unlike his malicious compatriots, he did not view Rome's rise to fame as the workings of chance or fortune, but, rather, as the result of her inflexible determination. "The Romans wanted world hegemony and achieved that goal" (1.63; 1.3–4). When comparing the Carthaginians and the Romans, he attributed to both a lucid awareness of what was at stake—world power. Once the Romans had achieved world sovereignty, they found themselves in a precarious position: they had climbed to the top of the ladder and now could only go downward.

Polybius was moved to reconsider his conclusions seriously out of fear of the end. He posed as an impartial observer, a dispassionate narrator who gathered technical and quantitative data, who scrupulously recorded accurate information on persons and places for the purpose of making history a useful instrument for future soldiers and statesmen. And yet, he felt a compulsive desire to clarify the vicissitudes of Roman history, to ferret out its beginning, to unravel its enigma, to relive its successive phases in order to explain them to himself; but above all, to predict what would happen on the basis of what had already happened. The problem of every historian is not the past, but the future. His most profound emotion is one of dismay at the frailty of every work created by man. In fifty years, the Romans had unified the Mediterranean under their laws. During those very same years, nations with ancient traditions, famous kingdoms, and free republics had lost their autonomy and sovereignty. But did this inevitably imply that Rome, too, would fall?

This question weighed heavily on the Roman leaders. Polybius echoed their anxiety even when he pretended to explain only documented facts or to describe familiar itineraries, or when he compared the length of Roman spears and swords to Greek lances, or the actual space occupied by a legion in battle formation with that of a phalanx, or meticulously described the details of battles, sieges, religious and funeral ceremonies. Whoever studies Polybius's writings for his economic notations and technical details, present to a degree that is rare in ancient historiography, will perceive the author's secret distress behind the facts and figures, the secret torment of a conscience that questions the legitimacy of any domination, the duration of any empire, and considers the probability that certain phenomena in the past are destined to repeat themselves, the possibility that the laws he tried to deduce from these phenomena may be constant.

Behind his moralizing and schematic theses, Polybius gives a sense of the real concerns of the Scipios and their circle. In those episodes where these men played a role, they reveal a surprising historical consciousness: they knew they were living through hours decisive for the world's future. They fully realized that the outcome of all those battles would be an unprecedented empire for the victors (15.10), and yet they were afraid of offending the gods with such victories.

Such ideas dominated public opinion in those years. The warnings that the ambassador of the King of Syria voiced to Scipio reflected the sovereign's sentiments as well, perhaps, as those of the Romans who listened to him: "The Romans should be careful not to challenge fortune too openly and not to extend their dominion endlessly . . . let them be content with Europe. It is so vast that nobody thus far has ever succeeded in subjugating it completely . . ." (31.14).

The words of Aemilius Paullus, riding the crest of victory after the defeat of King Perseus at the battle of Pydna, represent another variation on the theme of the frailty of human ventures. All around Paullus's tent gathered an immense crowd, curious to witness the humiliation of Perseus, that

proud monarch who, though a descendant of Philip and Alexander—"the men who had made Macedonia the greatest empire in the world"—came silently and in mourning to beg
mercy from his Roman conquerors. Paullus severely reprimanded him in Greek and then, turning to his troops, said in
Latin, "Here you see an outstanding example of the tran-
siency of all things human. I am speaking to you who are
young: conceit and arrogance are not befitting to the victor,
who should never take his fortune for granted, since nobody
can tell what will happen the very same night. . . ."

Both Polybius, who was a firsthand witness of the vicissitudes of this period, and Livy, who lived through the Augustan
era, sensed in those years the anxiety about death appearing
like a shadowy crack in the Roman wall of security. Syra-
cuse fell to the Romans in 213 B.C. after a three-year siege.
From a hill, Marcellus gazed down on what was perhaps the
most beautiful city of the time, and before the imminent massacre, in which Archimedes lost his life, "it is said that he
[Marcellus] wept, because of joy at having completed such
an enormous undertaking, but also because of the city's venerable glory. . . ."

Scipio Aemilianus, remembering perhaps his father's words
when Perseus surrendered, burst into tears when he ended the
Punic Wars and saw Carthage in flames. According to the
interpretation of a later historian, perhaps Scipio was thinking
of the legendary city of Troy, also destroyed by fire. But the
victorious Romans, in the opinion of their contemporary
Polybius, had a premonition that someday the same lot would
befall Rome.[39] Though tears may seem incongruous in a victorious commander who came from a merciless race, they
were consistent with his thoughtful approach to the tran-
siency of all human creations. Legend has it that when Scipio
was censor, he modified the formula of the public prayer that
besought the gods to enlarge the Republic; "It is large enough

as it is," he is reported to have said, "let us rather pray that the gods preserve its safety forever."[40]

In that withdrawn youth, who confessed to Polybius his feelings of alienation because he eschewed the oratorical competitions in the forum, we can catch a glimpse of the need to reconcile power with the ideal of justice; only on those terms could power endure. This meant a search for a reason behind history, and, therefore, in existence. Polybius's attempt to extract a norm from the tumultuous and incoherent reality around him reflects the religious and ethical problems of a century in which the fortunes of the individual and of nations were held in precarious balance: "You can see that the divine darts always strike the tops of the tallest trees. . . ."[41]

The Latin
Historians

As one reads the noble prose of the historians Sallust, Livy, and Tacitus, it is evident that despite a common matrix in Greek thought, despite their fidelity to stylistic models that cast situations and characters into stereotypes, each of the three has his own unmistakable tone. But underlying their measured phrases is the same echo of a secret fear.

They are timeless authors, pillars marking the boundaries of our own uncertain conceptual territories. Like us, they lived in periods of violence when traditional values were declining. Critical epochs in human affairs caused them to question themselves about the underlying reasons for these upheavals. Their insight into the social problems was ethical rather than political, a response based on the proud and absolute conviction that the past history of Rome was unique, that the men who lived under the stern, frugal regime of the City's early days were endowed with incomparable qualities.

That disdainful ethnocentricity had been crystallized into

axioms. It had helped the Romans overcome their insecurity in the early years, and accept their sovereignty as a mission. Though they occasionally deplored the methods necessary to exercise power, they never questioned the validity of their task.

Beneath the drapings of their togas they hid the vulnerability of men who, while deploring the conduct of their society, realized that they were not exempt from its faults or relieved from concern about its future. The more anxiously they examined the present, the more meticulously they scrutinized the future and its innumerable pitfalls. Finally they turned to the past as an exemplary yardstick by which to measure human action. The deeds of their ancestors no longer were confined to the simple realm of historical fact, but were seen to embody the idea of Rome, and their acts of courage and their dignity as free men were transformed into an ideal code of behavior just as the repertory of proportions characteristic of classical art became the golden rules from which the artistic canons of future generations were derived.

In the pages of these three historians, history unfolds against the background of an immense geographical area. However, its true province lies within the spiritual boundaries of Rome; the Empire is a private inheritance, which the forefathers had labored to amass and then passed down to their degenerate heirs. These writers had a humanistic view of history—events are determined by individuals, by their fidelity to or betrayal of established principles. They raised Roman history to a paradigm and sublimated its protagonists into symbols of lofty virtues or crass vices.

No hope sustained these historians. No celestial city rose as a viable alternative to the horrors of the era in which they lived. No political faith permitted them to forecast a better future. We, who also are unaccustomed to looking for supernatural solutions to the contradictions that beset us, who have experienced the failure of utopias, can easily identify with those lonely, farsighted ancients. The history of antiquity offers us no escape from the present, but it allows us to see contemporary problems against a millenary backdrop.

Common themes underpinned the work of these three writers: the Empire, the interpretation of its formative process, its possible duration, its historical function, and obligation: *Porro unum est necessarium* ("Looking ahead, one thing is necessary"). These are the themes common to all three writers but each views them from his own perspective. Sallust, a witness and participant in the civil wars, identified the causes for decline in this fratricidal strife. Livy pointed to the abandonment of those ancient virtues that, in his opinion, had sparked Rome's beginnings. Tacitus examined the crises in the imperial government and in the provinces; he identified internal despotism and poor colonial management as the primary factors behind Rome's disintegration.

These historians share the widespread conviction, so prevalent in today's society, that everything is on the verge of collapse. They observed a civilization on the brink of bankruptcy, overextended externally and internally torn. They wondered if ethics, political customs, and religion, so diffused and stretched beyond the purposes they were intended to serve, could withstand the strain. They questioned whether a culture could survive when ethnic and social groups break down the barriers that segregated them in order to adopt and at the same time dispute the premises on which that culture rests. Like seismographers, Sallust, Livy, and Tacitus measured the degrees of instability in Roman society and communicated to each other the warning signals; they are the ancient sentries who from their promontories alerted one another with signal fires to the impending dangers of storms and pirate ships, discerned in the distance, beyond the roar of the breakers and the gleaming waves.

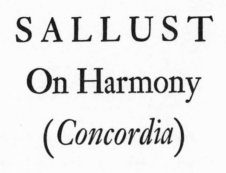

SALLUST

On Harmony

(*Concordia*)

B. C.: *Bellum Catilinae* (*The War with Catiline*)

B. J.: *Bellum Jugurthae* (*The War with Jugurtha*)

EP. AD CAES.: *Epistulae ad Caesarem senem* (*Letters to Caesar*)

EP. MITHR.: *Epistula Mithridatis* (*Letter of Mithridates*)

Oh sons, do not accustom your souls to such gigantic wars; do not turn such mighty forces against the father-land.[1]

—Vergil *Aeneid* 6. 832–833

The cause of all these evils was the desire to rule which greed and ambition inspire, and also, springing from them, the factiousness characteristic of party men.

—Thucydides 3. 82. 8

The scanty information we have concerning Sallust comes from later, hostile sources. We can find mention of him in openly defamatory works: an invective written by one of Pompey's freedmen, one attributed to Cicero.[2] Therefore, the selection of sources is risky. Nevertheless, it is important to locate Sallust within his age and environment. The key to any historian is to be found in the internal motivations and external pressures that cause him to reflect on certain events at the outset of his research.

Sallust's work reflects his reactions to events he had lived through and people he had met. He used these details as a springboard for broader considerations on human nature. Only in poverty and danger, he maintains, does man retain some of his intrinsic value; however, once he has tasted power and wealth, the most shameful aspects of his nature come to the fore.

Through Sallust, the Roman spirit took stock of itself,

identified itself with Cato's and Metellus's ancient morality and Caesar's pioneering vision. And perhaps the question arises whether it might not have been better had the City remained poor, obscure, and lusterless, rather than reach its height at the cost of so many lives.

Mala ambitio—ambition, an evil counselor—lured Sallust into politics upon his arrival in Rome from Amiternum, where he had been born in 86 B.C. These years were a period of uncertain truce between wars. The struggle between Marius and Sulla had just ended, and the rivalry between Caesar and Pompey would soon begin. Politics meant the readiness to abandon all scruples, all principles, and even all friendships, accepting compromises, blackmail, and even violence.

Inexperienced or rash, as the case may be, Sallust soon joined the ranks of those destitute, unprincipled, reckless nobles who populated Rome. Clodius, who could be correctly considered a typical example of that milieu, was perhaps a more enigmatic figure to his contemporaries than to later scholars. It was Clodius who, disguised as a woman, dared to enter Caesar's house during the secret rites that the matrons celebrated in honor of the Good Goddess (*Bona Dea*). Acquitted by a bribed court, Clodius then arranged to have himself adopted by a plebeian so he could run for the post of tribune, an office from which he was barred by his patrician lineage. Clodius was the type of aristocratic déclassé who could have been numbered among Catiline's accomplices. He was capable of rousing the rabble as long as power was at stake.

After the Tribune Milo had Clodius assassinated in a street fight at election time in 56 B.C., Sallust must surely have seen his naked body, exposed in the Forum so that the people could count all the wounds, while his wife screamed hysterically. And, on the Ides of March of 44 B.C., he probably saw the three slaves who, in icy silence, carried away Caesar's body, wrapped in a bloody toga. These were experiences that leave their mark.

In 54 B.C., Sallust was quaestor. Crassus, then proconsul in Syria, was planning his campaign against the Parthians, which ended in the catastrophe of Carrhae, one year later. Perhaps that event caused Sallust to reflect bitterly both on Roman misgovernment in the provinces and on the Parthian threat. We can find echoes of these two fears in his *Epistula Mithridatis* (*Letter of Mithridates*, to the King of the Parthians).

Sallust was tribune of the people in 53 B.C., but was expelled by the Senate in 50, on charges of immoral conduct. Caesar, however, reinstated him, with several military positions: in 47, he gave Sallust the praetorship, and in 46 made him governor of the new African province of Numidia, where the Jugurthine War had been fought sixty years earlier. He was accused of extortion at the expense of the local population and was arraigned on this charge. Once again it was Caesar who rescued Sallust, though this time it would appear that compensation was involved. Ironically enough, Caesar had done the same for Catiline twenty years earlier.

Sallust therefore knew all the secret levers of politics, all its connivances, and all its tortuous intrigues. He had ample occasion to ascertain the instability of a state that was not, however, as in his simplistic scheme, split between plebeians and patricians. This traditional division no longer reflected the far more complex social realities. The nobles, who were also the large landowners and the exclusive holders of public offices, still dominated the government; at the same time, the knights (*equites*), entrepreneurs, industrialists, financiers, tax collectors, builders, and merchants wielded considerable influence. Cicero would have liked to see this group flank the patricians, thereby forming a strong right-wing coalition; but more often than not, their interests were in conflict. Then there was the middle class, formed of petty-bourgeois landowners who were opposed to the claims of extremists and patricians alike. The army, which had, by then, become a permanent institution, was composed primarily of poor men. It was a hatchery for potential dictators, since the military, always eager for swift gain, supported anyone who favored them. There was a disproportionately high unemployment rate because the labor market had been saturated by the huge influx of slave labor. There were also the victims of confiscations and expropriations, impoverished aristocrats, frustrated or ruined politicians. The illiterate subproletariat survived as best it could on free-food distributions and welfare, and by means of prostitution and thievery. All these men were potential cutthroats, and all were weighed down by debts and harassed by usurers.

> No nation remains that we must fear . . . except ourselves and civil war.[3]
> —Cicero *Catilinariae Orationes* 2. 5. 11

Though Sallust could observe the protagonists of his era from a close range, not a single one made a positive impression on him. Each confirmed his pessimistic conviction that virtue gradually but inevitably deteriorates into vice under the corrosive influence of gold and power: love of glory sinks into a craving for publicity, an honest divergence of opinion is twisted into factiousness.

Only Cato and Caesar seemed to him worthy of admiration, perhaps because the author identified with them. The ambiguity of Sallust's judgment on them reflects the complexity of his spirit, not the uncertainty of his political choices. He let Cato and Caesar speak in a remarkable passage. These two men stood apart, isolated from the scum of profiteers and thugs that proliferates in moments of crisis. They almost seemed to demonstrate that Rome, though prostrate, could still breed sons equal to their forefathers. They represented a contrast that is not opposition between two parties; but, rather, the conflict between two types of human nature and two different ethical concepts.

The accusations of immorality and illicit enrichment hurled against Sallust seem incompatible with the puritanical disdain that pervades his works—a disdain that is, perhaps, dictated by hypocrisy or even by the presumption of a man who feels it unnecessary to make his conduct match his ideology. In the eyes of many critics, this ambiguity is strident in Sallust's harsh, sententious prose. To soften these accusations, it is only just to point out that political and forensic rhetoric abounds in more defamatory passages than Sallust's. Cicero charged Verres, Clodius, Piso, and Antony with ferocious, base crimes. Before Catiline had become the state's enemy and while he was a mere contestant in the 64 B.C. elections, Cicero publicly announced that Catiline was, in effect, the husband of his own daughter because of an affair he had had with the girl's mother, years before. Cicero also reported that after a Celtic platoon under Catiline's command had executed Marius Gratidianus, one of Sulla's political adversaries, Catiline walked through the city carrying the severed head in his hand.[4] Sallust skimmed over such obscenities and atrocities when he drew his concise, vigorous profile of this historical figure.

That Sallust had accumulated immense wealth is beyond doubt; the gardens of his villas would cover entire sections of modern Rome. After the death of his protector, Caesar, in 44 B.C., he retired to private life and devoted himself to his studies. For a retired public figure, history is the only substitute for politics. Reconstructing facts in conformity with one's principles and with one's frustrated hopes is the only way to continue the struggle. The declarations of impartiality that appear in the foreword of every historical work should make one wary of how tendentious eyewitness records are. In Sallust's time, however, the *otium* (leisure) of the intellectuals was still judged by many to be the sterile pastime of loafers. Therefore, Sallust wanted both to justify himself and to vindicate the dignity of his works: these, too, represented a service to the fatherland. He pleaded that history was his real vocation, that his temperament was more suited to meditation than to action. He even proclaimed that history had an educational function: "The State will draw greater profit from my inactivity than from others' activity" (*B. J.* 4.4).

Because of the very fact that he lived in an epoch of crises and was fully cognizant of it, he preferred focusing his research and meditation on these events rather than being their protagonist. Weariness and clairvoyance inhibited his desire to be a participant: what was the purpose of engaging in a race where less qualified men would emerge victorious? "It is pure folly to work to no advantage and to labor only to engender hatred . . ." (*B. J.* 3.1–4). Everything that surrounded him was rotten. He repeated a thousand times that the patrician oligarchy exercised power it did not know how to manage. But the men from the left, like himself, were not any better: their humanitarian slogans and their innovative programs hid their crass desire to snatch the lucrative positions: *furtim et per latrocinia* (by intrigue and fraud) (*B. J.* 4.7).

> . . . other enemies are within her walls, inside the very heart of Rome.
> —Sallust, *Bellum Catilinae* 52. 35[5]

Sallust chose recent events: the war against Jugurtha, the Numidian king who, after having murdered his two cousins, usurped the throne. The war lasted from 111 to 105 B.C. and was fought at the insistence of the left and against the judgment of the aristocrats in the Senate. After various failures by patrician commanders—except Metellus, who opened the way to victory for his successor—the conflict was finally decided in Rome's favor by Marius, the "popular" consul, the simple citizen from Arpinum who had risen from the ranks to become a top commander. Sallust's second monograph deals with an internal war: the *coup d'état* Catiline had prepared in 66 B.C., which ended in the execution of his accomplices in the Mamertine prison and his own death in battle, in 63. Catiline, an impoverished noble and former follower of Sulla, put himself at the head of a group of desperadoes in an attempt to overthrow the patrician oligarchy and establish a dictatorship by the extreme left.

In the two episodes that Sallust chose to examine in his monographs, some experts see the historian's desire to vent his hatred for a political class that had left him out in the cold, and to accuse it of ineptitude and venality. In my opinion, however, his criticism has a much broader base. Perhaps the Senate would have done well to take a firmer stand against the Numidian usurper and to keep watch over Catiline's subversive intrigues from the outset. But Sallust does more than criticize the Senate's behavior in these particular instances; he challenges the entire system, and in particular the party politics which forced opponents to lose sight of the ultimate goal that history had imposed upon Rome—namely, governing the empire. It was not a matter of wrangling over *who* would govern, but *how* it should best be done. The factiousness and growing bitterness of the political struggle produced a waste of vital energies and an erosion of trust among the Romans.

The Jugurthine War and the Catilinian conspiracy were, far more than patrician misgovernment, symbolic of the social malaise, the economic discomfort, and the moral decline that, in Sallust's opinion, had started with the fall of Carthage in 146 B.C. As soon as the enemy threat had disappeared, ambition and greed became rife, and created rifts. When the Gracchi made their first requests for more equitable land distribution, the Senate refused to allow even token concessions and instead toughened its already myopic conservatism. Convictions, exile, and every kind of iniquity followed (*B. J.* 42.4; *B. C.* 6–13). The incontrovertible duty of properly exercising power was forgotten, and men competed simply to secure power. In this light, civil war was the prelude of discontent in the provinces and other future uprisings, like the one led by Mithridates in Asia Minor.

Sallust linked the beginning of moral decline and lack of military discipline to the civil wars: he traced the first as far back as 146 B.C., and the second to Sulla's Asian campaigns, which ended in 62 B.C. (Other writers see the seeds of decline a full century earlier.) Sallust's purpose was undoubtedly to emphasize the ominous effects of wealth on the national conscience. In other eras, the Romans had "defeated huge armies with their tiny legions," whereas, after their recent victories, "greed generated pride, cruelty, neglect of the gods and total materialism" (*B. C.* 7.7; 10.4).

Sallust pronounced these judgments in a severe, melancholy tone, reminiscent of Cato. The nervous spareness of his prose contrasts sharply with Cicero's long, flowing sentences and metric cadences. In order to interpret the spirit of the *majores* (ancestors), Sallust adopted their vocabulary and their style. The formal side of his work reveals his inner conflicts: Sallust was a man of the people, a follower of Caesar, a "new man" (*homo novus*) who had come to Rome from a small Italic municipality and had no ancestors of consular rank to boast about. He belonged to that rising provincial bourgeoisie which, under Augustus, would oust the patricians. Marius, and Cicero before him, men from this same class, reveal the same inferiority complex and the same frustrations.

And yet, deep down, Sallust was a conservative who respected the ethical code of the aristocratic milieu, but, like the others, he was unable to formulate a new substitute. He was Italic, yet, at the same time, passionately devoted to Rome. He was a divided man, anxious and ambivalent in his reactions, tormented by his failure to disengage himself from a moral and political tradition, his inability to define the state in new terms. Except for the two *Epistulae ad Caesarem senem (Letters to Caesar)** in which he proposed a few reforms, he never pointed to people or classes that could undertake the task of re-establishing the state on a new basis. He always wrote *against,* never *for.* Though relentless in his harangues against groups wielding aristocratic power, he also criticized the social climbing and demagogy of his own social peers, and refused to back the proposals of the extremists in their attempts to oust groups with patrician economic power. He repeated Catiline's theses and arguments, which often coincided with his own views, or those formulated by the tribunes of his party, with the same words and the same indignation. Yet, Catiline was an enemy of the state and, for that reason, should be suppressed. Not for one moment did Sallust fail to respect private property, an attitude typical of a man coming from the country. He had a love of the law that was second nature to anyone who had attended the Roman schools, and a profound lack of respect for the masses—people, he wrote, of loose morals and who were violent and incapable of solidarity or cohesion *(Ep. ad Caes. 2.5).*

The hope for a supreme ruler who would bring about harmony among the social classes and resolve the contrasts is tacit, never explicit, in the two letters to Caesar—provided Sallust actually wrote them. The author, whoever he may be, made the typical requests of his day and proposed the very measures that Caesar later adopted. The latter fact seems to support the suspicion that these two letters may be patchwork jobs, compiled at a later date, or propaganda circulars, authorized by the dictator.

Their author, however, quite obviously reflected the views

---

* These letters were found without any author's name in a Vatican codex, and the debate on their authenticity has not yet been resolved.

of the democratic left. He is in favor of strict moral standards, civil order, and the elimination of any form of power monopoly. Wealth should not be a prerequisite for political power; the magistracy should be open to all citizens; the Senate should be rejuvenated with new men; the secret ballot should be abolished. He proposed that the urban proletariat, a serious threat to order and property, be scattered throughout new colonies and thereby integrated with peoples of different origins. Any subversive, once removed from Rome and set up in a comfortable little farm of his own, was bound to turn conservative.

By and large, Caesar enacted these reforms. In 49 B.C., Roman citizenship was extended to freedmen living beyond the Po, and to many Spaniards, Gauls, and Greek professional men living in Rome. The privilege of wearing the *laticlavium* (*i.e.*, a tunic with purple borders, worn by senators and members of their families) was extended to the non-Roman élite. At the same time, an Italian proletarian beachhead was created in Spain, Egypt, and Gaul: those colonies, made up of veterans and former slaves, were then granted the *ius italicum* (Italic law). To reduce the hordes of parasites that thronged the City, Caesar drastically cut the welfare program and imposed a limit on the number of slaves who worked the large farms. All these measures had previously been proposed by the Gracchi.

> One of the pillars of society and of the City is that private
> property remain both free and safe.[6]
> —Cicero, *De Officiis* 2. 22. 78

Caesar carried out these reforms with the utmost prudence, and kept a careful watch over both the masses and the property owners. After his victory over Pompey, he was distrusted in conservative circles. He was not expected to repeat the excesses of Sulla's regime but many feared he might enact the radical measures previously proposed by Catiline since in their view he had supported that conspiracy. The most serious measure would have been the abolition of debts. The reasons why many hoped for this abolition were sadly yet firmly expounded by Manlius, one of Catiline's followers, in a letter that Sallust might have underwritten (B. C. 33.1). In violation of ancient laws, the urban praetor, who was a reactionary, had imposed expropriation and even prison sentences on insolvent debtors. Caesar decreed that any interest already paid could be subtracted from the amount owed. This decision eased the debtors' position, and yet it did not completely cancel the public indebtedness,[7] which would have been tantamount to total expropriation, so far as the creditors were concerned. In Cicero's opinion, this had been part of Caesar's plans ever since he had plotted in Catiline's shadow. Worse still, the insecurity of one's private wealth would have weakened one of the fundamental principles of the state.[8]

In concluding, the author of the two letters appeals to Caesar for clemency, the virtue that most distinguished Caesar, especially during the civil war. In a letter dated 49 B.C., Caesar declared that he intended to exercise clemency and had no intention of following Sulla's punitive example.[9] Cicero praised Caesar's mercy, and Vergil hinted that it was perhaps a supernatural gift, that Anchises inspired him to adopt this attitude, so rare in the political battles of the day. When the old Trojan recognized Caesar's spirit in the Elysian Fields, centuries before his birth, he said, "You, blood of my blood, who are descended from the Olympian race, must forgive, and be the first to lay down your arms."[10]

Full of contempt, bitterness, and denial, Sallust's works lack a coherent line of thought. This explains why historians still subject him to a third-degree interrogation; they demand that he account for his work; they investigate his intentions.

While some critics define him as a partisan author or a mouth-piece for the proletariat, others maintain that he had been so corrupted by Caesar that he was forced to write a history of the conspiracy in order to exculpate Caesar from the recur-ring accusation of having been Catiline's accomplice. On the basis of a vulgar *Invective against Cicero*, attributed to Sallust, as well as his faint praise of Cicero's merits, other critics believe that the historian recalled the conspiracy, which had occurred during Cicero's consulship, to demonstrate the flimsiness of Cicero's alleged action in defense of the existing institutions.

As far as the history of the Jugurthine War is concerned, many scholars feel that Sallust's sole purpose was to glorify Marius, who was Caesar's uncle and his ideal precursor. Like Sallust, Marius was a *homo novus*, coming from the Italic provinces, and had risen to the consulship in spite of patrician opposition. Other historians label Sallust a cryptoconservative and are convinced that his real idol was Cato. Few indeed judge him on the plane of pure thought, or view him as a detached historian and patriot, rather than a libelist. Finally, some critics see him as a man of letters, intent upon writing for writing's sake.

The variety of arguments supporting these different theses demonstrates not only the ingenious skills of the philologists, but also the impenetrability of this great author, who may best be defined as obscure—and therefore unclear even to himself.

The web of our life is of a mingled yarn.
—Shakespeare, *All's Well That Ends Well*, IV, iii, 83

I should like to offer a different hypothesis—namely, that all these theses are partly true, and that we find in Sallust various contradictory tendencies. One can favor proletarian economic claims without subverting the state. One can hope for the renewal of society and the abolition of privileges without denying a tradition that has taken on perennial ethical values. One can, without abdicating one's supremacy, condemn colonial exploitation, which, aside from economic profit and national prestige, was viewed as Rome's historical duty, her civilizing mission. In Sallust, the theme of the *Empire* prevails over all the others. Social reforms, economic claims, power struggles, class wars could all be considered positive examples of the mode of life of a free people, provided they did not interfere with the fulfillment of Rome's primary duties—that is, the defense and administration of the provinces. On Sallust's scale of priorities, internal politics came second to world government. The realization of a new social stability, based on the overthrow of existing hierarchies, was a hypothesis viewed only as a utopian dream.

It is important to judge Sallust in this light. In the first place, he must be rehabilitated from the biased judgments that distort his character and falsify its dimensions. Then he must be judged independently of what happened after his death: specifically, the victory at Actium, Augustus's life term as prince, the Pax Romana through the ancient world. These are events that certainly would have altered Sallust's judgments, had he only been able to foresee them.

To imprison a man in a single stance, or to apply the criteria of our times to his is antihistorical. The traits of character and class attributed to Sallust are undoubtedly his, but they did not compel him to assume a position of intellectual coherence. Beyond their role in his life, they formed part of his spiritual make-up; they were present, but not determining. He was Italic, bourgeois, pro-Caesar, democratic, but in the face of the imminent Italic triumph over the social and doctrinary forces from the East, perhaps he felt that these traits were outmoded.

Maybe he acted for personal gain, or out of doctrinal conviction, or merely to serve the purposes of rhetoric, when he
labeled the agitators' humanitarianism as simple lust for
power. The Roman Senate had always looked askance at such
men. Take the example of Manlius Capitolinus, who had supported the poor and therefore was pushed off the Tarpeian
Rock six years after he had defeated the Gauls on that very
spot, or of Tiberius Gracchus. The low standards of the mob,
the overt ambition and arrogance of its exponents, did not
encourage the Senate to risk the stability of the Empire for
the sake of a proletarian revolution. Such a revolution seems
hypothetically plausible to those modern historians who judge
the ancients with their current ideological yardsticks, but in
Sallust's day, the situation was different.

It is only fair to believe Sallust, to recognize that his devotion to the Republic was not an alibi or a mask to cover up his
fear of imminent social collapse. If he joined in the condemnation of those extremists—many of whose demands,
however, he thought valid—this does not imply that he
wanted to hide his own revolutionary inadequacies under a
cloak of patriotism. It must be remembered that the loathing
he felt for that *dominatio* (dictatorship) which is inevitably
born of proletarian revolution had a long tradition in Greek
and Roman thought.

For a spirit like Sallust, who craved the absolute, revolution
was only sterile, murky confusion, a profane reality as against
the sacred cosmos resting on lasting values, the most basic of
these being veneration of the Republic. The modern historian
with a sense of professional and moral honesty cannot judge
Sallust's scale of values in the light of current criteria. Sallust
had different values, which made him prefer certain transfor-
mations over others in the *res publica*. But this should not be
considered as an example of bad faith.

Any motives that might have induced him to write tenden-

tious works had already disappeared. They had been supplanted by deeper worries and by preoccupations of wider
significance.

Sallust started writing in 44 B.C. and died nine years later, in
35. These years witnessed the conflict between Octavian and
Antony—a world conflict that involved mighty ethnic forces
and major ideological trends. The political struggle had swol-
len to such dimensions that being a follower of Caesar rather
than of Pompey no longer mattered. Cicero had already died,
and the nobility of his death had redeemed the vanities and
compromises that had sullied his life. Why stain his memory?

In the two episodes that Sallust chose for his two monographs, he pointed to the symptoms that sparked the two
great conflicts of his era. The Jugurthine War had brought to
light the conflicting interests between the middle classes and the
patricians—the former, the expansionists who favored increas-
ing investments in the provinces; the latter, the abstentionists
who, like all conservatives, were opposed to risks of every
kind. Marius was the leader and the mouthpiece of the former, while the patricians, a little later, supported Sulla's right-
wing dictatorship. The civil war that followed "upset every
divine and human law, and reached such a point of frenzy
that civic discord ended in war and the devastation of Italy"
(B. J. 5.2.)

Catiline's conspiracy, on the other hand, had demonstrated
the presence of other dangerous forces in Roman society—
forces, though still scattered, that were more numerous and
frightening than the Italic bourgeoisie. Unprincipled rabble
rousers could count on this support as they struggled to gain
power. It was imperative to nip these forces in the bud and to
try to satisfy, within limits, their demands if that single yet
sovereign mission which weighed on Rome's leaders was to be
accomplished: to govern the world with justice. This is the
peremptory injunction that echoes through Sallust's writ-

ings—all political competition may be considered legitimate provided it does not deflect from this goal.

> It is therefore true: fate has been unkind to the Romans who have been guilty of fratricide ever since Remus's innocent blood, a curse to his descendants, was spilled on the ground.[11]
>
> —Horace *Epodes* 7. 18–21

If we want to take psychological factors into consideration, then who can prove that Sallust did not project his own situation on the vicissitudes of the Roman state? He condensed, in his brief life span, the various phases that Rome had experienced over the centuries. He could measure the corrupting force of money, power, and pleasure in terms of his own experience of vice in the metropolis.

The years he dedicated to his historical meditations were years of inactivity, perhaps even isolation. In his splendid residence on the Pincian Hill, he had no future, except that of an old age without friends or glory. It was, therefore, the right moment for him to arrange his personal experiences in a systematic design so as to give meaning both to his past and to history. He had tasted the fleeting pleasures of success and power, and now grasped at literature as his last chance to gain eternal fame.

He undoubtedly thought about the place where he had been born: a harsh, desolate land where patches of snow still cling to the arid slopes even when the spring air is heavy with the scent of broom, thyme, and wild sage. The work in the fields is hard, and the harvests meager. He may have imagined life in the simple village that was to become Rome to have been similar to that of his birthplace, with its rustic setting and frugal habits. The cruel, opulent city that swarmed at his feet had, once upon a time, been a mixed community of Latins and Trojans: however, men different in race, unlike in speech, and of alien customs "were merged with incredible facility from that roving, heterogeneous band into a commonwealth through harmony" (*B. C.* 6.2).

Harmony—the word rings throughout Sallust's pages; it evokes painful responses, the longing, the frustrated hopes of the author who was born and lived during the civil wars. In one of the surviving passages from the *Histories*, he quotes the Consul Lepidus as saying to the Quirites (ancient Romans in their quality as citizens): "You have beheld even human sacrifices and tombs stained with the blood of citizens" (*Oratio Lepidi* 1.15).

As a child, Cato had seen the outlaws' heads displayed in Sulla's house. Cicero recalled five civil wars in fifty years[12] and as many outbursts of savage ferocity, all linked by a continuous chain of vendettas and reprisals. Each time political leaders competed for power, the excesses committed during the previous struggle were remembered. Sulla, who suffered from character assassination immediately after his death, became the bloody monster whose ruthless shadow still loomed over the City. According to Cicero, Catiline summoned him up from the nether regions. When the hostilities broke out between Caesar and Pompey, it was expected that one or the other would behave like Sulla. "*Sullaturit*," says Cicero of Caesar—he will behave like Sulla—a word that evoked atrocious memories and revealed a disheartened pessimism about human nature.[13]

To a man of Sallust's era, discord did not appear as a fleeting episode, but, rather, as a congenital vice in the human race, a curse that was transmitted from father to son—Cain and Abel, Eteocles and Polynices, Romulus and Remus. Fratricide, like an evil omen, weighs heavily on the origins of the human community. This ancient misfortune, which chained men of all eras to the same unhappy destiny, continued to blight life within the city. Fraternal blood might clot, yet all the rivers in the world could never wash away its stains.[14] For Sallust, discord assumed cosmic proportions. "Civil wars," he wrote, "flared up like telluric cataclysms . . ." (*B. J.* 41.10). In the words of Lepidus, the consul under Sulla (78 B.C.): "In these days, citizens, one either serves or commands, one either feels fear or inspires it; what human laws survive, what divine ones have not been violated?" (*Oratio Lepidi* 1.11).

Discord hung heavy over all men and pushed states toward ruin. "Since everything that is born must perish, when the hour tolls for Rome's death, her citizens will take up arms against one another until, exhausted and bled white, they fall prey to a tyrant or to a foreigner . . ." (*Ep. ad Caes.* 1.5). Then he sorrowfully added, echoing a passage from Plato,[15] that had they remained in harmony, "no coalition of forces, not even the entire world, would succeed in defeating and demolishing this empire. . . ."

The civil war had become a classical theme for the literati: Caesar had written his *De Bello Civili,* Lucan was to use it as a subject for an epic poem, Appianus was to write an account of it in Greek. The names of the great battles fought during the civil war—Pharsalus, Philippi, Actium—had acquired symbolic value. For Sallust, harmony was the only condition under which the state could survive. This word echoes throughout his pages as the word "peace" vibrates mournfully above the infernal winds in Francesca da Rimini's lament (see Dante's *Inferno, 5*).

> Kingdoms are clay . . .
> —Shakespeare, *Antony and Cleopatra,* 1, i, 30

At the end of the reigns of Rome's seven kings, the citizens of the Republic were stirred by a noble spirit of emulation.

Their *virtus* overcame every obstacle. They were frugal, hard-working for the good of the fatherland, loyal in their relations with foreigners: they lived "in the greatest harmony, almost without a trace of greed" (*B. C.* 9.1). This is the way the past looked to a man who lived in an era when, in the words of Cicero, "one was ashamed even of existing." "How many wars," wrote Vergil shortly afterward, "and how many countenances can evil assume?" The gloomy expectation that there would be a change "in things, in the times" weighed heavily on the Romans.[16] Sometimes their authors seemed to re-echo unwittingly the oracular literature of Jewish-Iranian origin, which Persia and Israel had always used as propaganda against the West. When Mithridates and, later, Cleopatra waged war against Rome, this literature flourished again and added an apocalyptic dimension to economic demands and requests for ethnic equality alike.

These ideas originated among the lower classes and through them filtered into the Roman world. Though the cultured classes pretended to ignore these warnings, they understood their message, which came to them by way of obscure channels: a foreshadowing of the end. Cicero considered the Catilinian conspiracy an eschatological disaster. That particular year had been forecast as fatal for the City and the Empire. The warning about an imminent civil war had been officially communicated to the Consul: "Haruspices from Etruria flocked [to Rome] to warn the populace of impending massacres, conflagrations, and the end of all legality; a civil war would break out in the city, and the hour of death for Rome and the Empire was drawing near. . . ." In apocalyptic tones recalling that prophetic literature, Cicero requested that the wicked be segregated.[17] He called on Jupiter Optimus Maximus to punish them, "both alive and dead, with eternal torments." Extermination of the unholy had been predicted in the Bible and in the prophecy of Hystaspes, which spread insidiously in Latin literature and was later quoted extensively by the Christian writers.[18]

The author of this prophecy is a mysterious figure often identified with some vague but venerable personage from the past to give greater credibility to these utterances. It was claimed that he was a king of the Medes, the father of Darius, or Zarathustra's precursor. By the time Mithridates headed the insurrection against Rome in the Asian provinces, his predictions had been widely spread. These prophecies always seemed to resurface in times of trouble. The fact that at a later date Christian writers were disseminating them shows that social classes that in the era of classical literature were not writing now joined the literary ranks.

This prophecy, as we have seen, was unearthed by Cicero at the time of the Catilinian conspiracy, and by other authors when Caesar's assassination seemed to signal the end of the world. They all speak of wonders that accompanied this event: "Such a thick mist rose," said Vergil, "that the people feared eternal night. . . ."[19] A comet was spotted—this, too, was confirmed by the oracle—and it was taken as the sign of war, famine, and death.[20] The news of the appearance of the *sidus Julium* (Julius Caesar's star) spread as far as the Jews in Alexandria.

Once again Rome feared an uprising by the plebeians and the slaves. In Cicero's view, those who had built an altar and erected a column on the spot where the dictator's body had been cremated were a despicable lot (*perditi homines*). These wretches and "bold, wicked, degenerate" slaves were a threat to Roman homes and temples alike. Among these outlaws appeared an individual who claimed to be Marius's son. In those tense, tragic moments, he instigated the rabble to ask the government for radical measures at the expense of the wealthy. He shared the fate of the other rebels, death.[21]

The fear of chaos, subversion, and conflagrations paralyzed

the Romans during those years. They feared invasion by the barbarians, who were watching Rome from afar, waiting for a propitious moment. "This is the second time," wrote Horace during the hostilities between Octavian and Mark Antony, "that Rome is torn by fratricidal strife. This City, which neither the Marsi nor the Etruscans nor Capua nor the blue-eyed Germans nor Hannibal nor Spartacus nor the treacherous Allobrogians could defeat, is pushed to the brink of destruction by an immoral war. Wild beasts will roam freely over Rome's lands; the victorious barbarians will trample her ruins under the clanking hooves of their horses and insolently scatter Quirinus' bones to the sun and the winds."[22]

They will take up arms, one against the other: greed for gold will be the City's wicked shepherd.
—*Oracula Sibyllina* 3. 464

He will hear that the citizens sharpened their swords, which they could have put to better use against the menacing Parthians.[23]
—Horace *Odes* 1. 2. 21–22

Sallust wrote during those troubled years. The war that was splitting the City reminded him of previous struggles and their dire consequences for the state. When Roman armies were fighting among themselves, he had the Consul Lepidus say, "Our arms are turned away from the enemy and against ourselves" (*Oratio Lepidi* 1.19).

Even in the letter that Sallust has Mithridates, King of Pontus and leader of the Asian insurrections, write to Arsaces, he depicts the king as well aware of Rome's internal strife. Mithridates allied himself with the rebel Sertorius, who had barricaded himself in Spain; he financed the pirates who infested the Mediterranean; he even planned to surround the Italian peninsula. This famous letter is certainly fictitious. Some scholars have read into it Sallust's approval of its anti-imperalist message and therefore his support of its contents. Others see in it his alarm in the face of the rising Parthian threat, or even his bitter admission that Roman misgovernment justified these yearnings for autonomy and the sudden outbursts of popular fury. Mithridates's accusations echoed those that Jugurtha had formulated in almost the same words (*B. J.* 81.1), and that elsewhere Sallust uttered in the first person.

The Parthian threat was a reality during the years that Sallust devoted himself to history. In 53 B.C., twenty years after Mithridates's death, Crassus suffered a tremendous defeat in the East. In 40, Labienus, a Roman official, had defected to the Parthians and, by subverting the Roman garrisons, threatened the security of the provinces of Asia Minor. Only the Italic Ventidius succeeded in wresting a victory from the Oriental forces in 38 B.C. His friend Sallust, another Italic, composed the speech that Ventidius delivered on the day of his triumph. In 36, Antony moved against the Parthians and lost 25,000 men in a disastrous retreat. The ghosts of Crassus's fallen soldiers were reawakened on the Syrian deserts. According to the oracle of Hystaspes, "The East will again rule, and the West will serve. Dominion will be transferred to Asia. The name of Rome will be erased." And Cicero, while recalling that war and the bold propositions of the king of Pontus, repeated this prophecy word for word: "The name of Rome was about to be erased from the face of the earth."[24]

Mithridates, clothed in the majesty of his ancestral royalty, appeared as the true antagonist of the Roman Empire. According to Sallust, the King had said, "We are suspected of being rivals of the Romans, and eventually avengers" (*Ep. Mithr.* 18). He based this claim on the conditions of social inferiority and economic exploitation that Rome had imposed

on her provinces. "Asia is waiting for us," says the King of
Pontus, "and cries out for help: the Romans have succeeded
in making themselves hated because of the greed of their
Proconsuls, the extortions of their tax collectors, the injustices of their magistrates. . . ."

The rising discontent in the provinces admitted by other authors, on a larger scale, the class hatred that was swelling up
inside Rome. Sallust, and after him Lucan, Juvenal, and Tacitus, joined the chorus of protest: "From a just and excellent
beginning, Rome's government has become cruel and intol-
erable" (*B. C.* 10.6). This is not a disillusioned abstentionist
speaking, this is not a simple question of human solidarity
with the oppressed. It is, instead, a gnawing fear that one day
these peoples will unite and will take the upper hand:
"Rome's enemies," as Sallust had the Consul Philippus say,
"lack only a leader."

In the provinces, Mithridates spread demagogic promises as
Catiline had done in Rome: citizenship to the freedmen and
the cancellation of all debts. As with everything that came
from the East, this insurrection had metaphysical overtones.
Cicero said that "they called him [Mithridates] father, the
saviour of Asia, God."[25] Mithridates had taken the title of
Dionysos Eupator. On the coins, his disheveled head, crowned
with ivy, recalled Bacchus or Alexander the Great, the young
king who had carried the message of brotherhood to the
world's peoples.

Even after Augustus, through diplomacy, achieved the formal reconquest of the East, the ideological conflict between
Asia and the West continued to concern the Romans. They
regarded the civil wars as all the more criminal inasmuch as
forces that would have been better employed to crush the
enemies in the East were dissipated. Horace, Propertius, and,
above all, Lucan[26] reiterated this thesis, which is deeply im-
bedded in Sallust's *Epistula Mithridatis*. The frontier along the

Rhine and the uncertain boundaries in Asia were the two great trouble areas in Roman foreign policy, and all of Rome's authors were aware of this.

> With that same spirit that wins every fight
> Unless its heavy body weighs it down.[27]
> —Dante, *Inferno*, 24, 53–54

History is to Sallust what family tradition is to the individual. How many times has he heard the patricians recall their ancestors' deeds or point to their portraits and wax masks in the atria of their homes. These mute presences spurred the grandchildren to valor: "It is the memory of great deeds that kindles in the breasts of noble men this flame that cannot be quelled" (*B. J.* 4.6). What this heritage of affection and examples meant to the gens (the Roman patrician family), the historical past meant to the entire people.

In Sallust's opinion the "great deeds" were actions performed for the good of the nation. His ideal pivoted around action and aimed at glory, the only form of immortality granted to men. Marius and Metellus, Cicero and Catiline, Jugurtha and Mithridates all thirsted for glory. Censure, however, was the lot of the unworthy.

But the fierce desire for power and wealth corroded the praiseworthy qualities of these potentially excellent men. It made them lose sight of the real goals worthy of their endeavor. Since man is composed of both matter and spirit, everything that is material or aims at this world is perishable. Sallust's vision of mankind, seen as prostrate and forgetful of the astral origins of its spirit, foreshadows the gloomy grandeur of Saint Augustine's: humanity contaminated by original sin, a *massa lutei*, a heap of mud.

For Sallust, this dualism had deep spiritual roots, possibly of

Pythagorean origin. It has been conjectured that among the strange, unsettling experiences of his disorganized youth, there figured initiation into some secret sect. Perhaps he had been influenced by the mystical undercurrent that in the dark days prior to Actium had colored even the skeptic Horace's poetry. Drowsy from the excesses of the previous evening, Horace wrote that "the body laden with external vices can weigh down the soul, that particle of divine breath, and nail it to the earth."[28]

Man, in Sallust's opinion, is composed of two parts, one that partakes of the divine and the other of animal nature (*B. C.* 1.2). Mortals, too, can be placed in two categories: those who are greedy and lustful, and the others, who are capable of dominating the whims of the senses. The material part of man is corruptible and finally dies: "The renown of beauty and wealth is fleeting; excellence of the mind is a shining and lasting possession" (*B. C.* 1.3). These ideas were perhaps drawn from Plato, directly, or indirectly through Posidonius's mediation, and would recur in Christian dualism. The world that Sallust saw before him had become so entangled in material interests, so lacking in any semblance of spirituality, that it convinced him of the approaching end.

Decay and death are inherent in all things that belong to this world. For the body, just as for the gifts of fortune, "there is an end as well as a beginning; everything that is born must perish, and everything that grows must get old: only the mind is incorruptible and eternal . . ." (*B. C.* 2.3).

Sallust defined immortality in a rationalist's terms. He did not speak of life after death, nor did he accept the Stoics' broad vision of a providence that governs the cosmos. He did not share the belief of Vergil and Livy that Rome's greatness had been preordained by the gods, and consequently he did not bother with prodigies or prophecies. In the debate in the Senate between Caesar and Cato, he had the former express a disdain of death that is typical of an Epicurean: "Death is a relief . . . not a punishment. After it there is no place for either sorrow or joy" (*B. C.* 51.20). While Cato, seizing upon the skepticism of his adversary as an example of the decline of the Roman conscience, replies: "Just a moment ago, Caesar spoke persuasively before this assembly, regarding as false, I presume, the beliefs about the nether world—where they say that the wicked take a different path from the good, and will end up in gloomy, desolate and frightening places" (*B. C.* 52.13).

Men like Cato and Sallust, who were open to philosophic thought, did not profess faith in immortality, except possibly in token homage to popular tradition or out of a belief in man's spiritual essence. "I am firmly convinced," we can read in Sallust's letters, "that a divine agency watches over the life of each mortal and that his every action, be it good or wicked, is recorded; therefore, by the law of nature, both the good and the wicked will receive their different rewards. And even if retribution and reward are slow in coming, each one knows by his own conscience what to expect . . ." (*Ep. ad Caes.* 12. 7, 8).

The author of the *Letters to Caesar* considers those actions as good which conform to religious precepts that as such are inviolable. This axiom held true for individuals and nations alike. "From what I have read and heard, I have learned how kingdoms, cities and nations have enjoyed prosperity and power so long as wise counsel has reigned among them; but whenever privilege, fear or pleasure take the upper hand, their strength rapidly wanes, their supremacy is wrested from them, and finally they are reduced to slavery . . . (*Ep. ad Caes.* 10). If one abandons the right path—namely, temperance and love for the fatherland—then the inevitable follows: "Whenever sloth takes the place of industry, lawlessness the place of self-restraint, arrogance the place of justice, then fortune keeps even pace with man's conduct, and power is transferred from the less to the more worthy . . ." (*B. C.* 2.6).

For harmony makes small states great, while discord destroys the greatest empires.[29]
—Sallust *Bellum Jugurthae* 10. 6

The war against Jugurtha started slowly, and since the Numidian usurper had corrupted the senators, it was conducted at a deliberately sluggish pace; it was finally won because of the tenacious will of Marius, a country plebeian. That, according to many critics, is Sallust's thesis. Undoubtedly, many facts seem to support this interpretation, but there were enough connections between the Roman nobility and the Numidian dynasty so that Jugurtha certainly did not have to buy their favor.[30] Sallust's accusation was based on the premise that ousting Jugurtha and placing his cousins, the legitimate heirs, on the Numidian throne was both a moral and a juridical obligation of the Roman government (an assertion that De Sanctis has since demonstrated to be unfounded). No treaty provided for such interference in the internal affairs of an ally. Intervention, however, became unavoidable after Jugurtha had killed the surviving cousin (the other had been murdered earlier) and the Italic residents at Cirta (modern Constantine) in 112 B.C.

Despite these events, the Senate still disapproved of engaging its military forces in an African war of attrition precisely when Rome was watching apprehensively the nations beyond the Alps and wanted to extend her power in those areas. In 118 B.C., the first Roman colony was established in Gaul, at Narbonne; in 115, a treaty of alliance was signed with Noricum (present-day eastern Austria). The first serious Roman defeat was in 113 B.C., in battle against the Cimbri and the

Teutones, the second in 109, the third in 105. In order to stop the barbarian advance at Acquae Sextiae (today, Aix-en-Provence) and Vercellae (modern Vercelli), Marius was forced to transfer to Gaul the Roman troops he had commanded in Numidia.

The reluctance on the part of the government to engage in a colonial adventure in Africa hardly seems unfounded. By sustaining a priori that intervention was necessary, Sallust revealed his attachment to the paternalistic policy, which relegated allies to the position of vassals. This is a typically aristocratic definition of power, and one of his inconsistencies.

Sallust did not minimize economic motives, and recognized that commercial expansion appealed to the Italic bourgeoisie. The Romans, who had been massacred by Numidian warriors at Cirta, by Jugurtha's orders, belonged to this class, and Marius counted on its support when he was running for the consulship. He joined them in disparaging the current consul, Metellus, the patrician he then succeeded, by promising that under his leadership the war would be over within a few days ("reasons that seemed all the more plausible since the prolongation of the war was damaging their [the traders'] interests: for greedy spirits nothing moves fast enough" (B. J. 64.6).

Had Sallust not selected the Jugurthine War as the subject of his monograph, it certainly would have received little mention on its own merits in Rome's history. It represented no threat to Italic security, nor did it reveal the existence of a future African threat. Sallust used the war as an occasion to discuss the class struggle within the Roman Republic, the competition for leadership, and the clash of interests. He watched as these dangerous forces threatened to undermine the soundness of Rome's century-old foundations. He even went so far as to declare that he had selected that particular episode because of its dramatic features and to bring out the fact that for the first time the arrogance of the Roman nobles had been humiliated.

According to Sallust's version, it was the Roman nobles who instigated Jugurtha to usurp the throne. He had been serving in Numantia as an ally of the Roman army when the nobles suggested that he become king. They even assured him of the tacit consent of the Senate by reminding him that "at Rome anything could be bought" (*B. J.* 8.1). Jugurtha returned to his country, and, though an illegitimate nephew, was adopted by the old king. Jugurtha immediately had the first of his two cousins killed. The survivor took his case to the Senate, but Jugurtha showered the senators with gold, and thereby won their favor.

This moment marks the beginning of a long series of procrastinations by the Romans: first they sent commissions, and then insufficient troops with inept commanders. Only Metellus, the third leader, had those traditionally Roman qualities *virtus* (excellence) and *gloria* (renown)—attributes that Sallust never applied to Marius. Metellus, however, had that fatal psychological flaw of *superbia* (arrogance), which characterized his class. He aroused Marius's rancor and rivalry to the point of goading him to throw himself wholeheartedly into the political fray. Marius then ran for consul, and despite his humble origins—he was a "new man" from the provinces—succeeded in snatching the consulship from his predecessor. His emotional make-up and behavior were marked by the plebeian vices of *cupido et ira* (greed and anger). He allowed discipline to slacken among his troops. He connived to turn the loyalties of the Romans in the colonies against Metellus, inducing them to write and tell their friends in Rome to call for Marius as a commander. He corrupted the Numidians with promises. These were the actions of an intemperate troublemaker. In contrast to Marius, Sulla, the young, highly cultured, perfectly mannered official recently arrived from

Rome, behaved like a true nobleman: "Unlike a man spurred by base ambition, he never tried to undermine the reputation of the Consul or of any good man" (*B. J.* 96.3).

Once consul and commander of Numidia, Marius engaged in dangerous and unnecessary sorties. In order to augment the number of soldiers under his command, and to circumvent the Senate, which was cautious in sending him additional troops, he found a new method that was to have serious consequences. He enlisted plebeian volunteers, and thereby created an army of his own. Out of loyalty, these men were ready to follow him into any action, even into civil war. The speech he delivered on this occasion was a model of rudimentary demagogy: he scoffed at the patrician sons who learned the art of war through manuals, not on the battlefield, as he had. He expounded a principle that was to become the cornerstone of Roman ethics: nobility depended on one's valor, not on one's birth. The titles of those vainglorious nobles derived from their ancestors' bravery. "No matter how grandiose your genealogy may be, your origins are still humble. The founder of your family, whoever he may be, was a goatherd or something else that I won't bother mentioning."[31] These are Juvenal's words, two hundred years later; this is the argument of Cicero and of all the other Italics who were conscious of their contribution to national security.

Marius knew that though he lacked an illustrious name, he was the legitimate heir of all those men who had played an important part in creating the Republic's greatness: "If the fathers of [the patricians] Albinus and Bestia could now be asked whether they would choose their own offspring or me as their sons, what do you think they would answer if not that they wanted to have the best possible progeny" (*B. J.* 85.19). Here speaks the proud yet illegitimate son of Roman society. He reasoned like Jugurtha, who knew that, despite his superior valor, he was excluded from the succession to the throne by reason of his birth. When Metellus learned that Marius was planning to run for the consulship, he echoed Scipio's counsel of moderation as he dismissed Jugurtha from Numantia. Though no legal obstacle could block Marius's election (the plebeians had gained the right to accede to the supreme magistracy as early as 367 B.C.), the patricians opposed this with a kind of scornful ostracism. All men, Metellus warned Marius, should not covet all things; Marius should be content with his own lot.

The revolt of the provinces would further extend the power of the new classes during the imperial era. The plebeian from Arpinum who became consul in Sallust's day was the counterpart of later emperors of foreign stock: Trajan, the Spaniard, and Septimius Severus, the African. The new classes and the foreign races had access to key government and religious posts, both previously reserved for the élite. They could also subscribe to the patrician moral principles and rules of conduct that distinguished this class from the plebeians. Though at a far remove from the principal stage of power, Jugurtha had nevertheless learned the patrician code based on the traditional values *virtus, animus* (courage), *gloria*. Marius had already made this code his own.

In Jugurtha, courage and ambition assumed the intensity of his fiery African temperament. He lacked Marius's rough good nature. A courageous warrior and fearless hunter, he was ruthless and arrogant when dealing with the first two consuls sent by the Roman Senate—two inept or corrupt patricians, Lucius Calpurnius Bestia and Spurius Postumius Albinus—and he became as suspicious and wary as a beast at bay when he sensed an implacable enemy in Metellus. He withdrew before Marius's pressing attacks, and fell into his hands only because the new quaestor, Sulla—subtle, correct, and astute—had succeeded in persuading the King of Mauritania to betray Jugurtha.

Sallust surveyed this war with an eye that scanned time. He judged the events that followed it as logical consequences of this struggle. Bitter feuds and conflicts were linked together in a twisted pattern of destruction. At times he spoke of Fortune as an occult, arbitrary power that preordained men's future, but more often than not he found the causes of the impending catastrophes in the protagonists themselves. It was useless to ferret out hidden reasons for decadence or to attribute the decline to the still-distant barbarian threat. This decline, when it came about, would be the consequence of the internal premises that Sallust had recorded in his works.

In a city so great and corrupt, Catiline . . .[32]
—Sallust *Bellum Catilinae* 14. 1

Just as a portrait painter does not limit himself to portraying the individual in his singularity, but looks for a type rather than a character, the historian represents, by extension, the consequences of universal situations.

Catiline stepped on the historical stage wearing a murderer's mask. Rather than persuade us of the verisimilitude of his character, Sallust described him as a type produced by a society that negated all moral values, in consequence of its experiences of a bloody dictatorship. Catiline, a man of raging ambition, lived in a state where the weak had no voice. On four separate occasions, the aristocratic coteries had banned him from the consulship. Had he been elected to this office, perhaps he would have proposed and brought about his reforms in legal ways; they had a basis in justice, but had been distorted by frustrations. He was dominated by greed in a society that had made wealth its sole yardstick of values. He was wicked, but this may have been the consequence of the injustices he had witnessed and suffered.

As a historical figure, Catiline evokes an aura of gloomy

grandeur. And yet, this rebel, this enemy of the state rose up in defense of the destitute. His opinions—even Sallust was ready to support them whenever they respected the constitution—coincided with those Sallust presents as his own or puts into the mouths of his fellow party members: "Ever since the Republic has fallen into the hands of a few powerful men, kings and potentates have paid tribute, and the people and nations pay taxes," Catiline is quoted as saying (*B. C.* 20.7). The popular Memmius repeated this same judgment: "Kings and free peoples pay tribute to a few nobles" (*B. J.* 31.9). "All the rest of us . . ." Catiline says, "have made up the mob . . . subservient to those to whom we should be an object of fear." The Tribune added: "You still fear those who should fear you." Sallust says: "The treasury, the provinces, public offices, renown and triumphs are in the hands of a few privileged men . . ." (*B. J.* 41.8).

This society was rotten, and had bred a large number of potential extremists: "The plebeians, desirous of change, all supported Catiline; this behavior followed the laws of nature since, in any group of men, the have-nots envy the good and exalt the base. . . . Rome, like a large sewer, had become the converging point for all who had gained notoriety for their shamelessness and impudence. Many, too, recalled Sulla's victory, when they saw common soldiers risen to high positions, and others amassing huge fortunes which permitted them to feast and live like kings. They, too, hoped for similar fruits of victory, each for himself, if he entered the field. Then there were the young men who earned a mere pittance as day laborers in the country and who had moved to the City because of public and private largesse . . ." (*B. C.* 37.1–7).

Finally, there were the politicians, the ideological opponents of patrician oligarchy. They were not motivated by a desire for justice or by a readiness to share more justly the rewards and cares of office. Their policy, in the bitter, farsighted words of one of their own kind, allowed for revolution as long as their party emerged victorious. The nobles, though heirs to the traditional uprightness and patriotism of their class, thought only about safeguarding their positions and wealth. What else could the party leaders—Caesar and Pompey among them—aspire to, if not absolute power? "They only seek power," wrote Cicero, "and both [men] want to rule"; their platforms do not represent an ideological conflict or a program to renovate existing institutions; they represent only a "power race."[33]

Sallust did not fail to see that social and economic factors were at play, but he transferred them to the sphere of morality. Unequal distribution of wealth, depopulation of the countryside, veterans' demands, unemployment, and excessive taxation were all phenomena characteristic of a society whose economy was based on slave labor and governed by a few landholding families, unprepared to comprehend the magnitude of the state and its innumerable problems. Sallust worried that these evils, like weeds, might overgrow and eventually choke the Romans' positive qualities.

Against this background of abuse, favoritism, special interests, and gross inequalities, Catiline loomed sinister and powerful. Sallust omitted some of the details of Catiline's private life and viewed him with cool detachment, as he would later be seen by posterity. He was a figure of large dimensions, a fearless, vigorous, true patrician. Sallust was influenced less by the speeches Cicero delivered at the moment of the conspiracy than by the orator's thoughtfully just commemoration three years later: "Who was more rapacious than he [Catiline] and yet, at the same time, more generous?"[34] And as Sallust repeated, who was more "greedy of the wealth of others, yet [so] liberal with his own"? Catiline thus remained a man racked by fiery ambitions, tortured by unattainable goals, but always willing to fight alongside his men, like a simple soldier (B. C. 20.16).

Frustrated in his ambitions, Catiline may have taken up the cause of the oppressed in order to defeat Caesar at his own game. Perhaps Catiline even aspired to found a more audacious party than his rival's, and thereby unite the volatile, tumultuous masses into a legitimate force. When his aims were discovered and he was consequently forced to leave Rome, one of his followers goaded him to make the final gesture of appealing to the slaves: this would have been tantamount to unleashing wild beasts during a public debate.

Catiline's campaign was violently demagogic. He promised to satisfy the ancient, recurrent demands, "abolition of debts, proscription of the rich, pillage . . ." (*B. C.* 21.1, 2). He found support among the provincial Etruscan farmers who were weighed down by debts, among ex-veterans, and victims or followers of Sulla. Cicero described him as "surrounded by a crowd of farmers from Arretium [modern Arezzo] and Faesulae [modern Fiesole], and perhaps some ex-followers of Sulla; [he was] violent, arrogant and threatening: 'those who are poor and downtrodden,' he orated, 'should not trust the rich and powerful . . . there are two bodies in the state— one is fragile and has a head that is quite worthless, while the other is strong but completely lacking a head; as long as I live, the latter party will have its head. . . .' "[35]

The Romans feared he would adopt radical measures: expropriations, and the liquidation of capital invested in loans— in short, the very same reforms that they were to fear from Caesar fifteen years later. Cicero's letters to Atticus in 49 B.C. repeat these alarming rumors: in the eventuality of Caesar's victory, there would be massacres, outrages against private property, abolition of debts, a left-wing, egalitarian dictatorship. In order to enrich himself, Caesar would not have to confiscate the state's revenues, but could simply expropriate the citizens' private wealth. Caesar even recruited his followers from the same social strata as Catiline: dissolute youths, debtors, all those who had little or nothing to lose.

The Senate feared the actions of the headstrong masses, especially that they might march on the jails to free the inmates. To prevent such an eventuality, Cato urged immediate emergency measures and sentences of execution without appeal. The Consul Cicero took upon himself the responsibility for having Catiline's supporters killed before his very eyes in the Mamertine prison.

> But the army of the Roman people gained no happy or bloodless victory.[36]
> —Sallust *Bellum Catilinae* 61. 7

Cicero viewed Catiline's attempted coup as an attack on private property. Quelling the conspiracy meant blocking agrarian reform, confiscation and land distribution to the peasants. These were the measures he succeeded in foiling; Catiline's supporters were preparing to slay those in authority and the rich, and to set homes and temples afire.

Sallust's vision, however, was broader and less limited by contingencies. His constant concern was Rome's *decline and fall*. At the same time he, too, considered the conspiracy a danger for the propertied classes, and consequently tried to dissociate himself and Caesar from such radical demands. He stressed the uniqueness of Catiline's undertaking, which, in itself, exposed the ferocity of the political struggle. For the first time in Rome's history, a bold man, perhaps more frustrated than wicked, had tried to undermine the state's security. In Catiline, Sallust sees the prototype of all rapacious adventurers who are emboldened to strike because others aspire to totalitarian power. In Catiline's shadow, unscrupulous men like Pompey, Crassus, and Caesar were secretly plotting, men who cautiously eluded personal danger, but were always ready to seize the propitious moment.

Catiline conspired, and conceived reckless projects precisely because he had been born in a lawless society. In another era, he would have channeled his frantic vitality into serving his country. His unrealized gifts were recognized after his death. ("He had," according to Cicero's dispassionate judgment, "more than a few seeds of worth that were potential, though not manifest."[37]) As soon as Catiline knew that he had been condemned and exiled, he wrote his friend Quintus Catulus—Sallust asserted that this letter was authentic—and entrusted his wife to his friend's protection. He explained that he had had recourse to arms rather than passively endure the indignity of the humiliating ostracism he had repeatedly suffered when the Senate, for one reason or another, had not only rejected his candidacy for the consulship, but would not permit him to run again. The unworthy, he said, had been elevated to the very honors that were his by right (*B. C.* 35.3). He justified his actions with personal reasons. Caesar noted that the same reasons prompted the civil wars,[38] namely, offenses to *dignitas* (personal worth).

Catiline had an additional motive: according to the ancient code, it was the patricians' duty to protect the poor. Here he assumed the tone of a man conscious of the moral obligations imposed by his ancient lineage. The Gracchi brothers and even Caesar were nobles. Upon hearing the first accusations against him in the Senate, Catiline was surprised to find himself mistrusted: "He was a Roman patrician sprung from such a family . . . who, like his ancestors, had shown, on many occasions, largesse to the Roman plebeians. Why should he want to overthrow the state—to have it saved by Cicero, a resident alien in the city of Rome?" (*B. C.* 31.7).

One of the conspirators repeated that protecting the poor was a duty incumbent on the nobles; whoever could not pay his debts would see the little he had taken away and would lose even his personal liberty: ". . . but, once upon a time, your ancestors, moved by pity for the Roman populace, issued decrees that lessened this misery . . ." (*B. C.* 33.2). Sallust expected the patricians to create a government geared to the people's needs, open to the most qualified, and yet continuing to be faithful to Rome's best traditions. It would have been so easy to follow these precepts and live happily: "All the conquered nations from East to West paid homage to the Roman people: there were no wars . . . and riches flowed into the city . . . but there were still citizens who persisted in bringing ruin unto themselves and the Republic . . ." (*B. C.* 36.4).

Those accomplices of Catiline who had requested support from the Allobrogian legates were betrayed by them and then condemned to death by the Senate. When Catiline learned that they had already been strangled in Cicero's presence, he tried to escape to Transalpine Gaul, even though many of his supporters had deserted him. Pursued and encircled, he spoke these final words to his few remaining faithful followers before their last battle: "Two armies, one toward Rome, the other toward Gaul, block our passage. . . . We are battling for country, for freedom, for life, while the others fight to defend privilege."

True to his beliefs, he went on foot into the open battlefield, had the horses taken away so that no man could flee, and placed himself in the front rank, alongside his best soldiers. He "stood with the freedmen and the farmers under the eagle which, according to legend, Marius had fought under in his war against the Cimbri. . . ." Like Caesar, he called upon the Roman hero to vindicate the political aims they held in common.

It was a fierce and bitter battle. When Catiline realized that only a few of his men were still alive, he "remembered his lineage and his ancient worth, plunged into the thickest of the fray, and there fell fighting" (*B. C.* 60.7).

Here Sallust pauses in his narration to contemplate the

battlefield littered with corpses. Each man lay where he had
fallen, each one wounded from the front. Catiline's body was
found far in advance of the others. He was still breathing and
wore the same expression of "indomitable spirit." The victorious soldiers who examined the bodies after the battle "recognized here a friend, there a guest, there a relative. . . ."

Although Sallust describes the scene with icy precision, an
undercurrent of passion vibrates throughout his prose. The
voice is that of a man who has watched other victors recognize friends or relatives among the dead. On the day of that
ominous battle, he already foresaw the fratricidal wars that
would follow the Catilinian conspiracy. Beyond the battlefield on the hills of Florence, he glimpsed Pharsalus and Philippi. And throughout his lugubrious narration sounded the
mournful echo of his yearning for *Concordia* (Harmony).

> Whoever does not propose to change the current state
> of society is a good man and a good citizen.[39]
> —Macrobius *Saturnalia* 2. 4. 18

Sallust's dilemma, and that of the Roman spirit as a whole,
is symbolized by two personalities, diametrically opposed
across the benches of the Senate—Caesar and Cato. Whoever
wants to reconstruct rhetorical battles between famous an-
tagonists can name Marius and Sulla, Caesar and Pompey,
Cicero and Catiline, Octavian and Antony. With a keen sense
of history, Sallust contrasts the positions of two politicians on
the issue of the conspiracy. It was not antipathy that made
him belittle Cicero's work or deride his motives—"prompted
by anger and fear," he says of him—or the fact that the Consul praised his own merits fulsomely himself. It was, rather,
his evaluation of what Cato and Caesar represented in the
period of crisis as Rome passed from a city-state to a universal
power, from city particularism to Roman universality. Cato

was the essence of republican thought. He had the mentality of the aristocrat who viewed power as the monopoly of a restricted class on the basis of its proven experience and rectitude; he naturally applied this criterion to Rome's dominions. Caesar, on the other hand, realized that a great nation, composed of heterogeneous countries, needed a unified legislative system. Cato knew very well that the premises that justified a government of the élite over the other classes and nations no longer corresponded to reality, since that moral supremacy, symbolized in the very words—*aristoi* (aristocracy) and *optimates* (élite)—had long since ceased to exist. And yet he remained tied to the old city because, he maintained, the highest truth of the Roman spirit was contained in its values and principles.

Cato the plebeian from Tusculum walked in the shadow of his ancestor Cato the Censor, who had also scourged degenerate nobles. In Caesar's wake, the barbarians from *Gallia comata** were already distinguishable, and they would be welcomed in the Senate one hundred years later by his descendant Claudius. These are the two perennial aspects of the Roman spirit—colonialism and the overcoming of social and racial barriers. Caesar the politician, alert to the needs of the day, could not afford to ignore or misinterpret them if he wanted to stay in power. He recognized the changes he had to support if he was not to be overwhelmed by them; was aware of the tremendous responsibility of a man who, whether from fear or rancor, created a precedent through recourse to cruelty.

Sallust gave such parallel yet impartial judgments that scholars are still arguing over his preferences. He pointed to a certain narrow-mindedness in Cato, but in the same breath

---

* Long-haired Gaul, the newly conquered area north of the Alps, in contradistinction to *Gallia togata,* "toga-wearing Gaul," the southern part of the province, in the Po valley.

hinted at Caesar's ambiguity and subtle cunning. To each man he gives distinct speech habits and a stylistic and intellectual unity, which perhaps reflected the historian's actual knowledge of the original speeches rather than his literary abilities.

With insinuating flattery, Caesar recalled a famous precedent of clemency—the Senate's pardon to the inhabitants of Rhodes, who, a century earlier, had betrayed Rome.[40] And ironically enough, it had been Cato the Censor, the ancestor of Caesar's antagonist, who had proposed clemency. While trying to dissuade the Conscript Fathers from what would have been considered, at least from the legal point of view, an exceptional measure, Caesar did not minimize the gravity of the offense. He fully realized that he was suspected of complicity with Catiline. According to other historical versions, Cato did not hesitate to reproach him for this. Caesar did not forget, however, that the Senate had condemned the Gracchi precisely with a similar exceptional procedure. By petitioning for a regular trial, with appeal to the people, he called for positive legislation against uncertain legal rules and customs (*incerto jure et consuetudine*)[41] that lent themselves to arbitrary interpretations; he demanded the application of laws with universal validity as opposed to the rudimentary and static precepts of archaic law. The Decemviri had been entrusted with the delicate task of compiling the juridical norms so that—according to the *Digest*—"the city would be founded on laws."[42] It was a solemn moment in Roman history when human rights were affirmed over arbitrary power and privilege. Ever since that moment, the lower classes, in their steady advance, had secured some guarantees. Caesar simply asked that these guarantees be respected, if for no other reason, he added, than recognition that, in the face of an exceptional case, the death penalty itself would be an inadequate punishment.

Cato brusquely entered the discussion, dispensing with ora-

torical flourishes. He pointed out that this was no simple debate on political or financial issues, but that the stability of the
state was at stake. Catiline's conspiracy was an unusual crime,
and therefore justified emergency procedures and exceptional
measures—*supplicium more majorum* (punishment in accordance with the customs of our ancestors). The rigid application of that harsh, archaic penalty had been relaxed during the
past centuries, and Livy reported that as early as the sixth
century B.C., the condemned man had the right of public appeal to change the death sentence to exile. This *provocatio ad
populum* had been one of the plebeians' most important
democratic conquests. Both Cicero and Livy defined it as the
stronghold of liberty, the safeguard of democratic institutions. Polybius judged it to be a cornerstone of Roman law,
one of the most civilized among nations.[43]

Cato, however, opposed indulgence, and argued that this
conspiracy involved high treason. Just as Caesar had dissoci-
ated himself from Catiline, who represented the extreme conclusions of his own thought, Cato likewise, from the beginning, scornfully distinguished his position from that of the
conservatives. He seemed to say that governing the state be-
fitted a Senate composed of men of a different ethical fiber. In
order to shake the senators from their moral sloth, he reminded them, with biting sarcasm, of their houses and art
collections, which they valued more highly than the Republic. Let them awaken, at last, if for nothing else than to save
those dearly prized possessions.

But he did not share their mundane values, for his position
was purely ideological, free from all self-interest; his is Socrates's view, as it is stated in the *Criton.* He was not concerned
with the economic content of the demands advanced by the
conspirators, and left Cicero with the task of exaggerating
their implications so that the wealthy would panic. In his
opinion, a coup would be tantamount to abolishing a political

tradition which coincided with that moral code he so zealously observed, with those values of which he, among so many degenerates, considered himself the depositary and guardian.[44] If the ancient order was destroyed, then the Empire would inevitably fall.

The death penalty Cato proposed was as harsh and explicit as one of the Twelve Tables.* It was one of the most ancient, and had sacred origins. It was reserved for those guilty of high treason or parricide, or for a vestal virgin found guilty of common crimes (she was buried alive if she allowed herself to be seduced). By advocating a return to this archaic punishment, Cato refused to come to terms with the democratic conquests that mitigated the rigor of this law through the right of appeal. He simply cited examples where discipline had been inexorably applied so as to keep the state's authority intact: a consul had even condemned his own son to death on charges of insubordination. Now, however, he said, indulgence is called understanding, and the waste of public money is termed generosity. The use of such ambiguous terms derived from an insidious confusion of ideas, an uncertainty of principles, and faltering in the application of the laws. In Cato's words, we can sense the bewilderment of a man who feels himself increasingly isolated because he upholds the moral values of another epoch. "We make no distinction between scoundrels and honest men . . . we have long since lost the true names of things."

Sallust placed these two politicians before the Senate and posterity. The prominence he assigns to them is undoubtedly due to the influence of pamphlet publications of that period. The myth that made Caesar's name a title and Cato's a moral

---

* *Lex XII Tabularum*, twelve tables on which a code of laws was published (traditionally dated *c.* 451 B.C.).

category was beginning to take form. In his comparison of the two men, Sallust sees them as embodiments of conflicting historical forces. The uncertainty of later scholars in establishing his preference for Cato or Caesar gives additional proof of the historian's objectivity and, perhaps, reveals his own inner torment. Sallust shared both Cato's anger and Caesar's understanding, but he did not himself know which side of the Roman spirit was more noble, more efficacious in safeguarding the state and Rome's domination over the world. He appears to have sensed the dichotomy that would last for centuries. The contemporaneous but opposing positions of the two men who clashed in the Senate that evening became synonymous with the idea of Rome: the Empire versus the Republic, collectivism versus individualism. Everything that Rome signified for future generations as the source of eternal moral categories can be traced back to Cato or to Caesar, in equal measure.

By absolving Cato from the "sin" of having defended the privileged classes, Sallust implicitly recognized that the moral heritage of the élite should be preserved. In dissociating Caesar from Catiline, he established the former as the prototype of a democratic ruler determined to erase all disparities, but also fully cognizant of the particular moment and the particular milieu in which he acted. Augustus may have pondered these pages and understood the necessity of fusing the two positions. Clearly he tried, in his own person, to reconcile Cato's ideas with Caesar's.

But at the time of Sallust's writing, all he saw around him was vindictive wrath. As the people watched Caesar's triumph in silent sorrow, the shades of Cato, dying from self-inflicted wounds,[45] must have joined the defeated barbarians brought to Rome in chains.* A few years later, Sallust saw Caesar

---

* After Caesar's victory over Pompey, whose cause Cato had taken against Caesar, Cato committed suicide, in 46 B.C.

bleeding from twenty-three dagger wounds. The two greatest men of his day had fallen, both the victims of civil war.

In his portrait of Cato and Caesar still living and actively
engaged in the Senate debate, Sallust, as it were, also pronounced their funeral eulogy and with it the eulogy of what
they represented and what was disappearing with them—free
political expression.

LIVY
On Virtue

I have transmitted many of [our] forefathers' examples, long since fallen into disuse, so that posterity will imitate them.[1]
—Augustus *Index Rerum Gestarum* 8

The gods were present when Rome was founded and [thus] her worth will not diminish.[2]
—Livy 1. 9

After Augustus's death in A.D. 14, his final wishes were read before the Senate. His will, which had been kept by the Vestal Virgins, contained a list of bequests and the order to return any estates left to the Emperor by private citizens to the legitimate heirs.

Then four volumes were carried in and read to the senators. The first contained a complete list of all of Augustus's accomplishments as emperor,[3] and specifically commanded that they be engraved on the bronze columns to be placed around his tomb. The second and third volumes discussed the military situation in the Empire and gave a report on the finances, the treasury, and the administration in Italy and the provinces. There was also a series of orders to Tiberius and the entire population; in particular, the injunction not to extend the Empire beyond its current boundaries: it was already too large, and any further expansion could threaten its very existence. Many years earlier, Scipio Aemilianus had expressed the same idea, a view consistent with the pacifist trend that dated back to Numa, the pious king who had built a temple to the god Terminus[4]—the divinity that watched over the borders.

The last volume contained directions for the funeral, which was celebrated according to the Emperor's precise wishes, with a triumphal celebration, apotheosis, a sacred performance, a final public declaration of his thought, and the goals he had pursued since 31 B.C. This was the year he had defeated Antony at Actium, the year he had ascended the imperial throne at the age of thirty, the year he had assumed, singlehanded, the responsibilities of world government.

> He shall rule a world to which his father's virtues have brought peace.[5]
>
> —Vergil *Eclogue* 4. 17

According to an ancient custom described by Polybius (6.53), the relatives of the deceased took part in the funeral procession. They were carried on the bearers' shoulders in curule chairs and wore the ancient decorations of the civil and military offices held by the dead man's forefathers. To make the links with the past even more evident, the family members wore their ancestors' wax masks, which were religiously preserved in little wooden cabinets in their atrium. It was as if they had left, that day, the misty realm of the afterworld to welcome the dead, and thereby confirmed that he had lived up to their moral expectations and ideals. For every Roman patrician, the family name was a sort of password and imposed a special kind of behavior. The supreme measure of valor was to follow the example of one's ancestors. "My conduct has epitomized the virtues of my stock." These are the words that one of the Scipios had engraved on his tomb. "I have received approval from my *majores* [forefathers], so they can rejoice that I issued from their loins. . . ."[6]

But, in Augustus's case, the *majores* who accompanied him to his tomb and recognized him as their worthy successor were not limited to his forefathers by birth. He was accompanied by a series of imposing shades who proclaimed that he had continued their service to the fatherland. Among Augustus's ancestors were numbered the most remote heroes of the Roman nation—Aeneas, Romulus, the great men of the Republican era—and, in more recent times, even rivals from opposing factions, such as Pompey, whose image was surrounded by that of the nations he had annexed to the Empire, as far as the shores of the Caspian Sea. In this way, it became clear that all past antagonisms were resolved in the person of the Princeps, and that after the civil wars and partisan hatreds had abated, Rome alone mattered. Thus, Rome's two fundamental characteristics, her Latinity and her perpetuity, were brought into focus.

The day of the Emperor's funeral, *imagines* made of lightweight material which traditionally followed the cart drawn by white horses in triumphal processions now were paraded behind his coffin. These images confirmed the principles he had formulated iconographically in the major artistic undertaking of his reign, the Forum of Augustus. A high tufa wall, built to protect the Forum from fires, still separates what remains of those monuments from the *suburra* (a lower-class district in ancient Rome).

In the center of the Forum stood the temple dedicated to Mars Ultor (the Avenger), god of the double vengeance: one against the tyrannicides (consummated in 42 B.C. at Philippi); the second against the Parthians, who had defeated the Roman legions in 53, 40, and 36 B.C. At both sides of the temple, two hemicycles bounded by porticoes opened; bronze and marble statues of ancient Roman heroes had been placed in niches in the semicircular walls and between the columns. The smaller forums of Republican times had also been filled with statues—the first Sabine king, Pythagoras, Alcibiades—but these personalities had been selected at random and honored according to the occasion. In contrast, the architectural plan that governed the Augustan buildings was organic and coherent. Here for the first time the famous men of the past were offered to the meditation of passers-by in a definite chronological and ideological order.

Before leaving the stage, Augustus had wished to reconfirm his definition of the Empire, which was based on a philosophic interpretation of its formation, a juridical stoic view. He saw the Romans as shepherds: in the past, they had tended herds, and in his day they tended the world. This task had fallen to them because of their courage, loyalty, self-sacrifice, not because of their craving for power or through the whims of Fortune. In Livy's words, "the expansion of the Empire was due more to the misdeeds of Rome's enemies and rivals than to the City's ambition" (41.1).

Power, then, was the just reward for merit. If a sober, tenacious people had won this power through their *virtus,* the men entrusted with safeguarding this legacy had to be equally meritorious.

Livy, who shared this point of view, proposed to illustrate it in his *History of Rome.* He had made history his religion. To the ever-recurring question as to the causes of the conquest and the reasons for its continuing success, Livy responds by pointing to the trials overcome by the builders of the Empire. Pausing to contemplate the extent of Roman dominion after the Second Punic War and the First Macedonian War (178 B.C.), he observes: "In their successful ventures and the prosperity that rewarded them, the Romans were more distinguished for their prestige than for despotism; dealing with foreign nations, they prided themselves on using authority rather than violence or terror." The Empire was secure because of the praiseworthy conduct of the men who conquered it and then governed it with firmness and justice: ". . . the only guarantee of loyalty—obedience to their betters" (22.13).

It was essential to demonstrate the truth of this axiom; to illustrate the conduct of individuals and nations in war and peace; and to gather a sufficient number of exemplary actions to prove that man's worth could be measured only by deeds. The historian, who was the interpreter of the emperor's thought and perhaps even its inspirer, recognized an intrinsic order in events, a beneficent providence, fate, or will of the gods that had preordained in its own inscrutable way the grandeur of Rome. But this was the extent of his concessions to the metaphysical sphere: those fateful premises had been carried out by men.

Livy's vision of history was humanistic and, at the same time, eschatological; in Vergil's view, fate plays a dominant role. In the *Aeneid*, he traced Rome's predestination as far back as Olympus. Aeneas sailed from Troy to the distant shores of Latium to fulfill a preordained mission, which he only gradually came to understand. Unlike Ulysses, he would not be allowed to return to his fatherland, nor would he share the throne with Dido, as Antony did with Cleopatra, another African queen. Her proud, sumptuous city of Carthage, which one day would become Rome's enemy, had been founded by a wicked man, who was "blinded by lust of gold." The angry gods watched as Aeneas, adorned with a purple cloak and jeweled sword, helped build towers and palaces. They enjoined him to leave because Carthage was not his city. The Urbs, the ideal city which his descendants would found on the seven hills, would be built on different principles: frugality, equity, endurance. It would not resemble Troy, the city that had been burned by the Greeks. Troy, too, had been opulent, haughty, and, therefore, short-lived: "The Trojan riches, that unfortunate kingdom." The references to this wealth seemed to point to the city's doom. Priam's fifty sons lived in the sumptuous palace with their respective wives as guarantee of a long future with numerous and valiant progeny. The doors of the palace were covered with gold, and all the rooms were laden with precious trophies, taken from the enemy. All this wealth, however, foreshadowed an impending destruction, which Vergil emphasized through the expressive power of the verb *procubuēre* ("were laid low").

Arrogance and conceit—vices engendered by power and gold—arouse the gods' anger. This was the persistent somber preoccupation of whoever paused to consider human power and tried to elucidate the mechanisms behind its formation and the chances for its duration. If Aeneas wanted to found a state that would be dear to the celestial powers and therefore enduring, he should not concern himself with walls and palaces, but instead should tend to the spirit of his people. This was to be a people not disposed toward the arts of philosophy, but endowed with moral qualities enabling them to govern the world. If they resisted the "ominous hunger for gold,"[7] then their dominion would last forever.

Upon Aeneas's arrival at the mouth of the Tiber, Evander met him and invited the Trojan refugee to his humble home. Together they climbed the hill that had been a god's abode. Here, Evander uttered a supreme warning to Aeneas: "Dare, my guest, to scorn riches; only in this way will you be worthy of the god."[8] This god was Hercules, who had undertaken every kind of strenuous task—the so-called Herculean labors (*labores*). To Vergil, the omen marked the beginning of the admirable Roman race.

The Romans' deeds are the theme of Livy's *History*, and represent his solution to the major problems preoccupying the Roman mind—namely, the Empire, its causes, its formative phases, the responsibilities of its government, the means for guaranteeing its stability and duration. Livy was less interested in predestination than in the Romans' dedication, their untiring industry, their resistance to danger, discomfort, and setbacks, which were not chance events, but trials sent by the gods. His narration is a series of variations on the theme of *integra et immobilis virtus* (the full and unchanging worth), the ideal of a social and cultural élite. Through the work of the Latin authors who praised this ideal, it became the nation's ethical code, the essence of the Roman spirit, and, finally, a philosophy of history. Rome's *virtus* had seduced even blind, fickle *fortuna*, and therefore it provided the one and only guarantee of *aeternitas* (eternity).

> The City, founded for eternity . . .[9]
> —Livy 4. 4; 28. 28

In periods of uncertainty, poets and prose writers returned to the theme of the City's perpetuity; it was engraved on coins and appeared in inscriptions. Jupiter reassured Venus, concerned about the future of her son Aeneas after his escape from Troy. The king of the gods pledged to her that as soon as Aeneas landed on the shores of Latium, he would rule for three years, his son Ascanius for thirty, and the Alban kings for three hundred. Furthermore, the people, who would take their name from Romulus, were destined to overcome the limits of time and space: "To them I have granted an Empire which will know no end."[10]

"No end": this was the wish, the blind faith that sought to deny the evidence of history. Vergil regularly contrasted the *res romana* (the Roman state) to the other transient powers (*periturăque regnă*). It appears that while expressing this proud assurance on various occasions, Livy's true intention was to give warning to the man who had made himself guarantor of Rome's eternity, rather than following his guidelines.

In Livy's choice of examples, we can sense another conviction: that Rome's duration is coextensive with her liberty—liberty defined as a progressive extension of rights to underprivileged classes or peoples. When the Tribune Canuleius defended the plebeians' demand to marry into the patrician families, he recalled the changes that had been introduced into the constitution throughout the centuries: the advent of the Republic, the creation of new public offices and sacerdotal orders to fill the needs of an ever-growing population. This city, founded to last eternally, must continue to accept changes in order to keep pace with its expansion. Thus, liberty was conceived to be dynamic in its power to expand and to render a society more just (4.4, 445 B.C.).

This juxtaposition of liberty and eternity, inseparably linked, appears in the words of another tribune, Lucius Furius, when he speaks of the necessity for alternating public offices. Intolerant of the procrastinations of Camillus, who still retained the command despite his years, the younger tribune burst forth: "A city destined to last forever cannot depend on the mortal body of one man, and cannot grow old with him . . ." (6.23, 381 B.C.). Scipio echoed the same thought when he reprimanded his troops, which had revolted upon hearing the false news of his death: "Jupiter Optimus Maximus would never allow a City, which has been founded to last eternally, to be conditioned by the vicissitudes of my fragile, mortal body" (28.28). On this occasion, even the great Scipio renounced the halo of a man of destiny that on other occasions he had laid claim to. Here he openly admitted that though men will perish, Rome shall endure. This episode was perhaps meant as a lesson to the Emperor Augustus. Unlike Romulus or Castor and Pollux, who were all deified only after death, the Princeps was worshiped during his lifetime, and furthermore was declared superior to all men in the present or in the future.[11]

Livy, unlike the poets of his day, does not appear to be a fervent admirer of Augustus. The books dealing with the Emperor's long reign have been lost, but in the extant books, the historian did not exalt Augustus as a cosmic and providential ruler. Livy merely approved of the Emperor's political direction. He mentions him only two or three times: as the man who closed the doors of the Temple of Janus* after his victory at Actium—an event that had not occurred since the end of the Punic Wars; who pacified Spain, the most rebellious of the provinces (28.12); and who furnished him with a precise datum concerning the rank of Cornelius Cossus when he offered the *spolia opima* (the armor of an enemy leader defeated in single combat) to Jupiter Feretrius in 437 B.C. (4.20). This last example gave proof of the Emperor's passionate interest in Rome's ancient history. On this occasion, Livy also praised Augustus for having restored that sanctuary and having reopened, in all, eighty-two sanctuaries that had fallen into disuse and disrepair. The Emperor prided himself on this accomplishment, and listed it in his will with his other innumerable deeds that deserved recognition from the people.

From what little has come down to us about Augustus in Livy's *History*, not even a trace of flattery toward the Emperor is discernible. Augustus jokingly called Livy a "Pompeyan,"[12] because of his favorable opinion of Pompey. It would appear that Livy, rather than joining the chorus of court poets, chose the role of mentor. An obscure provincial, he devoted himself to history, not to fulfill political ambitions or to back his party's platform, but simply out of love for his country. His purpose was to remind all Romans, including the Princeps, that Rome's miraculous deeds had been achieved in a climate of liberty.

The palaestra, where free men could display rhetorical skill

---

* The doors were kept closed during times of peace.

or military valor, had not yet been moved inside the imperial palace; however, a pall hung over it, dimming the features of men and muting their voices. Beyond it, the future lost contour in an atmosphere of apprehensive uncertainty.

> Our Republic is not the work of genius of one man alone, but of many. It was not created during the life span of one individual, but built up throughout the centuries.[13]
> —Cato, in Cicero De Republica 2. 2

Who chose the subjects for the statues in the Forum? What texts were used as documentation for these episodes? Who composed the eulogies that were engraved on the pedestals?

We can imagine a series of meetings in which political and military advisers, Agrippa, and the ever-present Maecenas gathered around the Emperor Augustus and discussed such matters. Perhaps we might even find among them Livy, who was then barely thirty and had just moved to Rome from Padua, where he had been born in 59 B.C., or even Vergil, who, frail and reserved, was intent on tracing the Trojan legends back to their origins.

These were the years immediately following Actium. The danger that the East would demand parity with Rome—or perhaps even superiority—appeared to have been averted. After a century of civil wars, the doors of the Temple of Janus had been closed, and the coins that Augustus had minted bore this symbol as an auspice of lasting peace. The barbarian danger seemed remote. The fear, anguish, and all-pervading sense of precariousness that had characterized the preceding years were replaced by the hope that the Empire would last. It appeared possible to continue the Empire's unifying mission and to block the disruptive forces, provided Roman power could be anchored to the ideals of its formative period, could be rescued from the mounting tendencies toward theocratic and egalitarian absolutism.

The deeds of the legionaries and the social work of tribunes and legislators were re-evoked in order to counteract the tendencies that challenged the Romans' right to world rule. The imperial Romans looked back to their plain, sober ancestors with the tender respect of rich grandchildren who look fondly upon the plain houses of their forefathers, their rudimentary tools, and their simple mode of life. These humble examples were the only ideals that the theoreticians of imperialism could propose to justify Rome's expansion.

The work of the sculptors paralleled that of the literati. The *Aeneid* was begun in 29 B.C., Livy's *History* in 27, the year that Octavian took the title "Augustus." As soon as the land for the new Forum had been expropriated and the houses demolished, the Emperor started the construction of the monumental complex, which was solemnly inaugurated twenty-five years later—possibly the same year that Livy stopped writing. Although a funeral inscription found in Padua would lead us to believe that he died in his home town in A.D. 17,[14] the final page of his books (of which we have only brief summaries, the so-called Epitome) deals with the year 9 B.C.

The meaning of Livy's dual messages, the figurative and the literary, was unequivocal. The Empire had not been created by ambitious, arrogant men, or by fortune. Since it had been governed fairly, it could not incur the disfavor of the gods. The stern, valiant nature of the ancestors proved the truth of these assertions. They embodied the Romans' positive qualities, which contrasted with the negative traits of the aliens and of the heterogeneous, undisciplined plebeians, lacking roots and moral tradition, who made up the bulk of the Roman citizenry.

The *imagines* in the Forum and those that were paraded in the Emperor's funeral procession also appeared in the *Aeneid*. In the Elysian Fields, Anchises pointed out to Aeneas the spirits of those Romans who were destined to achieve lasting renown. These men were saturated with *virtus* even before they were born: Camillus, Torquatus, Cato, the Decii, the Drusi, the Gracchi, the Scipios, Fabricius, Cincinnatus, Fabius Maximus. Venus, also, showed her son these figures and related their deeds, which had been carved on Vulcan's shield; the cycle began with the twins nursed by the she-wolf, the seven kings, the heroes. All of Rome's illustrious forebears were present, even Cato, Caesar's unrelenting opponent. All of them were counted by Augustus as his illustrious precursors.[15]

It was hoped that the men who contemplated those austere faces and read about their deeds would be stirred to emulation and would define good and evil according to their scale of values. Though those values were still valid for a man like Livy, who was descended from a conservative, provincial family, this was not the case for a society that had been decimated by civil wars. During the years of fratricidal strife, the Roman component had been submerged by an overwhelming number of immigrants and foreign slaves, who brought with them all sorts of novelties—doctrines, gods, arts, customs, games, fashions, and vices.

What the Augustan poets, faithful to the dictates of a moral and conservative policy, had condensed into a few hexameters, Livy expounded with such a wealth of detail that he is undoubtedly the most frequently cited author in any field of history—economic, juridical, religious. His goal, however, was not to provide accurate, quantitative, and chronological data or to publish unknown documents. Instead, he explored the causes of Rome's development from a small agricultural community to the capital of the world. He underlined the uniqueness of this evolution, and emphasized the characteristics of the Roman spirit.

Livy's history is so dramatic, so rich in battles, psychological insights, and pathos that it can be enjoyed as a record of events, but in a deeper sense it is like a choral composition in which characters representing abstract values are grouped in symbolic combinations. Livy found solace in evoking these events, he enjoyed the company of these noble spirits, he yields to that romantic yet didactic nostalgia for the pure, simple customs of a bygone era. It was a nostalgia originating in a historical and metaphysical anxiety: his is a dismay over the recent fratricidal struggles that had spread economic dislocation and unrest in their wake, scorn for a skeptical, lazily self-indulgent society aiming only at the undisturbed enjoyment of its wealth, even at the price of servility. He shares the Romans' inferiority complex with regard to Greek culture and an undefined restlessness spread by the wave of oracular literature, most of which has since been lost or destroyed.

From that vast array of people and events, Livy evolves a knowledge of what constitutes the good. The past revealed to him the eternal laws for growth, and from them he extrapolated the rules for man's conduct.

Mankind was guided by fate, a fate that bore the imprint of a stoic, providential nature; it identified with the gods, or was even stronger than they. Fate had presided over Rome's foundation: "But the Fates were resolved, I think, on the founding of this great city and the beginning of such a vast empire, next after that of Heaven" (1.4). We can sense the tone of Livy's entire history from his opening remarks. It was fate that made Camillus massacre the inhabitants of Veii (5.19), and Marcus Manlius disobey the Consul—a rash decision that cost him his life (8.7). Again, it was fate that encouraged the Gauls to pounce on Rome precisely when Camillus was far away (5.33). Sometimes, however, events were decided by fortune, which was just as unpredictable and inscrutable as fate. Though fortune collaborated with *virtus*, she often bestowed her gifts on the unworthy. As Aeneas said to his son Ascanius, "from me, you can learn *virtus* and deeds, from the others, *fortuna*."[16] "With a good commander fortune was of little moment," said Fabius Maximus (22.25).

The will power of the ideal Roman was so strong that even when overwhelmed by supernatural forces, he was not subjugated by them. He could overcome them, in time, by bearing suffering and sacrifice with steadfastness. A few years later, Seneca, pondering over Livy's *exempla*, wrote that "Mucius Scaevola was stronger than fire, Attilius Regulus stronger than the cross. . . . Cato defeated the death he had imposed upon himself with his own sword. . . ."[17]

Livy was aware of the rivalry between Greece and Rome, of the hatred that Alexandria and Judea bore the City, and of the Parthian and Germanic threat. He recognized the hostile propaganda spread by Hellenic literati and by the Egypto-Judaean oracles for what it was. In the previous three decades, Rome had changed the geography of the world. Pompey had quelled the revolt instigated by Mithridates in the Eastern provinces, and had annexed Judea and the Middle Eastern lands up to the shores of the Caspian Sea. Then Augustus annexed Egypt. Rome pushed her armies as far as Ethiopia and Arabia, appointed kings in Armenia, sent colonies of veteran soldiers to Asia and Syria, and extended the Illyrian borders to the Danube. And according to Augustus in the *Testamentum Ancyranum*, his last will, all the while ambassadors arrived in Rome from India, from the Sarmatians, the Scythians, the Parthians, and the Medes.[18]

The East looked upon Rome with hatred. As had always been the case, it communicated its tragic sense of history to the victors. History was reviewed as a cyclical drama built on recurrent disasters in which one event—perhaps an imminent one—would change the future for all the world's peoples.

Livy was conscious of various forces undermining Rome—the apocalyptic predictions of doom exploited by a politics of demagogic egalitarianism, the alienation of discontent and sloth, subtle subversions rather than open opposition which provided the basis for the disintegration bound to occur with the passage of time. In one of Cicero's finest pages,[19] Scipio looks down on the Empire from the heavens, and finds it a paltry construction compared to the universe. The disparagement of the Empire by the philosophers unintentionally strengthened Rome's adversaries.

Livy observed a shift of values. Deeds, great works are no longer regarded highly, and yet he is unable to define what has taken their place. A sense of melancholy came to tarnish the sparkle of new victories; it distracted the Roman spirit from the ambitions and glorious objectives of former times; it discredited the guardian divinities. This insidious state of mind derived from a lack of interest in the *res publica*, and was latent not only among the oppressed classes and races but also among the upper classes. These subtle changes did not chronologically follow the compact civism of the Republican era, as one phase succeeds another. They simply spread. Starting at the lowest social levels, they flowed from countries that contributed to Roman culture doctrines and ideas rather than treasure. They had seeped into the Roman spirit and had dampened its sturdy vitality.

There was a need for solitude and meditation, a thirst for direct contact with the divine, a feverish receptivity to mystery, which extinguished the desire for action and stripped their meaning from victories and glory itself. Each man was absorbed in the mission he felt incumbent on him: to save that small particle of light imprisoned within sordid matter. The citizens felt solidarity with members of the same sect, participants in the same mysteries, or victims of the same tax collectors, rather than with members of their own race, born in the same city. Turning from the feverish construction of terrestrial cities, they longed for their heavenly home. Religion was dissociating itself from politics.

Disinterest in the state or escape into the artificial paradises of ecstasy seemed equally condemnable in the mind of anyone who viewed man as an instrument for perpetuating the Republic's greatness. Livy hoped to build a dam stemming these tributaries of dissolution. Stone by stone, he extracted from the shapeless heap of the past only what would best serve his needs. And then he skillfully arranged these pieces to arrest the flood.

> Proud Rome is broken by her own opulence.[20]
> —Propertius 3. 13. 60

Whoever sets his ideal in the past implies in every sentence and in every episode a covert comparison and views the present with pessimism. In Livy's view, history is intrinsically the story of decline. From the introduction to the end, his work is dominated by the same perspective, which confers to the actions and utterances of his characters an ideal coherence. The historian wanted to reconstruct Rome's development from her modest origins to a majesty now so extensive that "her very size is a burden to her." Readers, he says, surely want a new interpretation of recent events, but he was almost relieved whenever he could take refuge in the security of the past, because "recently one can witness how a formerly valiant race is destroying its own strength."

The phenomenon he denounced was not an isolated occurrence. "There is no great city," said Hannibal to the Carthaginians, "that can survive in peacetime for long . . . the same holds true for robust individuals: one might say that they are immune to external harm, but instead are weighed down by the burden of their own strength . . ." (30.44). Other factors can accelerate or halt this gravitation toward decadence: "Cities," Romulus's messengers argued, "like everything else in this world, start from nothing"—and here we sense the stoic, humanistic, and providential scope of Livy's historical vision—"but achieve great power and renown by their worth [*virtus*] and divine favor . . ." (1.9). This favor will be denied, however, every time *virtus* fails. The Romans, when asked to help the city of Clusium, sent ambassadors to negotiate with the Gauls, who had swept down into Etruria (391 B.C.). Instead of using diplomatic means, the Romans behaved as imperiously and arrogantly as the barbarians. Fate, overhanging the city, induced them to forget the diplomatic responsibilities of their mission, and thus to disregard the rights of nations. Instead of remaining neutral, the three Fabii joined the melee on the side of the Clusians, and one of them with his sword struck down the commander of the Gauls (5.36). For this breach of faith (*fides*), Rome was sacked and burned the following year (390 B.C.).

Equally serious calamities strike anyone who acts inconsiderately or is guilty of arrogance, *hubris*, or *temeritas* (fool-hardiness)—the typical plebeian vices. The defeat at the Trebia (218 B.C.) was the result of the rash behavior of the Consul Sempronius, bent on distinguishing himself for the upcoming elections (21.63). The defeat at Lake Trasimenus was the fault of another plebeian consul, Flaminius, who was imprudent and, worse still, irreverent to the gods. Upon various occasions he had disobeyed the Senate and had neglected the proper religious rituals. His vulgar pride blinded him to the impending dangers forecast by three frightening omens: on the day of his induction, the sacrificial calf had fled, bleeding, from the altar, his horse reared as he was preparing to attack the enemy; the herald could not pull the standard from the ground. But with the impulsiveness characteristic of vulgar men, Flaminius nonetheless dashed into the field and was severely defeated (22.3, 317 B.C.). A third vainglorious plebeian, Consul Varro, joined the revolt he had instigated, then forced his colleagues to assent to marching on that village,

"Cannae, whose name would be remembered for the massacre of the Romans that took place there" (22.42-43, 216 B.C.).

The verification of Rome's grandeur causes the historian to reflect on that achievement with certain misgivings. After the Romans had conquered the neighboring peoples, they started to move against the Samnites. Here Livy paused a moment to describe the growing dimensions of the war theater, the distance from the fronts, the duration of the campaigns, the numerical make-up of the enemy, and commented: "How vast a series of events! How many times the extremity of danger was incurred so that our Empire might be exalted to its present greatness, hardly to be maintained . . ." (7.29).

This greatness, as Romulus had solemnly declared after he had ascended to heaven, had been the will of the gods (1.16). Sometimes, however, the very same men who pursued this goal also contested its validity. In the first conflict between Rome and Alba Longa, the Alban dictator Mettius Fufetius proposed resolving this rivalry through a duel among three champions from each city in order to avoid useless bloodshed. At the same time, he recognized the inanity of that power race: "since we are not content with unquestioned liberty, but are proceeding to the doubtful hazard of dominion or enslavement . . ." (1.23). These are Livy's feelings, dating back to the seventh century B.C. The two armies watched the duel among the six champions with trepidation, and were fully aware that "empire was staked on the valor and good fortune of those few . . ." (1.25).

Upon other occasions, the City's imperialism was condemned by her enemies. Sallust made Mithridates and Jugurtha speak out against Rome, tacitly agreeing himself. Tacitus was to do the same with the rebels in the European provinces. Antiochus wrote to the King of Bithynia that "the Romans come to destroy all kingdoms so that there will be no other dominion in the world except Rome" (37.25, 190 B.C.).

In Livy's day, that goal had been reached, but the new power had produced alarming changes in Rome's spirit and her customs. The historian noted the restlessness of his times with concern, though he could not guess in what direction the population would channel its spiritual vitality. Loyal to the ancient values, he praised the Romans of bygone days: "Never did one see such a strong, virtuous state nor a people that learned greed and vice so late and honored poverty and frugality for so long. . . ."

"So late" and "so long": these terms presuppose that decay is a process inherent in all living things. And Rome was no exception, although evidence of her decline appeared very gradually. The Romans learned to appreciate beauty; they became collectors and connoisseurs of art, lovers of antiques, gourmets and epicureans. They imitated the lordly manners of the East and the gracious art of living, which refined their spirits but, at the same time, destroyed their old customs. ("Lately," observed Livy, "the variety of pleasures offers every possible occasion for squandering.") The first signs that the Romans were weakening and yielding to luxury dated back to the end of the Macedonian Wars, when the legions returned home. It was then that the Romans started dining to the music of the harp and lute: ". . . things that caused a scandal in those days, but were nothing compared to the luxuries that followed later on" (39.6).

Livy evidently agreed with the position taken by Cato the Censor, and supported the latter's famous speech against the abrogation of the Oppian Law, which had severely limited the luxuries of the Roman matrons: "As fortune shines on the Republic and as the Empire expands, we have been owned by our possessions, rather than owning them—ever since we have gone to Greece and Asia and have captured kings' treasures" (34.4). This new love of art turned the Romans away from their ancient terra-cotta idols, which still kept benevolent

watch over the City. It also awakened two apparently contradictory passions—greed and prodigality, "vices that have
dragged the most powerful empires to ruin. . . ."

Decline was inevitable. Livy denounced this decadence in
solemn, melancholy tone as he piously cited the complete
archaic rituals. "I do not feel that it is extraneous to my
undertaking to relate these things exactly as they were originally formulated and transmitted, although today every memory of these former sacred and profane uses has been obliterated; now everything that is new and foreign is preferred to
the ancient customs of the fatherland . . ." (8.11).

The poets transformed this nostalgia for the past into a
vague regret for a mythical and pastoral epoch ("then one did
not hear the blaring of trumpets nor the ringing of swords on
the anvil").[21] The historian, however, regarded the decline as
a change in spirit and in customs. Once upon a time, nobody
was envious of a person who excelled. Both the mother and
the wife of Coriolanus earned fame when they stopped him
from leading enemy troops against the city. "So free was life
in those days from disparagement of another's glory," commented Livy (2.40).

The change had taken place in man's spirit rather than in
the world around him. After the long struggle between the
patricians and the plebeians, the latter finally obtained a further increase of their political rights, but they were careful
not to abuse these new privileges. Livy observed: "Today
where could you find even one person who would show the
same wisdom, the same magnanimity, the same rectitude as
the entire population once demonstrated?" (4.7). The young
men agreed to vote a second time when the Consul, who had
been honestly elected with their support, declared that he was
unfit to take office for reasons of health: "Vote again," he
said, "and remember that the Punic War is being fought in
Italy and that the enemy commander is Hannibal. . . ."

Those young men not only accepted his plea, but even consulted with their elders about the choice of the best candidate. Livy's bitter comment was "Let them come now to scoff at ancient times! Even if that Republic of wise men, which our intellectuals imagined without ever having seen it, were really to exist, could one find among those in authority leaders more austere and unsullied by political ambitions, or a more disciplined electorate? That the younger generation wanted to ask the opinion of the older men in their choice of the best candidate seems incredible in this century, when even parental authority over their children is despised and weak . . ." (26.22, 211 B.C.).

> History is very close to poetry; it is, in a certain sense, poetry in prose.[22]
>
> —Quintilian *Institutio Oratoria* 10. 1. 31

Drawing on sources deeply rooted in Greco-Roman civilization, Livy records legends like that of the she-wolf, which modern critics have branded as a myth typical of a totem society or, on the basis of comparative psychology, linguistics, and ethnology, have classified among the archetypes of the subconscious, or among the mental categories characteristic of all primitive societies. These are Greek myths that contain references to a common ethnic origin, to divine ancestors, such as Hercules and Evander, who preceded Aeneas from Greece to Latium, to judges whose names were recorded on the linen pages of the *libri lintei* (which antedate the *Fasti*, of which only marble fragments remain), and to those meteorological and commodity data that the Pontifex Maximus had recorded on the *Tabulae Dealbatae*, white-painted wooden tablets, documents that were destroyed by fire during the invasion of Rome by the Gauls in 390 B.C.

Livy recalled everything that happened before that date

with affection and reverence. Occasionally the authenticity of those immemorial sources is recognizable when he quotes them in their original simplicity: "Under the Consulship of Marcus Valerius and Spurius Verginius there was a shortage of grain because of inclement weather" (3.31). In general, however, the facts are diluted in rhetorical prolixity. Sometimes he repeats ritual formulas in their entirety, as, for example, the exchange of questions and answers in their prescribed form between the victor and the heralds of the vanquished in the *deditio*—the unconditional surrender according to which the victor, after he had ordered the messengers to declare their office, their powers, and by whom these had been conferred, asked if they were ready to surrender themselves, the people, city, lands, water, boundary marks, shrines, utensils, in short, everything they possessed (1.38).

In another example, we find a declaration of war pronounced by the Pater Patratus, the leading priest of a religious order (the Fetiales), which handled differences with foreigners. He recited the warning formula at the border of the enemy's territory, at the gates of the city, in the market square. After invoking the gods of the fatherland, he demanded satisfaction for the offenses suffered and added, "if what I ask is unjust and unholy, may I never see my native land again."[23] The Romans allowed the enemy thirty-three days in which to comply. If by that time they had not received a satisfactory answer and if the King and the Senate had voted in favor of war, then the priest returned to the borders. As he pronounced a similar formula, he threw a spear into the enemy territory (1.32).

The details of Decius's *devotio* (dedication) were also recorded in this solemn, severely liturgical style. In order to guarantee a Roman victory, Decius, having consulted the priests on the forms of the ritual and the exact formula of recitation, dedicated himself and the enemy army to the gods of the underworld. He put on the *toga praetexta* (the national dress of the ancient Romans, worn by curule magistrates and even adolescents, up to the age of seventeen) and stood on a lance that had been placed under his feet. These excerpts are of archaic rigidity, and reinforce the evocative power of the historian's account.

Livy found other information in the reports of the senatorial meetings and in the private archives of the great families, which in some cases had been transferred from the level of ancestral records to that of history: Fabius Pictor, Valerius Antias, Claudius Quadrigarius (all authors cited by Livy) had written histories that favored their respective families, the Fabii, the Valerii, and the Claudii. There were also commemorative poems, like those of Livius Andronicus, Naevius, and Ennius. In those years, like everything that belonged to ancient Latium, they had become fashionable, part of a nostalgic nationalism. "Today any poem about bygone times is sacred," observed Horace, who considered these rustic compositions unsophisticated at best.[24] Other biographical sources were undoubtedly the funeral eulogies, often amplified for the sake of fame and not immune from interpolations, lacunae, or other changes (8.40), as Livy well knew.

He mentions many authors, the most famous being Polybius, but makes no effort to indicate systematically the sources or verify their reliability. He notes discrepancies, and often doubts statements that might have been motivated by patrician pride or political tendentiousness. Whenever possible, he compares texts. He deliberately changes facts for one purpose only: the glorification of Roman *virtus*.

Attempts have been made to identify the members of that "vast company of authors" with whom, in his Introduction, he admits measuring himself "not without qualms." Only fragments remain of some of these authors; of others, nothing but the names. These indistinct faces and invisible presences are concealed behind the impersonal formulas: *traditur; constat; fama est* (it is reported; it is known; it is said).

The Punic and Macedonian Wars had awakened in the Romans a desire to transmit the story of their important deeds to posterity. The first compositions, annals in Greek written in poetic form, were perhaps echoes of archaic *chansons de geste*. Even today, the suggestive hypothesis formulated by Niebuhr at the beginning of the last century is still under discussion. According to Barthold Georg Niebuhr,* some of the most dramatic episodes of Latin historiography probably derive from convivial songs.[25] As the poets entertained the dinner guests with their songs, they also acted as a link between daily reality and the experiences of men who in these sagas assumed the statuesque immobility of the gods, and thereby became perennial guiding images for the common people. Tacitus said of the Germans: "They celebrated their heroes through song, the only form of history they know." This is a common practice among all peoples who have reached a certain degree of cultural development, and thus, at least from the ethnological point of view, Niebuhr's hypothesis seems plausible. Cato knew that these rudimentary compositions had existed. He regretted, however, that they had been lost because, in his opinion, the pontifical chronicles, which listed only food prices and eclipses, could not be considered history.[26]

Perhaps the compositions of these troubadours were absorbed into the epics, annals, and tragedies by osmosis. Although Aristotle had defined them as distinct genres,[27] history and poetry often treated the same themes, drawn from the same mythological sources. Legendary elements lived on in history, while historical data crept into poetry. The tone of moral edification made the two genres very similar.

---

* Nineteenth-century German historian.

All of Livy's work is permeated with this moral spirit. His heroes talk in axioms and know, without a moment's hesitation, what maxim to pronounce, what precedent to cite, to which ethical code to adhere. Scipio, the typical example of Roman continence in opposition to Numidian lust, admonishes Massinissa with the accents of a spiritual leader and chides him for having celebrated his marriage with Sophonisba in record time: "The danger, these days, does not come from the enemy's arms, but from the pleasures that assail us from every side. Whoever can succeed in overcoming them with temperance wins honor and a greater victory than we won over Syphax. . . ." When, on other occasions, he returned a captive virgin to her betrothed and relatives, he spoke like a boring, sanctimonious hypocrite (26.1). The ethical fortitude of his character regularly prevailed over vaster historical factors. *Virtus* was becoming an ideological tool.

Faced with a hazardous trial or a conflict of duty, the first thing a Roman did was to consult the spirits of his ancestors. A particular kind of moral behavior, a distinct way of defining *virtus* is discernible in the history of each patrician family. At intervals of a few years or of centuries two Bruti suppressed a tyrant, two Decii offered their lives to the gods in order to save Rome, three Valerii proposed to law of appeal whereby the people could change a death sentence into exile, two Gracchi were killed because of their love of the people, two Catos rose up as champions of ancient austerity. Despite changing conditions, the Scipios and the Fabii behaved like their ancestors, almost as if they were a single individual who continued to live on for centuries. Political ideas, merits, and faults were transmitted as if by a hereditary law. The arrogance of the Claudii, the stubborn enemies of the plebes, was deplored by Livy, who considered their systematic opposition to all reforms pernicious to the cause of liberty and progress (2.27-29). Their "fierce and arrogant" spirit was passed on from father to son, and made them odious to the people and detrimental to the stability of the state. And yet they were held in high esteem by the conservatives, who sang their praises every time they gave proof of "not being unworthy of their race" (4.48).

When Lucius Lentulus was forced to persuade the consuls to submit to the shamefulness of the Caudine Forks,* he bitterly recalled how differently his father had acted in a similar situation. The father dissuaded the Senate from submitting to the humiliating delivery of the gold that Brennus† had demanded. "If we had the possibility of attacking the enemy, even on unfavorable terrain, then I would not fail to live up to my father's example: surrender is a disgrace. But the fatherland is so dear that, in order to save it, we must be ready to serve it not only by dying but even with ignominy . . ." (9.7). Titus Manlius condemned his own son to death because he had fought outside the lines, against his father's orders (8.7, 340 B.C.). A second Manlius opposed ransom for the soldiers who had fallen prisoners to the Carthaginians at Cannae "because they comported themselves neither like men nor like Romans" (32, 217 B.C.).

This patrician ethical code, transmitted from father to son, had become imbued with Stoic doctrine, from which it derived a wider scope and the validity of an ethical doctrine peculiar to the Romans. Augustus takes up this mandate, and Livy, drawing on Stoicism, interprets the past in a manner that often sounds oracular. He creates a portrait gallery of superhuman figures, of majestic, static beings who are not to be seen as historical personages but, rather, as representatives of an inner truth. Livy wrote a long vast funeral eulogy to a

---

* A small plain between two mountain passes (in the vicinity of Capua) where the Samnites had entrapped a Roman army in 321 B.C. See page 115.
† Commander of the Semnones, who had seized Rome (except the Capitol) in 390 B.C. When the ransom was weighed, he put his sword on the scale, exclaiming, *Vae victis!*

kind of man and a set of ideals which were disappearing. He reduced history to a selection of dramatic "moments," chosen for their impact.

> Ah, here are the minds whose company I should have shared![28]
> —Rousseau

Livy fails to mention the providential and egalitarian aspects of Augustus's reign, which reflected the trends of the day; he culled only the conservative traits based on republican and hegemonic values. The characters in his epic are meant to serve as a reminder for contemporary men of the duties incumbent on the ideal soldier and the ideal citizen who, confronted with cosmopolitan concepts and the relativity of all principles, had lost their bearings. The historian's entire work was built on the premise that the Empire could be saved only if certain virtues were respected and exercised. But what were these virtues?

In Livy's work there is no catalogue of virtues, but each episode illustrates an unequivocal concept of duty. Livy's vision is one-dimensional: he does not cover up ambiguous sympathies or interior conflicts. His is, above all, a civic conception: man does not count per se, but only as a member of the community. Man's passions hold interest for the historian only if they unleash wars or revolutions. Thus, Tarquin's precipitous entrance into Lucretia's bedroom was important only because it marked the beginning of the Republic. The adultery between Tullus Hostilius's daughter and her brother-in-law was simply a connivance between two people motivated by ambition, not by love. Tarpeia betrayed her country because of greed for gold. The virtuous characters were just as stylized. Coriolanus's mother rejected her son's embrace ("Let me first know whether an enemy or a son stands before me . . .") (2.40). Here Livy, as is often the case, adds a detail to accentuate Roman steadfastness, whereas according to Dionysius of Halicarnassus, Coriolanus's mother simply wept (8.45).

Tormented and complex figures such as Othello, Medea, and Orestes do not exist for Livy. Since his choice of examples was meant to be a school for greatness, feelings were relegated to a secondary plane. Contrasting virtues typify certain classes: rashness is a trait of the plebeians, prudence of the patricians; the plebeian *temeritas* of the two consuls responsible for the defeats of the Trebia and Lake Trasimenus contrasts with the disciplined steadfastness shown by the patrician Fabius Maximus. He resisted both the contemptuous provocations and the ambushes of Hannibal, exasperated by his rival's elusive tactics ("but in the silence of his heart he was troubled by the thought that he would have a general to deal with by no means like Flaminius or Sempronius") (22.12, 217 B.C.). Fabius withstood the defamatory tactics and the open accusations of his officers, who were intolerant of his caution. His answer to anyone who rejoiced over the outcome of an uncertain skirmish was "that he feared success more than adversity." When the soldiers' discontent and the plebeians' anger reached Rome, and he was publicly criticized in marketplace and Senate, the dictator did not bother to justify his actions to the masses "since it is not a matter for their competence." Instead, he went directly to the Senate and presented the suspicious Conscripted Fathers with his philosophy of action rather than with a justification for his actions: "If his authority and strategy were allowed to prevail, he would soon let people know that with a good commander fortune is of little moment; that mind and reason were in control" (22.25). Fabius expressed the same principles in his warning to the Consul Lucius Aemilius Paullus when the latter left for the war. The Consul was endangered by the rashness and demagogy of his plebeian colleague Varro more than by Hannibal. Fabius told the young Roman: "Make reason, not fortune, your guide" (22.39), but Varro goaded his troops to insubordination and swept the army to the disastrous defeat at Cannae.

Solemn, sententious, the Romans showed what heights of heroism can be reached with composed dignity. The day the Gauls were about to storm the city, "in Rome everyone in the citadel was ready for the defense." After the Romans had decided to abandon the dwelling area to the enemy, "the old people, firm in their decision to die, returned to their own homes to await the enemy. Those who had held offices in the magistrature donned the solemn vestments of the charioteers of the sacred chariots or of the triumphant victors, so they would die wearing the honors earned through valor and the insignia of their former rank. Thus attired, each man sat in the ivory seat placed in the center of his house. According to some sources, the Pontifex Maximus even recited the ritual formulas that consecrated victims who had given their life for the fatherland and for their fellow citizens" (5.41, 390 B.C.).

The noble conduct of these old patricians, *simillimi dîs* (altogether similar to gods), who knew how to die without flinching, was paralleled by that of the proud legionaries on the battlefield. Forced to submit to the disgrace of the Caudine Forks, at first they railed against their consuls, whose rashness and cowardice had put them into such a shameful situation. "As they uttered these complaints, the fateful hour of their humiliation came, an hour far more bitter than they had foreseen. First, they were ordered to come out, unarmed, clad only in their tunics. . . . Next, the lictors were commanded to stand apart from the Consuls, who then were stripped of their generals' cloaks, a thing that inspired such compassion in those very men who only shortly before had cursed them and had declared that they deserved to be given up and put to torture, that every man, forgetting his own mortification, looked away from the degradation of so majestic an office as though it were a spectacle of horror" (9.5, 321 B.C.).

Livy's point of departure is a rigorously conceived and unifying principle: individual and collective examples of discipline, sacrifice, and civic pride are arranged and illustrated in turn. He infuses such passion and such poetry into his prose that even generic personifications acquire a forceful individuality, and stand out vigorously against a dark historical backdrop. Through concise sentences and suggestive silences, he constructs a moral truth that asserts itself independently from the verification of his sources and the exactness of his data. Critics have analyzed, compared, confuted, and often demolished Livy's narration; they have assiduously tried to reconstruct the true history of Rome from other sources, often fragmentary or secondhand. Though they may deny Livy's version, they cannot suppress it. Even if it was pure invention, it would still be authentic and important for the reasons that led him to write it—namely, the recent discord, the incessant barbarian rumblings at the borders, the restlessness in the provinces, and the economic and social demands. A vast tide was spreading and submerging the very foundations of the Empire.

The figures that Livy immersed in a rarefied, remote aura towered within this ominous landscape. Throughout the centuries, they were a source of inspiration to the young, an object of meditation to those athirst for glory, symbolic names to patriots. They were omnipresent in the repertory of the classical theater, provided actors with opportunities to display their interpretative talents, and painters with themes for their experiments in color and volume—the clash between Horatii and Curiatii, battles, triumphs, Sabine virgins in disarray and tears. The adjective "Roman" evoked severely draped togas, powerful muscles, glittering helmets, burnished shields, rearing horses, vertical lines of lances and standards juxtaposed to horizontal cloud formations and fallen soldiers. These clean-shaven faces were meant to illustrate typical Roman qualities to the amorphous masses inclined to put everything in doubt, ready to accept any belief, and to serve anyone as long as they could live in peace and feel directed and protected.

For centuries the myth of Roman patriotism has tinged Italian history with emotional warmth and passionate nostalgia.

> *O how adventuresome, dear and blessed were*
> *Those ancient times when men*
> *Sought death in throngs for their beloved country!*[29]

The vision of Roman greatness, based on deeds, not ideas, is the leitmotif of Latin literature; however, this nostalgic longing for ancient sternness and frugality also constitutes its inner weakness. Livy and the writers of his day asked the same question that had tormented the Scipios. They still pondered over the first solution given by Polybius, Panaetius, and Posidonius, who all had invoked Roman moral and political superiority as justification for Rome's dominion and as a guarantee for its duration. The Latin inability to imagine anything "greater than Rome" (Horace *Carmen Saeculare*) was the key to the Empire's spiritual insufficiency, the weakness from which it suffered from its beginnings, ideological deficiency. In historiography, it derived from a social insensitivity and short-sightedness in the face of the plurality of the historical phenomenon.

> To act and to endure valiantly is the Roman way.[30]
> —Livy 2. 12

At this moment the definition of the Roman spirit was crystallizing, and the idea of the fatherland was being replaced by a cosmopolitanism that viewed tradition and religion as useful instruments for conserving the supremacy of one class and one race and for stimulating competition. The intellectuals became aware of the importance of ethnic values and wore them as a badge of honor. In 37 b.c.—ten years before Livy started his *History*—Varro was writing *De Re Rustica*, a work that reflected Catonian influence and later served as a model for Vergil's *Georgics*. The agrarian origins of the Roman race were becoming a source of pride.

Frankness and honesty were considered the outstanding Roman traits. Camillus scornfully rejected the proposal of the Faliscan tutor, who offered him as hostages the youths entrusted to his custody: "Between the Faliscans and us," he answered, "there are no pacts founded on men's covenants, but only that human solidarity we both respect. . . . I shall conquer them [the Faliscans] as I conquered Veii—with the Roman arts of valor, toil, and arms . . ." (5.27, 394 b.c.). After Mucius Scaevola missed his target, he placed his right hand in the flames, saying, "To act and to endure valiantly is the Roman way" (2.12).[31] Fabricius explained to King Pyrrhus how Roman principles differed from those of the Greeks, and denounced the deserter who had offered to poison the King (39.51).

The enemy nations parade across Livy's historical stage with their stereotyped characteristics. It was invariably the others, the "aliens," who luxuriated in rich vestments and splendid armor. The King of Veii stood out in the distance because of his opulent mantle (4.19). The Sabines had tempted Tarpeia with heavy golden bracelets, and had made her betray her country (1.11). The Samnites wore superb helmets and carried magnificent shields (10.40), as can be seen in the decorations of the Lucanian tombs in Paestum. The Gauls always wore their *torques* or golden necklaces. In fact, Titus Manlius Torquatus acquired this surname because he was the first Roman to kill a Gaul in single combat (6.42).

After Scipio's victory over the Gaulish Boii in 191 B.C. the Romans collected 1,471 *torques*, 247 pounds of gold, 2,340 pounds of silver—in part worked and in part in ingots (36.40); Marcellus gathered similar war trophies after he defeated the Insubrian Gauls (33.36).

Italy had her first contact with the Gauls in 390 B.C., when the barbarians savagely raced down the peninsula. The endurance of these fierce warriors "with long tawny hair, huge shields and enormous swords" did not match their arrogance, and they were quickly broken by the Mediterranean climate and by exertion. Livy contrasted their blind violence with the constancy and measured rationality of the Romans: "Nature has endowed these people, who advance in hordes, with bodily size and courage, great, indeed but vacillating . . ." (5.44). When the Romans again met the Gauls, two centuries later in Asia Minor, where some of the tribes had migrated, they found their old enemy unchanged: "They move into battle screaming their war chants over the deafening din of clashing metal, but their bodies are soft, and their spirits are also soft when their fury abates . . ." (38.17).

Likewise the *perfidia punica* (Punic perfidy) was contrasted with the *romana fides* (Roman loyalty). The Carthaginians stole from their treasury (16.6) and did not respect treaties (34.31), whereas in Rome the old senators actually scorned the diplomats' tricks: "Loyalty and frankness, not Punic perfidy or Greek cunning, are the Roman arms" (42.67). Livy hinted at unnatural loves in the Punic army (21.3), and described Hannibal, the great enemy of the City, as the antithesis of the Roman leaders. The historian stressed the fierceness of Hannibal's African temperament, just as Sallust had done with Jugurtha. While Hannibal's courage, his skill, his adaptability, and his endurance of discomfort and hardship were praiseworthy, these exceptional qualities were accompanied by monstrous, typically barbarian vices: "Inhuman cruelty, perfidy worse than Punic; nothing was sacred to him; he had no fear of the gods, no reverence for the oath, no religious scruple . . . (21.4). By contrast, the various consuls who led the operations against the Carthaginians were distinguished by their religious observance, their prudence, their steadfastness.

When he writes of Eastern peoples, Livy contrasts their tendency to excessive indulgence in pleasure with Roman sobriety. As a consul told his legionaries, "You will find that the Gauls have become weak and degenerate after their long sojourn in Asia . . . by now they are nothing more than Phrygians wearing Gallic armor . . . they are no longer the Gauls of former times . . . ever since they moved, many generations ago, to this opulent land with its mild skies and gentle people, their fierceness has been undermined . . . you, who are sons of Mars, by Hercules, hurry up and escape from Asian charms; here pleasure is so strong that it can extinguish the vigor in one's soul . . ." (38.17).

Civic conscience, the Romans' most salient trait, was completely lacking among the Asians, who were accustomed to despotism. "In the place of laws," Livy wrote, "they have always had kings" (37.54). The typical Roman characteristics were reinforced through these comparisons to the discredit of the Eastern nations. According to Cicero, "Jews and Syrians" were "nations born to serve. . . ."[32]

Give me one Cato for three hundred Socrates.[33]
—Annaeus Florus *Epigramma* 8

This biting comparison sprang from the burning sense of inferiority that the Romans felt toward the Greeks, whose futile vainglory—*levitas*—was invariably juxtaposed to the solid Roman character. Whoever wants to remain a Roman—this was told of Cato, Marius, Augustus, and Tiberius—refuses to speak Greek, even if he knows that language. It almost appeared as though this was a way to avoid contagion from its insidious fluidity. "Words," said Cato, "come from the Romans' heart, [but] from the Greeks' lips. . . ." Cicero wrote to his brother that the Greeks "for the most part, are frivolous, deceitful, and because of their prolonged servitude, most adept in agreeing with you with excessive enthusiasm."[84] And Livy wrote that "the only thing that remains of their past glory is their arrogance . . ." (31.14). "They are ever ready to listen to agitators, and nowhere are there so many of the latter as in Athens" (31.45); "they wage war with their mouths and pens, the only things in which they excel" (31.45).

Thus the Romans reacted to Greek superiority in thought and culture, and thus they countered the cold war of the East. Latin authors repeated the contemptuous judgments once pronounced by the Greeks upon the Romans. "The Romans' language, their customs and laws," said King Philip to the representatives of the *pòleis* who had gathered for the Aetolian Diet, "separate us from them more than the miles of land and sea that lie between us . . ." (31.29).

In an attempt to refute the Greek historians, whose accounts were hardly flattering to Rome, Livy wrote the only diffuse digression in his tightly knit narration of events and personalities. It was directed against those *levissimi ex Graecis*, whom he did not further identify. "These people," he wrote, "go around saying that Alexander could have routed the Romans had he turned his armies westward instead of eastward, and they even dare to assert that the Parthian forces are superior to the Romans'. . . ."

Scholars have tried to identify who was the target of Livy's passionate refutation, whether it is complete or fragmentary, and whether it refers to *fortuna* and *virtus* as agencies in the growth of the Empire—the Greeks favoring the first and the

Romans the latter. Here, it does not matter whether Livy's target was the Greek Timagenes, a friend of Augustus's indomitable enemy Asinius Pollio, or some other person. What is certain, however, is that Rome's denigrators represented a strong current, as can be seen from the works of Pompeius Trogus and, later on, the apologists. Their biting criticisms must have been insidiously effective if the Emperor's official historian deemed it necessary to refute them with such sternness. Livy juxtaposed the unsung self-sacrifice of countless Romans with the legendary heroism of the incomparable Alexander; "He has become famous for the simple fact that he acted alone and died young, at the pinnacle of his career, without having known a single defeat." But there were many Romans endowed with as much "talent and courage as he, and who had been trained in a school of war originating with the City, so that the army had by then become a profession."

Even if Alexander, with his mighty armies and subtle strategy, may have been superior in the theory of warfare and more adept in his choice of battle sites and arms, he would have had to admit that the Roman army differed greatly from that of Darius, weighted down by its retinue of women and eunuchs, its treasure of gold and precious vestments. And how different Italy would have appeared to him in contrast to India, which he invaded with an army of merry drunkards. In Italy, he would have clashed with a real army, not with the servile, cowardly Eastern hordes. In these comparisons, Livy describes the compact discipline of the Roman legions and the harsh nature of the Apennines; he recalls the arduous wars that Rome had fought during Alexander's lifetime to unify Italy: wars against the Sabines, the Aequi, the Volsci, the Etruscans, the Campanians, the Paelignians, the Picenians, the Apulians, and the Samnites. Here, he has a moment of emotion, but soon takes hold of himself and confronts the present; he dispels the discouragement and dismay that weigh him down: "The Romans conquered a thousand armies stronger than those from Macedonia, and they will do so again provided this peace lasts, and we preserve civil harmony. . . ."

The two most acute problems of Augustus's day appear in this excerpt—namely, harmony as a vital factor for stability, and Rome's cultural rivalry with Athens and Alexandria. Rome could win this battle only if she took pride in her humble origins, her simple past, the scantiness of her legends. The early inhabitants of the City, Livy admits, may have been a motley crowd of coarse shepherds, and it was a good thing that they drove out their kings after they had acquired ethnic cohesion and a political consciousness. From that moment on, Rome's history became the history of free men.

> Freedom, a word sweet to the ear.[35]
> —Livy 24. 21

All Livy's work is a demonstration of Rome's history as the history of *libertas*. It is a chronicle not only of victories, acts of valor, and territorial expansion, but also of a fruitful class struggle that produced a growing sensitivity to democratic values and made for continuous social mobility throughout the centuries.

Originally *libertas* was juxtaposed to *regnum*. In practice, this liberty belonged to a small privileged class, the landowners in the Senate, who viewed the absolutism of a tyrant and the economic improvement of the plebeians as an equally dangerous threat to their own freedom. This class firmly believed that whoever proposed giving lands or political rights to the poor coveted power. Spurius Cassius was sentenced to death for high treason because he had presented the first project for agrarian reform, in 486 B.C. To punish him and his family, his house was razed (2.41), while his fellow consul predicted the nefarious consequences of the first agrarian law in an almost prophetic trance: "Their fields would become instruments of enslavement for the very men who received them; they would open the way to royal power. . . ."

The rich equestrian Spurius Melius distributed grain to the poor during a famine (4.15, 440 B.C.). For this act of generosity toward the hungry, he was sentenced to death, and his house was also razed. Manlius Capitolinus, a third example, was doubly guilty in the eyes of the Senate because he was a patrician. He freed, at his own expense, four hundred plebeians who had been imprisoned for debts, but his greatest civic act was that of having driven the Gauls from the Capitoline Hill. Out of pity for the poor, who were harassed by the usurers, he defended the plebeians and incited them to what today we would call "class consciousness." Neither his illustrious name nor his good deeds nor his battle scars nor the plebeians' favor could save him from patrician condemnation in the Senate. He was hurled down from the Tarpeian Rock (6.20, 384 B.C.): such zeal in protecting the humble classes could only be explained by his desire for kingly power.

The tradition that colored the behavior of kings with moral weakness, intrigue, arrogance, and licentiousness had patrician origins. Tolumnius, King of Veii, treacherously kills the Roman legates and thus provokes a long war (4.17, 437 B.C.). Tarquin, the proud king of Rome, is the first to promote electoral intrigues and to deliver demagogic speeches (1.51). When the Roman legions march into the East, the behavior of the Eastern monarchs is stereotyped: Philip of Macedon is irresolute and emotional; Perseus, his son, is untrustworthy, suspicious, and cruel; Antiochus is a servile *débauché*. The kings were assigned stereotyped emotions—wrath and greed—and were supposed to indulge in equally conventional sins—cruelty and lust. But, most important of all, they acted with complete disregard for the laws, which, for the Romans, constituted the first democratic conquests and the first safeguard for the people. When Tarquin's courtiers schemed for his return to the throne, they explicitly expressed this concept: "The law is a deaf, inexorable thing, more salutary and serviceable to the pauper than to the powerful" (2.3).

Order within the limits of legality is what distinguished *libertas* from *regnum*. It defines liberty from the people's point of view. The severity of the rulers is not what counts: what matters is that they really know the precise limitations of their power. Livy specified that "the power of the Consuls is not inferior to that of a king," but the fact that Rome had two consuls, elected for not more than one year, was indicative of the City's greater liberty (2.1). The words that Livy chose to describe the Brutus who drove out Tarquin the Proud ("avenger, founder and custodian of liberty") could not help but evoke, in the minds of the historian's contemporaries, that other Brutus, who had recently killed Caesar. Not even twenty years had passed, and yet his name, along with Cato's, was on the altars where republicans honored the Empire's opponents.

To the first Brutus, the Romans swore a binding oath that they would never stand for another king, "nor anyone who might pose a threat to their liberty" (2.1). When Porsenna, King of Clusium, tried to reinstate Tarquin on the throne, the Senate sent authoritative messengers: "The Romans were not living under a monarchy but were free. They had resolved sooner to open their gates to enemies rather than to kings; and they were all united in this prayer that the day which saw the end of liberty in their City might also be the City's end" (2.15). According to Livy's narration, Scipio rejected the title of king offered him in Spain: "Elsewhere," he said, "it is a coveted title, but in Rome it is not tolerated" (26.19). This is one of the many cases where Livy, for illustrative purposes, differs from Polybius, who had stated that Scipio had solicited the royal title. Though Livy felt that the great Roman general had some weaknesses, such as fostering the rumor that he was inspired by Jupiter, still Scipio would not allow statues to be erected to him in the Forum or his image in triumphal dress to be carried outside the Temple of Jupiter (38.56). Livy probably intended these examples as useful precepts for Augustus, who was undoubtedly the first to read the books of the *History* as they were published. The Emperor was gradually gathering the reins of the state's powers with icy determination, while displaying, at the same time, the most scrupulous respect for legality. He introduced the deification of his person as an extraconstitutional support for his office, but he abstained from flaunting the titles of the Eastern monarchs, or from adopting such titles as *rex* or dictator, of dismal memory. All the while, however, temples were being built in his honor along the Elbe and in Narbonne. In Rome, a priestly order bearing his name was instituted.[36]

It is not difficult to pinpoint the warnings that Livy, supposedly Augustus's docile mouthpiece, gave the sovereign in his *History*. In addition, a careful study of the *Testamentum Ancyranum* suggests that Augustus heeded them. Once the Emperor had freed the seas from the pirate threat, quelled the civil wars, extended and consolidated the imperial borders, distributed thrones to princes of his choice, re-established the Empire's prestige in Asia, annexed Egypt, he proclaimed the Empire's majestic unity to the world. However, solid republican ideas underlie this hymn of triumphal domination. For the Romans, every attempt to create or extend an office beyond its established duration or to accumulate additional powers was a crime that endangered democracy—a *crimen regni* (2.7; 3.8; 6.20; 13.9). The examples that Livy cited in his *History* are innumerable and not encouraging; and here Augustus stresses the fact that he had never exercised extraconstitutional functions or powers that exceeded those of his colleagues. (Respect for the collegial rights of offices was another typically Roman trait.) The Emperor refused in turn both dictatorship and life consulship, and only accepted the *Tribunicia potestas perpetua* (the power of a tribune for life), which, however, had been granted him *per legem* (by law). If he dominated everyone, it was by virtue of *auctoritas* (authority), an indefinable influence of moral rather than practical force. He accepted recognition of his exceptional merits from the nation—for example, the golden shield that was placed in the Basilica Julia.[37] His report, although it reflects pride in achievements, is nonetheless humble inasmuch as it is an account of them rendered by a retiring administrator. He lists his actions in the service of the state, the *labores* that had benefited the community, as meritorious as those of Hercules, the god, who had inspired him. *Virtus* became an attribute of the sovereign, just as his *pietas*, his *gloria*, his *res gestae* (religious devotion, glory, achievements).

Augustus's primary goal seemed that of proving that nothing in his reign resembled a monarchy; at the same time, however, he demonstrated that all the Empire's successes were due to him alone. Under his leadership, which the poets fervently supported, political contrasts dwindled, debates assumed an academic character, commanders fought in his name. This realization undoubtedly influenced Livy as he wrote his *History*.

There is no liberty without laws.[38]
—Livy 37. 37

Augustus's insistence on the legal character of his reign had origins in Greek doctrines, but it also shows the influence of Roman ideas as embodied in a series of examples. From the cases that Livy cited, we can deduce that the idea of liberty meant freedom from the foreigner, freedom from arbitrary power wielded by a despot or a faction, from the supremacy of one class, from pressures of the populace. Liberty was, above all, the exercise of rights and duties in a climate of strict legality. Obeying the laws was synonymous with being free. Conquering new nations and aggregating them to the state with the corollary of gradual recognition meant extending to them the privilege of this liberty. This thesis produced a subconscious identification between "Roman" and "free":[39] "it is against the divine law for the Romans to be slaves, since the gods wanted them to rule over all the nations."[40]

Whoever tried to escape the rule of law committed an outrage against liberty. Spurius Melius was suspected of trying to subvert the state's power when he distributed grain to the hungry; consequently, the dictator (extraordinary magistrate) appointed to settle the case sentenced him to death. Spurius freed himself from the lictors, who had presented him with a summons, appealed to the plebeians whom he had helped, and urged them to riot. In the brief fray that followed, he was killed by the commander of the public forces. This was the end he deserved, explained the dictator to the disoriented crowd, which was torn by conflicting emotions. Even if Spurius had not coveted absolute power, he still deserved capital punishment, because he had tried to subvert, by seditious means, the workings of justice (4.15, 440 B.C.).

The very same motive induced Scipio Africanus to end his days in voluntary exile in Liternum, far away from his "ungrateful country." "His spirit was so proud, so accustomed to excessive glory, that he could not bear the thought of being called guilty and submitting to the humiliation of justice" (38.52). He was disliked more for this attitude than for the suspicion that he had personally appropriated the gold of Antiochus, instead of delivering it to the Roman treasury. "No citizen," whispered his slanderers, "can climb so high that he can ignore the law. Nothing is more essential in preserving liberty than the obligation to appear before the court; this holds true for every man, no matter how high-placed he may be . . ." (38.1, 187 B.C.).

The rule of law is stronger than the rule of men, and is the basis of civil liberty. Rome became a *libera civitas* (free city) when each man had the possibility of knowing exactly what sanctions he might incur and what rights he could enjoy. "A city is not a city," said Cicero, "if the laws are not enforced and if the courts are idle."[41] Being free, therefore, was synonymous with being a citizen. Giving a city "its freedom, its laws," as the Romans did in Locri in 204 B.C., meant granting it autonomy. After the victory of Cynoscephalae (197 B.C.), Titus Quintius Flamininus gave the Greek cities a memorable gift: the Romans solemnly pledged to withdraw their garrisons, not to impose proconsuls or fiscal agents, "so that all Greek cities, both in Europe and in Asia, could be free and govern themselves by their own laws" (33.30).

After the crier had announced the extraordinary news to the crowd that had flocked to Corinth for the Isthmian games, the grateful Greeks, for days on end, extolled this action of the Romans as that of liberators rather than conquerors. "They have crossed the seas," it was said, "so that no land may bear the yoke of iniquitous domination, and so that law, justice, and legality may reign everywhere" (33.33).

When taking leave of the delegates, the Consul defined and circumscribed this liberty, in terms inspired by Roman *prudentia* (prudence) and Stoic self-control. "Let them make a moderate use of liberty," he paternally warned his listeners. "When it is temperate, it is healthy for individuals and states; if it is excessive, it can damage others, because it knows no limits and races toward destruction. Let them cultivate harmony among the cities, among the classes, among all men, because if they are united, there will be no king or tyrant strong enough to harm them" (33.49).

Without liberty, Livy warned Augustus, not even sovereignty over other peoples could be considered valid. When the Decemviri exercised tyranny, they were always surrounded by lictors armed with axes, while the people no longer had their tribunes. Liberty seemed lost forever. The City's neighbors began to despise the Romans and to be enraged that "a people that controls an empire has lost its own liberty" (3.38, 449 B.C.). Whoever was not master of himself in his own home did not have the right to rule others; power had been entrusted to the people, not to one class or one man (4.5; 6.18).

The liberty that the patricians had gained through the deeds of the first Brutus lasted until Caesar. After the second Brutus had killed the tyrant, there followed a period of transition and readjustment. Livy lived during those times, and consequently had the opportunity to observe at first hand, perhaps with tacit alarm, the progress of Augustan autocracy.

Though freedom from the kings had enabled the patricians to establish an oligarchy, the plebeians had gradually gained economic concessions and civil rights during the incessant tension between the two classes: the tribuneship and the quaestorship in the fifth century (2.32; 4.54), the consulship in 367 (6.42), the censorship in 351 (7.22), the praetorship in 337 (8.15), the priesthood in 300 B.C. (10.9). This liberty had stimulated *virtus*, and had slowly extended equality of rights to aliens. Perhaps Livy's insistence in recalling the lofty function of liberty reveals his fear that the Emperor was about to suppress it.

> Those princes and republics that want to keep themselves free from corruption must, above all, maintain their religious ceremonies free from corruption.
> —Machiavelli, *Discourses on the First Ten Books of Livy*, I, xii

In Livy's ideal themes—civil dignity and moral strength— we sense the nostalgia of a man who was an eyewitness as Rome, the wealthy, powerful City, morally abdicated. In his work, Livy condenses Western ethics: he affirms the superiority of a people's qualities as against foreign ones. He laid claim to a liberty untrammeled by both external and supernatural forces. Livy's hero was religious, respectful of omens, and faithful to the rules of the ritual; but he threw himself wholeheartedly into the fray, always aware that while fate is unavoidable, fortune helps the bold.

An unconscious inner vitality impelled this hero to put his capacities to the test each time. His every action was animated with dramatic energy. Livy felt ill at ease in his own times, and took refuge in Rome's past when that small, yet intrepid nation had conquered an empire. He said, "In some inscrutable way my soul became ancient." After having finished his long exposition of the Punic Wars, he felt relieved, "almost as though I had been living myself those dangers and tribulations" (31.1). His commitment to a world populated by men of towering dimensions reflected his weariness of the present and his fear of the future. He may have asked himself whether the values of that distant past were only temporarily obliterated or whether they were buried forever; whether that heritage could be revived and recovered, or whether it represented only an ideal and a flight from reality.

Livy's philosophy was nourished by a Stoicism that guided man in his conduct and encouraged him to rely on his own resources in conformity with the divine laws and the intentions of an inscrutable Providence. Other doctrines, which did not exalt action, were moving to the forefront, however; they considered life as a long waiting period, a tension toward a supernatural realm.

These concepts were alien to the Roman religion, which was based on the strict fulfillment of formal precepts, on the observance of propitiatory rites, on the interpretation of injunctions sent by the gods through prodigies and signs that only the augurs or the haruspices could unriddle. Religion was an inseparable part of civil life. Politics was colored with sacred terminology: the tribune of the people was *sacrosanctus*, meaning that his authority and his person were equally inviolable. Whoever threatened either was considered *sacer*— that is, consecrated to the infernal gods—and to kill him would not constitute a crime.

Livy never omitted mention of presages or portents; and this because of his scruples as a historian, his respect for the ancient sensibilities, and his emotional attachment to a faith that he no longer shared on the rational level but which, nonetheless, still seemed beneficial: "I cannot help noticing," he wrote, "that nowadays, because piety is lacking, some people deny that the gods wish to communicate with men through prodigies; omens are no longer mentioned, and in historical works these phenomena are not even recorded. But as I write about distant epochs, in some inscrutable way my soul becomes ancient; a pious reverence compels me to include in my history those prodigies that the sages in other times thought cause for propitiation" (43.13).

Earthquakes, stones raining from heaven, and the birth of hermaphrodites were no longer considered messages from the gods, they evoked no reverberations in a generation of skeptics or in those who sought miraculous regenerations or tended to withdraw from society into a life of private study, of pleasure or contemplation—in effect, into sterile isolation.

For Livy, however, the only metaphysical value was love of the fatherland. He rejected mystic annihilation and occult rites; he had no use for prayer or purification; he did not grant anybody the right of immediate communication with the deity without the mediation of the state's religious order. He hoped that the national cult would be saved. Ever since it had been instituted by Numa, it had served as a civilizing instrument for a nation born to violence and arms. Religion had an instrumental value: it acted as a moral restraint and a means of cohesion among the citizens. It could even be used to

placate or propitiate gods who were vaguely conceptualized
in names given to various aspects of the divine in the cosmos:
gods who, unlike the god of Israel, did not actively intervene
in human affairs, did not punish the wicked, did not reward
the good, but gave the offended party a chance, and sometimes the strength, for vengeance.

This was the purport of a speech that Marcus Manlius
Capitolinus addressed to the plebeians, inciting them to a genuine revolution: "How long will you remain ignorant of your
own strength? . . . Count up your numbers, and the number
of your adversaries. . . . What can I expect if my enemies
grow bolder? . . . The gods will never come down from the
heaven on my account: rather, let them inspire in you
the courage to prevent [my death], just as they gave me the
strength to defend you, both in war and in peace, from the
barbarity of your enemies and from the arrogance of your
fellow citizens . . ." (6.18, 384 B.C.). In fact, the gods did
not stir on the day that generous agitator climbed the Capitoline Hill that he had defended from the Gauls and was
hurled over the Tarpeian cliff.

"The gods never extend an avenging hand to the guilty,"
said a tribune to the plebeians when he accused the consuls of
causing the defeat at Veii. "It was enough if they armed with
an opportunity for vengeance those who had been wronged."
When the soldiers stumbled through the city gates and fled
full of fear and covered with wounds, they accused neither
fortune nor the gods, but their leaders (5.11).

The City was filled with sanctuaries, images, and sacred
buildings. Every corner awakened memories of ancient legends, prodigious warnings, arcane voices, and apparitions. An
official ritual punctuated the calendar with liturgical dates. In
order to build a temple to Jupiter on the Capitoline Hill,
Tarquin Priscus had desecrated and destroyed the existing
sanctuaries, and had transferred the images elsewhere. The

gods, who had been consulted through the augurs and haruspices, had agreed to the move. Only one, the god Terminus,
had answered negatively, by means of a flight of birds: "The
fact that the seat of Terminus was not moved and that of all
the gods he alone was not called away from the site consecrated to him was a sign that the whole Kingdom would be
firm and steadfast . . ." (1.55).

According to Ovid, February 23 was the day sacred to
Terminus. On that day, the borders of private property were
reconsecrated. In Rome, a sheep was sacrificed at the sixth
mile of the Laurentian road, the road that led to the shores
where Aeneas had disembarked, the event that foretold
Rome's future. The god Terminus promised the City stability
and set her boundaries to coincide with those of the entire
world.[42]

Religion was part of the fiber of Rome's civil life, as Ancus
Marcius, who restored the public cult, knew instinctively,
while Tullus Hostilius, prey to suspicious fears, gave himself
up to occult rituals and sacrifices (1.32). Devotions held in
secret were a sign of moral weakness or emotional instability,
and appeared mostly in periods when plagues, famines, or
enemy threats fostered unrest. The Senate had always repressed such forms of escapism, in which it sensed social subversion. In 428 B.C., it prohibited soothsayers and astrologers
from questing from house to house, promoting new gods or
new rites which might work to the state's disadvantage
(4.30); the same sanction was repeated in 213 (25.1). These
decrees revealed an increasingly strict government control
until 186 B.C., when the denunciations against groups practic-
ing the cult of Dionysus resulted in their repression
(39.7–17). In those secret rites—and, later on, the same would
be said about the Christians—the participants supposedly gave
themselves up to sinful ecstasies, collective orgies, and atrocious crimes. In 139 B.C., Scipio persecuted the Jews and the
Chaldeans for spreading foreign sciences.

Livy certainly recognized the spirit of those stern guardians of the cult in Augustus, who prohibited the Egyptian religion, expelled astrologers and seers alike, and ordered that all the Sibylline Oracles be confiscated from private houses and then burned.[43] Augustus's actions were prompted, as were those of his forerunners, by considerations of public order, since those oracles, reflecting Asian and Egyptian propaganda, spoke about the East's imminent retaliation against Rome. The end of Roman supremacy would be near when a woman reigned. Maybe this woman was Cleopatra, called the "Widow" because, like Isis, she has lost her husband, Ptolemy XIV. At her sumptuous coronation in Alexandria in 34 B.C., she wore the attributes of Isis, while Antony appeared in the Eastern provinces as a new Dionysus, the divinity of the Asian proletariat, rather than as a Roman proconsul surrounded by lictors. In Alexandria, he had founded an Eastern empire antagonistic to the Roman Empire, open to alliances conflicting with Roman policy, with the Medes and the Parthians. His marriage to Cleopatra appeared as a wedding between divine beings, which would shower beneficent gifts upon mankind. He called his children Helios and Selene—that is, Sun and Moon, the two divine stars which cast their light over all human beings, not over one city or one élite class or one race of conquerors.[44]

All those regal trappings seemed to point to a cosmopolitan and egalitarian theocracy, which would have placed Alexandria and Athens on the same level with Rome. In order to compete with that policy, Augustus wanted to turn the mystic expectations of the restless masses to his own advantage, and to give the Empire a unifying and providential character, while in Rome he adhered to the traditional images.

These were years of tension and fervor, the years when an obscure prophet was born in Judaea. It is not important to identify the mysterious child that Vergil referred to in the *Fourth Eclogue*. The messianic contents of his poem and the

oracular tones with which the poet announced the arrival of a
new golden age certainly reflected the sentiments of his times:
the earth would spontaneously produce fruit and grain, goats
would bring milk to the houses, the herds would no longer
fear the lions.[45] These promises echoed Biblical texts and ancient prophecies.

The hopes that followed the sufferings during the civil
wars transcended national boundaries. They had a universal
appeal, an expectation of cosmic renewal. Augustus was too
shrewd not to understand this hope for the Millennium, and
within limits he utilized it in specific ways. From the poets, he
accepted hyperbolic eulogies that came close to deification; in
the Eastern provinces he permitted his name, which was engraved on the coins, to be followed by the title "God the
Saviour"; in Egypt, his name appeared among those of the
gods.

In the West, as he well knew, it was essential not to depart from tradition, since repudiating Rome's heritage meant
suffocating her spirit and destroying the reassuring certainty
that the gods watched over the City's safety. This protection
would be lost, however, if the Romans neglected the cult of
their ancient gods. Thus when Christianity became the state
religion and the Empire was subsequently invaded, it almost
seemed as if the angry gods had abandoned their neglected
sanctuaries and left the impious, ungrateful City to its unfortunate destiny. Or perhaps these gods had been weakened by
the lack of sacrifices and incense. We can deduce the number
of people who must have believed this from the passionate
fervor with which the Christian authors repudiated these accusations.

In the dualism that divided the Empire—the Eastern theocratic demands and the Western Republican tradition—Livy
took it upon himself to defend the latter. He raised ancient
Rome to the realm of myth. "Even if Plato's dream were

realized," he wrote, "and that republic of wise men, which the
Greeks had imagined in the abstract but never seen, were
created on this earth, still the greatness of Rome and the
merits of her citizens would never be equaled" (26.22).

His ideal was still the *pòlis* (city), set up by him as a moral
system. But he looked only at the past. Everything that the
politicians augured for the future of their country and fought
to attain had, in Livy's opinion, already come to pass. It was
useless to gaze upon utopian visions or to project demands for
justice into the crystal-clear realm of metaphysics. It was useless to try to quench in religious mysteries the thirst for the
absolute, which tormented the soul. The only solution was to
draw from the pristine source of energy, to revive the spirit
of past ages. History concentrates around individuals, and is
conditioned by them.

At the threshold of the future, Livy seems to withdraw. It
is symbolic—though accidental—that his books about the
events of the most recent past are lost and have come down to
us only in the summaries of the *Epitome*. The last episode of
Livy's work describes the death of Drusus (in 9 B.C.), who
died beyond the Rhine in the heart of Germany, a land that
would remain, throughout the centuries, indomitable and remote from the Latin spirit. This event was judged by Livy's
contemporaries as an evil omen and became surrounded by
portentous legends.

The body of Drusus, son of Livia, was taken to Rome by
his brother Tiberius. "He was buried in the tomb of Caius
Caesar. The funeral oration was pronounced by his step-
father, Caesar Augustus. Many other ceremonies were added
to the usual ones" (*Epitome* 140).

According to an undocumented source, Livy ceased writing in the year A.D. 9, when he learned about the Roman rout
at the Teutoburg Forest. Savage hordes were repulsing the
Empire, the standard-bearer of civilization, and threatening

the admirable construction whose phases of development he had carefully illustrated. Though alarmed by the changes that had taken place within the Empire, the historian was still confident about the inviolability of its borders.

Livy's characters, like the exemplars of *virtus* chosen by Augustus to represent the Empire's builders and eternalized in marble, continued to live on for the Romans of future generations, set apart in an aura of piety and awe. They were objects of undisputed respect and were cited by classical and Christian authors alike, even though the Christians challenged the essence of the Roman spirit in denouncing glory and power as fleeting, illusory values and imperialism as ignominious banditry.

Even Saint Augustine, in the fourth and fifth centuries, still evoked these exemplars—then more remote and, for that very reason, even more imposing—in his *City of God*, the most persuasive refutation of Roman thought and ethics ever written, despite a tinge of the author's Punic nationalism. Augustine's conception of an interior and otherworldly City of God completely negated the proud, sinful city of Rome, which claimed to rule the world with its rods and axes. His idea of Grace was the opposite of Roman merit. But his final rejection of the Roman ethical code, which saw deeds as the only road to glory (or to heaven), came only when, as champion of orthodoxy, he realized that the Pelagian heresy had been fostered by those very principles.

Before that violent theological contention with the heirs of the Latin ethical and juridical code, he did not deny the Roman virtues. Their example, he stated, could be beneficial even to those aiming at different goals. The desire to achieve and the passion for praise and renown were the only faults in those otherwise exemplary beings; however, this vice, as he, with his insight into the human psyche, admits, is extremely difficult to eradicate from the heart.

Saint Augustine did not exorcise these phantoms from the past, which continued to stimulate his imagination. He referred to them more often than to other pagan authors who had played a more influential role in his cultural formation and even in his conversion. He cites Lucretia to comfort the women who had been raped by the invaders of Northern Africa, he cites Cato in his condemnation of suicide; he respects the cult of law in Brutus and Torquatus, the devotion to his country of the statesman and soldier Camillus, the steadfastness of Mucius Scaevola and Attilius Regulus, the self-sacrifice of Decius, the voluntary poverty of Fabricius. He is aware of the veneration surrounding these figures. He understands that they represent sparks of the divine for men who knew no religion loftier than duty. He has no wish to disown those generous personalities: they, too, helped add another stone to the structure of the Church, to the image of his celestial city.

It was God who rewarded the Romans with His gift of the Empire. It was God, Saint Augustine wrote in a private letter dated 412, who showed, in the rich, illustrious Roman Empire, "what heights civic virtues could reach even without true religion." It was an act of Providence that this power had been granted "to men who, out of love for honor and glory, did not hesitate to place the safety of the fatherland ahead of their own, to subordinate greed for money and many other vices to one single weakness—the desire for praise."[46]

TACITUS
On Power

A.: *Annals*

H.: *Histories*

G.: *Germania*

AGR.: *Agricola*

DIAL.: *Dialogus de Oratoribus* (*A Dialogue Concerning Oratory*)

> Therefore I hated life; because the work that is wrought
> under the sun is grievous unto me.
>
> —Ecclesiastes 2 : 17

A dim foreboding courses through the centuries, like a dark current, underneath the stone-paved streets and the marble floors of Rome. Tacitus caught its murmur and turned it into an articulate voice—the last and noblest voice of Roman conscience, raised in an impassioned outcry. After the turn of the second century, his words were drowned out by the shrill eloquence of the panegyrists and by the anathemas of the seers.

He no longer felt a need to explain the Empire; he wanted instead to examine its government and the attempts by both rulers and subjects to preserve it. His theme was the problem of power viewed from a moral perspective. Tacitus observed absolutism and its effects on nations and individuals alike; he recorded Rome's transition from principate to tyranny, her shift from compliance to acquiescence. He diagnosed the Empire's degeneration as cancer, the cause of Rome's death.

A nameless fear induced him to bring onstage protagonists

and extras, barbarians and citizens, in order to probe their souls. The dregs of society which populated the City spread their contamination from the center. Juvenal threw open the windows and caused a pitiless light to shine on the triclinia, the bedrooms, the brothels; he denounced moral shortcomings, secret vices, private perversities. Tacitus decried public faults. He sensed in every proconsul a greedy, lustful, petty tyrant, in every senator a base spirit, in every emperor the living proof that man could resist deprivations, threats, tortures, but not power. A building whose foundations are sunk in mud and blood cannot last. His indictment sprang from this bitter knowledge.

Tacitus and Juvenal responding, a century later, to Livy and Vergil seem to say: See what has happened to the model city founded by Aeneas; see in what manner she wields the universal power the seers had prophesied for her, which Romulus had enjoined upon her before ascending to the heavens; she is sinking in her own iniquity.

> That dull patience they call life.
> —Keats

Almost everything we know about Tacitus is obscure and fragmentary.[1] His very name hints at his chief characteristics: discretion and ambiguity. He is reticent in the very brevity of his fulminations. As his words flash against the dark backdrop of his terse, restrained prose, he implies more than he writes.

He rarely uses the first person, almost never expresses wrath or grief: *raram occulti pectoris vocem* (*A. 4.52*). But each word vibrates with contained emotion: contempt, regret, shame, pity. He is silent about his private life—about his birthplace, his marriage, the number of his children, if any. Scanty reference is made to his career, which progressed in an orderly fashion under Vespasian, Titus, Domitian, and reached its peak under Trajan and possibly Hadrian. We find no mention of his residence, his financial situation, the occasion for his writings or their dates.

His judgments are so contradictory that they have lent themselves to various interpretations. His opinions are those of a man who lived in an epoch of violent contrasts and moral bewilderment, who had read and echoed many authors, since lost to posterity, who had practiced law and had thus slipped into the hyperboles of forensic oratory as he pleaded alternately for the prosecution or for the defense. Consequently his religious beliefs, his political views, his philosophical doctrines, his literary tastes, and his friendships can be deduced only from fragmentary writings that stand out like mutilated ruins in a desolate countryside.

If we try to visualize Tacitus as he pronounced orations that were elaborate to the point of artifice, we see a man who gives away little of his secret cares; his look is stony, his gestures spare, his deep voice level: Σεμνῶς, an adjective used by Pliny (*Epistolae* 2.11.17) to describe his friend Tacitus as he addressed the Senate and to define his severe, solemn eloquence. Now and then he would raise his eyes and flash out a look charged with meaning, a look to unlock the depths of his soul and strike an answering chord in ours. He commented, when writing about Germanic customs: "It is fitting for women to weep; for men to remember" (*G.* 27.1). *Flere decet* exudes an almost perceptible plaint whereas the smoldering vengeful thought, the contempt for those who forget are revealed in the verb *meminisse*, which has all the force of a whiplash. When Otho conspired against Galba (A.D. 69), Rome was filled with rumors about the plot, but the Prefect dismissed them (Shakespeare was later to recall this quirk) because "he was opposed to any project, even the best, which he had not himself thought up" (*H.* 1.26). When Augustus died, calm reigned within the Empire and on all its borders:

"were any left who had seen the Republic?" (*A.* 1.6): it was the silent crumbling of the old guard. Here Tacitus, with admirable economy, conjures up a moral and political climate.

Since many of the minor works that Tacitus probably used as references have disappeared, it is difficult to single out his sources. Behind his togaed figure stretches a road dotted with names of writers whose works have been almost completely lost to us. He claimed to have consulted every one. He found them all vitiated by flattery when they wrote about the ruling monarch or by rancor when they dealt with his predecessor (*A.* 1.1). Actually, Tacitus started his history with Tiberius. Cato and Sallust were quite clearly his ideal precursors and stylistic models; like theirs, his style is compact, his tone mordant, his verbs uninflected. A deep love for Rome and her semimythological past, which he absorbed from Livy, flickers through his desolation.

The great writers who had celebrated the *res gestae* (noble deeds) of the Republican heroes had long since vanished. The principate had become a monarchy. Retracing the years when his native land was torn by factions, when neither morality nor legality (*non mos, non ius*) was respected, when a great number of decrees were promulgated not for the good of all but for the benefit of only a few, Tacitus concedes that Augustus had brought back peace along the frontiers and order—if not harmony—within the Empire. But what bitter irony he betrays in the words: "Augustus, secure now in his power, repealed the rights of the triumvirs and laid the groundwork for peace and a prince" (*A.* 3.28). Lucan was to echo the same thought: "this peace comes with a master."[2] But Tacitus expresses it with greater subtlety.

Despite internal peace, security on the borders, administrative efficiency, and cultural unity, there was no real liberty in the Empire. The term was used for a vague, changeable concept containing juridical and political overtones, literary reminiscences, and iconographic inspiration. By Tacitus's time, the opposition had turned these themes into hagiography. *Leiber-tas*, in its archaic spelling, had been engraved on the coins of Brutus and Cassius. In the *Testamentum Ancyranum*, Augustus repeated the very words that Caesar had spoken at the Rubicon,[3] to the effect that he had given liberty back to the Republic, which had been oppressed by one faction. *Libertas* was the password among the conspirators who planned to murder Caligula. The word evoked populist images: Harmodius and Aristogiton, Lucretia and Virginia, the first and second Brutus, the elder and younger Cato. Symbols and gestures—a Phrygian cap, a raised arm holding a dagger—were to remain valid and sacred throughout the centuries. But, as Seneca had already pointed out, it was absurd to try to exhume liberty when the conditions essential for its survival no longer existed.[4]

> . . . I will follow your name, Liberty, even when it has become only a vain dream.[5]
>
> —Lucan *Pharsalia* 2. 301

In Tacitus's day, liberty connoted more than just the opportunity for distinguishing oneself, the justification for Republican institutions, the abolition of ethnic and social discrimination, and the restoration of order and harmony; the term had acquired new meaning and subtle nuances.

Some, realizing that their ideals were no longer shared by their contemporaries, that customs had changed, became a prey to boredom and listlessness, which lured them to a surprising indifference toward death. For them, liberty meant quiet withdrawal from the political fray and from a society that imposed tedious contacts and social obligations.[6] Position, honors, ambition, competition presented obstacles to the development of their inner needs. For them, the only road to freedom was solitude.

This world-weariness had not yet led men to escape into the desert or into the seclusion of the monastery. However, this mental climate aroused a romantic curiosity and empathy toward primitive peoples and stimulated an idealization of their way of life.

In Tacitus's opinion, liberty was incompatible with power. Liberty was possible only under a government that was not based upon progressive stages of subjugation: *patientia* (endurance), *adulatio* (flattery), *servitium* (servitude). His concern was with political ethics. In his long meditation on the limits of power, he gave more weight to the essence of political life than to juridical or constitutional questions. In theory, he did not oppose the monarchy, which he judged necessary. Nor did he dream of an impossible restoration of the Republic; he was fully convinced that ancient mores and the past no longer fitted the realities of imperial Rome. He did not challenge the principate per se, he merely hoped that it would become less dictatorial. As a form of government, it was a historical necessity, springing from the Romans' primary task, that of governing the Empire. Thus, it naturally followed that the Republican concept of liberty—that is, a government in which the senators were free to dissent, to argue, to stand out—did not respond to the Empire's new needs. Despots have always preferred mediocre men.

Tacitus here condemned the futile self-immolation of the Empire's opponents, the Stoics, who calmly slashed their wrists. At the same time, however, he characterized their behavior as an example of "liberty," since it reflected an inner liberty, one of the spirit, that was neither political nor juridical. As they lay dying, they succeeded in freeing themselves at last of cowardly silences, connivances, and servility.

Their spurt of independence, followed by death, conferred upon them the ultimate freedom. Faced with these two extreme solutions to the dilemma, Tacitus refused to make a choice. He wondered whether there was still a place for human dignity in the huge bureaucracy run by a despot, or whether the only remaining freedom depended upon the Emperor's good will and clemency. "It is your spirit," Pliny said to Trajan, "which curbs and contains a power that knows no limit."[7] Thus, liberty became a gift from the Emperor: "We shall be free if you order us to be so."[8]

Under these conditions, a historian of the imperial period felt a constraint that was mirrored in his prose. Unlike the chroniclers of ancient Rome, who wrote of shining deeds and heated exchanges, the imperial historian assumed an inglorious, narrowly circumscribed task (A. 4.32). In listing a series of sentences, passively accepted, of denunciations, of secret accusations, complicities, abominations, he ran the risk of incurring imperial wrath. Within Tacitus's lifetime, Tiberius had condemned Cremutius Cordus to death because of his eulogy of Brutus (A. 4.34), and Domitian had pronounced the same sentence on the authors of eulogistic biographies of Nero's victims.

Nevertheless, during the new climate of peace under the emperors Nerva and Trajan, Tacitus turned to history with the explicitly didactic purpose of recording for posterity examples of exceptional nobility or depravity (A. 3.65). The chronicling of these details was to make them serve as points of reference for those who, without them, could not distinguish right from wrong (A. 4.33). For this reason, he did not allow even the smallest such detail to escape his attention; he scrutinized denunciations, testimony, sentences, and innumerable cases that other historians had glossed over either because there was too much material or because they were ashamed to paint for their descendants a repellent picture of their own era; such decadence might not have seemed credible (A. 6.7).

Like Cicero, Tacitus viewed the writing of history as "the testimony of the times . . . the teacher of life . . . based upon a scrupulous impartiality,"[9] but, at the same time, he considered it a work of literary and stylistic merit. One still wonders upon which of these goals he concentrated and which one he attained.

Sallust, who had lived in an age when action was judged the supreme virtue, apologized for having sought fame through an idle though instructive activity like the writing of history.[10] In the opening pages of the *Agricola*, Tacitus vindicated himself, but only for his concern with certain values. Writing, under the guise of a belated eulogy, an encomium for a man who had served his country with honor, the historian realized that he was following an obsolete model—his eulogy was incongruous "in times cruel and hostile to virtue" (*Agr.* 1.1), as indeed they were, even though Nerva, and later Trajan, had allowed "two heretofore incompatible institutions—monarchy and liberty" to coexist (*Agr.* 1.3).

That the virtues of private individuals were celebrated shows to what extent the Roman scale of values had changed. Agricola offered an example of this evolution. His superiority consisted in the wisdom with which he carried out imperial directives and in his scrupulous sense of responsibility. Henceforth, military success was to hinge upon the guidelines (*auspicia*) provided by a farsighted ruler who, without stirring from Rome, engineered the action. Subordinates could no longer distinguish themselves by a *beau geste*, an outstanding sacrifice, or a brilliant initiative; the age of the hero was over. A new élite had stepped into the places once occupied by patriots, consuls, and tribunes. These new men were either bureaucrats or martyrs.

Tacitus's chapters on Caligula have been lost; those on Tiberius and Nero are still extant; the shadow of Domitian hovers over his *Agricola*. But through all his works the crushing influence of the *Lex de Imperio*, which although never specifically alluded to, is almost palpable. The *Lex* was the vehicle through which Vespasian, albeit respectful of the Senate's political and administrative functions and reluctant to assume an autocratic stance, had carried to its logical conclusion the whole of Augustus's authority. He had couched imperial control in constitutional forms. By availing himself of the powers conferred upon his predecessors, the Princeps declared himself in substance above the laws and therefore free to form alliances, negotiate peace, declare war, appoint magistrates, and shift borders.[11] The principate became *dominatio*, not through the aberrant claims of a tyrant or the rise of a new ideology, but because the fabrication that conferred upon the Senate a pretense of authority had finally been worn through. The Flavian dynasty assumed new prerogatives, which were reflected in their titles. Domitian was the first to use the title "Dominus." Pliny regularly used it in his official correspondence with Trajan. Legitimized despotism had gradually laid aside its mask and had openly become a monarchy, the only form of government suitable for the protection of the Empire's flimsy stability. Under the circumstances it was prudent to abstain from speaking about the present. "Let us see," wrote Juvenal, "what I shall be allowed to say about those who are buried along the Via Flaminia and the Via Latina."*[12]

During a period of absolutism, all politicians are forced into retirement, ritual appearances in the Senate notwithstanding. This held true for Tacitus as well as for the others. However, he did not use historiography as an excuse for expounding party platforms or wreaking vendettas; he used it to probe the genesis of events. He paid particular attention to those rulers under whom absolute power had become a reality: Tiberius, who was Augustus's heir; the three competitors for the imperial purple: Galba, Otho, and Vitellius, who, through their power struggle in A.D. 69, paved the way for the Flavian dynasty. Each ruler was observed in the light of his predecessor. Though replete with traditional ideas, Tacitus's justly fa-

---

* The highways leading out of Rome, such as the Flaminia, going north, and the Latina, running southeast, were lined with tombs of famous men.

mous prose remains unique. His style gradually grew more compact and powerfully expressive through the use of antitheses, assonances, parallels; his powers of evocation were prodigious: his use of archaic words conjured up concrete images (*pectus* for soul, *civitas* for state), or poetic ones (*senecta* for *senectus*). The use of all these devices made of Tacitus's Latin a fit subject for literary debate, a model for other prose writers, and a source of torment for translators. His prose is made up of commonplaces and inconsistencies, delivered portentously; yet what results is a masterpiece: his observations were informed by intuition; he was a great artist who, tersely and swiftly, captured the universal man. He recorded with great finesse the gradual evolution of the personalities he studied, carefully registering the influence upon them of those with whom they came into contact and, despite his tortuous complexity, managed to situate them in a hierarchy of morality. And there they have remained, transfixed through the ages.

His reputation as a historian who was both judge and adjudicator is unshakable. Malevolent despots, predaceous, dissolute women, collaborators, informers, cutthroats, all stand out so clearly against the dark backdrop of his stage that no amount of revisionism can rehabilitate those doomed souls. The tragic masks that Tacitus affixed on them have indissolubly turned into their own physiognomy. No effort can now separate the mask from the original. Whoever contradicts him will reap discredit. A case in point is Velleius Paterculus whose eulogy of Tiberius is wholly discounted even today.

In an attempt to find in the men of the past that linear coherence which they seek in vain in their contemporaries, scholars have tried to pinpoint Tacitus's key themes and guidelines: *virtus* (virtue), *senatus* (the Senate), *patria* (the fatherland), *libertas* (liberty). They have described him as a man who nostalgically upheld ancestral customs, supported provincial demands, praised the frugality of the Italic municipalities, promoted imperialism; a pacifist, a politician, a moralist, a republican, a spirit open to the concept of a universal empire, a misanthrope, and an idealist. Psychoanalysis delving into his subconscious has brought to light a guilt complex which supposedly derived from all the death sentences he heard pronounced—even those for which he had not voted, having somehow managed to remain neutral despite his hatred for Domitian.

There is undoubtedly some truth in all these theories, and in others as well, because Tacitus's greatness does not rest upon his political vision or, even less, upon the originality of his ideas; it stems from his ability in brilliant synthesis, the passion that lights up his pages, the disquietude that pervades them and imparts to us a sense of his anguish and bitterness.

Tacitus lived in an epoch of moral and social transformation; he witnessed an irreversible decadence which filled him with dissatisfaction with himself as well as with others, and allowed him few certitudes. One of these was the futility of all constitutions and laws; even if originally good, they soon degenerated because of man's nature. The primary cause of the rise of the monarchy was precisely the discredit into which laws had fallen because they had been "deranged by violence, by favoritism or by gold" (*A*. 1.2).

"Only a politician," Polybius had written centuries earlier, "makes use of history, and only a politician is capable of writing history; not because he is better informed than others or has access to secret documents, but because his experience enables him to understand the hidden working of events, the motives behind every action. Therefore, it is through history that he expresses himself, his tendencies, his reflections on past trials, his problems."[13] Even when Tacitus refers to military or political actions, and condemns or praises the men he has seen act—or abstain from acting—he expresses his doubts and his anxiety for the future, not just the future of Rome or of her Empire, but for that of mankind. He records the dismay characteristic of every period of transition. He wonders whether it is possible to reconcile Rome's two orientations— tradition and universality—and extend to the masses a culture and a moral code that had been created by the few for the few; whether a new civilization could arise from the fusion of Rome's dual spirit—the *Urbs* and the *Orbis;* whether the dissonant voices of the masses could be harmonized on an instrument with a limited sound range. Could the institutions and structures of the City be stretched to absorb that vast, restless multitude racked by economic discontent, social demands, and ethnic claims? Would it be possible for someone spiritually belonging to the past to become, without feeling disloyal to it, a part of the present?

The history Tacitus wrote is not important for the information he gives us. He does not satisfy our curiosity for reliable detail. His text is tendentious and technically defective. It is not the fruit of painstaking research, but, rather, the outlet for his tormented thought and unresolved conflicts. It reflects his need for inner clarification.

History, viewed as an abstract of the social, military, and economic situation, did not reflect either the tastes of his period or his personal inclinations. The places, dates, and numbers he mentions are usually imprecise and incomplete. He rarely remarks on financial questions, food crises, or social phenomena. He completely disregards the masses, and seldom takes into account the factors that enabled new classes and new ethnic groups to participate in the government. He notes the preponderance of barbarians in the army, but does not bother to ask the reasons; he simply deplores the fact and fears the worst.

One thing only appeared to be clear for Tacitus: it was the duty of everyone to resist the decline of values and the corrupting influence of power and money. There was not even any need for heroic action; all that was required was that everyone behave with dignity.

For Tacitus, the substance of history was primarily a question of the individual conscience, not in the sense of tormenting spiritual or doctrinal crises attended by passionate conflicts, but in the sense of making a choice when confronted with power. In order to preserve his power, Tiberius, acting with calculated hypocrisy, exterminated the family of Germanicus. Power exacerbated Caligula to the point of madness, Nero to matricide. Again, it was power that, in A.D. 69, drove the three contending emperors to kill one another in turn, and Domitian to murder his brother. Power degraded some men to the point of turning them into informers; raised others to martyrdom, and humiliated all of them by reducing them to servility. Moderation in the exercise of power was a supreme virtue to be hoped for in all princes; it was considered a miracle when they succeeded to some degree in permitting power to coexist with liberty, its naturally incompatible opposite.

All of Tacitus's writings are variations on the theme of power. At that particular moment in history, panegyric was no longer just an occasional public speech; it had become a literary genre which dwelt on the superhuman virtues and achievements of the reigning emperor. The first Latin writer, and the only Italic one, to hold such views in Tacitus's time was Pliny.

Cicero had already added a touch of the miraculous to Roman virtues by attributing supernatural good fortune to Pompey, clemency to Caesar, "almost divine" wisdom to young Octavian. Pliny enlarged upon the seminal qualities of power, and presented them in a metaphysical light. Trajan, his *Optimus Princeps*, was faithful, as a citizen, to the laws, but "chaste and holy, and altogether godlike."[14]

Tacitus held aloof from this theory of the transfer of im-

perial power from the secular to the divine. He stressed the
Emperor's behavior as a man, and soberly recognized that the
community as a whole benefited when decisions were taken
by one man—provided he was *sapientissimus*—rather than by
many inexperienced men (*Dial.* 42.4). But the difficulty lay in
finding this *sapientissimus et unus* (one man who is the
wisest), and in preserving him as such when there were no
checks on or criticism of his actions. Tacitus gradually came
to the conclusion that this was impossible, and therefore
called upon barbarians and Romans alike to join his indictment of despotism at any time, under whatever guise or name.

Tacitus's views are diametrically opposed to Machiavelli's.
For the latter, the individual's actions are not moral or immoral per se, but become moral or immoral depending upon
their political frame of reference. Tacitus, on the other hand,
judges politics by the conduct of individuals. An emperor
would be unable to transgress the boundaries of his power if
there were checks written into the constitution, but the chief
curb would be the moral resistance of the citizens. Unruly
legions would not confer authority upon an ordinary corpo-
ral unless they had reason to expect favors in return from him.
He himself ought to refuse the leadership unless it was sanctioned by a ruling body. For example, when Germanicus was
elected by his troops on the Rhine front, he was indignant, "as
though he had been made an accomplice to a crime" (*A.*
1.35).

Histories (*Historiae*), according to Servius, were a narration of recent or contemporary facts, for example, Tacitus's
analysis of a short-lived political crisis in A.D. 69; *Annals*
(*Annales*) dealt with more remote events. As the word implies, it was a year-by-year chronological recording of events,
as they occurred. And true to republican usage, the year was
identified by the name of the magistrates of that year, since
these, unlike the emperor, were elected officials.

In his very titles, Tacitus shows his deference for custom. Furthermore, in his readiness to summarize even inconclusive debates and to record speeches, he writes as a man of the Senate. Wherever it is possible to compare Tacitus's transcript with a still extant text, it proves to be exact, as in the case of the Emperor Claudius's speech (A.D. 48) in favor of admitting to the Senate the élite from *Gallia Comata* ("Long-haired Gaul," annexed to the Empire later than *Gallia Togata*). The Emperor's words, a genuine pronouncement in favor of racial equality, were immortalized in bronze by the grateful Gauls in the capital of the province, Lyons, the birthplace of Claudius. Centuries later the inscription was unearthed, almost intact.[15] Although Tacitus's rendering was more concise and elegant, it did not substantially depart from the original.

The monographs—*Germania, Agricola*, and *Dialogus de Oratoribus*—contain the nucleus of Tacitus's thought. While some scholars view them as digressions that were later singled out and expanded, others maintain that they were short essays inspired by Sallust's models. The *Dialogus* is an inquiry into the reasons for the decline of oratory. Actually, this debate on rhetoric reveals a more serious preoccupation: the effects of political power on culture and, therefore, on man's conscience. A dictatorship ensures perfect order; all is calm and covered with a film of ashes: "What is the point of delivering lengthy orations in the Senate when the best men are soon in agreement? Or of lengthy harangues to the people, when political questions are settled not by the ignorant multitude, but by one man who is the wisest?" (*Dial.* 42.4); at first sight, this may appear to be a positive judgment, the consensus voiced by one of the interlocutors. In reality, it was the expression of spiritual impotence of an age that had witnessed the precariousness of liberty—a liberty that had soon degenerated into license, and it was the admission that an opposition unable to provide remedies, nurtured as it was by nothing but sterile regrets, was quite useless. It was stupid to offend the powerful by eulogizing a Republican hero like Cato when neither professional duty nor the defense of a friend called for it (*Dial.* 10.5–6). The new social reality, Tacitus seems to say, demanded a revision of ethical patterns. With Vespasian's accession, the process of democratization in the national life, an adjunct of the Empire from its beginnings, was reactivated. With the rise of the bourgeoisie and the provincial class, patrician privileges began to disappear, and the structure of the economy, which depended on large estates, began to change. Society had new requirements, and anything that harked back to the old Roman ideals exuded only nostalgia.

All these changes were reflected in literature. Style, according to Seneca,[16] mirrors the customs of the times. "It is an oft-repeated adage that the Greeks have made into a proverb: As a man speaks, so he behaves." Truncated sentences, archaic language, and a terseness bordering on obscurity revealed Sallust's innermost feelings. His style was in direct contrast to Cicero's elaborately flowing periods, as was Tacitus's, who copied Sallust's use of the infinitive, his archaisms and dramatic concision.

Eloquence is based on strong feeling and is sensitive to fluctuations in the level of education. During the Empire, it had become a topic for lectures and panegyrics. Rowdy trials were a thing of the past. The Forum and Senate no longer echoed to the sound of virulent charges and passionate countercharges. The low level of the cases argued mirrored the intellectual deficiency of the men of the times. This had by no means always been so. There had been a time when the atrocity of the crimes and the forceful personality of the accused fired the imagination of the speakers: "How much ardor the political assemblies and the universal right to attack the powerful used to kindle in the orators!" (*Dial.* 11.1).

When the civil wars had ended and greedy, ambitious figures no longer loomed over the flames of civil discord, a decline in a dense climate of torpid calm set in: "The long peace, the unbroken tranquillity among the people, the inactivity in the Senate and rigorous discipline had silenced everything, including eloquence . . ." (*Dial.* 38.2). The famous Pax Augusta, which had re-established order and security in the Empire, destroyed man's inner vitality and oppressed his conscience. No longer were there occasions for polemics or clashes of opinion. "And where they create a desert," observed one of the provincial rebels, "they call it peace" (*Agr.* 30.4).

In the silence imposed by imperial authority, political crimes ceased. The peace kept the political classes from excesses as well as from all public life. It was a moment for rhetoricians, functionaries, for those who had given up. Words like *inertia* (slothfulness), *desidia* (apathy), *taedium* (boredom), which had rarely appeared in Latin prose, were used more frequently now and reflected moods that often led to suicide. The only way to stand out from the common herd was through death, which need not be physical extinction: "Even *inertia* had its own sweetness; although one may start out by disliking inaction, eventually one comes to like it."

Tacitus gives a preliminary sketch of his fundamental problems in two short pieces, the *Germania* and the *Agricola*. In the *Agricola*, he outlines the conflict between absolute power and the individual, a problem that he later expanded in the *Annals*, the masterpiece of his maturity. The *Agricola* appears to be Tacitus's counterbalance to Cicero's oration against Verres. Here he expounds the principle that Rome's dominion was legitimate and would not be threatened if all the governors and officials were of the same fiber as his father-in-law, Agricola. The theory is presented with both the hyperbole characteristic of the funeral *laudatio* and the tendentiousness of a political argument.

Agricola was a provincial Gaul, brought up in Marsilia (Marseilles), with typically small-town frugality, under the watchful eye of an admirable mother. His upbringing met all the requirements of Tacitus's ethical and pedagogical standards. Agricola gave up his study of philosophy out of a Roman sense of duty, that is, the compulsion to serve, and upon the advice of his mother. All too often the pursuit of philosophy tends to stimulate an arrogant complacency about one's own moral superiority. Here we find the beginnings of Tacitus's theory, that exemplary conduct does not necessarily call for empty, theatrical acts of heroism—an allusion to the Stoic martyrs about whom he would later write more fully. Agricola devoted himself, with humble perseverance, to the service of the state, the only acceptable path to glory for a true Roman (4.3).

It was this high-minded man who put an end to twenty years of bitter guerrilla fighting in Britain. Agricola was sent there in A.D. 77, the year in which Tacitus married his daughter. He succeeded in quelling various revolts through a series of military operations which lasted until A.D. 84. He explored the coastline, and was the first to verify that Britain was an island. He tried to introduce Roman customs and culture to the natives, thereby conforming to the noblest dictates of enlightened colonialism. Tacitus, however, deplored this cultural interference, and labeled it a corrupting intrusion. Liberty, in this case, meant preserving one's own tradition against the intrusion of foreign customs. "Return to the customs and manners of your fathers, cut off those pleasures which give Romans more power over their subjects than their arms" (H. 4.64). This has always been the chief tenet of autonomists.

According to Tacitus, Agricola's worthiness aroused Domitian's envy more than his gratitude. As soon as Agricola returned to Rome, he was politically ostracized and forced to retire. As a result of this imposed inactivity, he went into a decline and died a short time later amid general mourning. True to his philosophy, he met his fate serenely. Other men had paid with their lives for their opposition, even when it was directed not against the regime per se but against the personal vices of the man who represented it. Others sought safety in prudent silence, and hoped to survive by keeping in the background. When the dictatorship ended, and they had drawn up a balance sheet of their lives, they realized they had been cheated of their most productive years, "we few survivors not of others alone but of ourselves" (*Agr.* 3.2).

Here Tacitus outlines the choices open to nations and individuals living under absolute power. The former could choose open war or slavery; the latter heroic withdrawal or servility. A third choice straddled the other two: to accept, because of its advantages to the community as a whole, a government in conflict with one's political views. This was the choice made by Agricola, Tacitus, and many others; they made the salvation of the state their primary objective, and subordinated their ideological views to the realization of that goal. The motto of these men was *patientia*. The price they paid for their decision was high: mute renunciation, ingenious connivance, forced acquiescence, smothered contempt, and, worst of all, a slow disintegration of their conscience.

> My tears for the vanquished and my hatred for the victors.[17]
> —Corneille, *Horace*, I, i, 94

As for colonial power—that is, economic exploitation, abolition of indigenous customs, and imposition of the victor's culture, which was axiomatically judged superior—Tacitus expressed warm understanding, if not open solidarity, toward anyone who viewed such measures as oppressive, an attitude that did not stem from his opposition to colonialism or his underestimation of the Roman ethical and cultural values, but from the firm conviction that, in his day, those values no longer had worthy representatives. Only in the case of the Jews did he call their resistance "obstinate superstition" (*H.* 2.4). Here, however, Tacitus conformed to the prevailing Roman prejudice: that Oriental peoples, and especially the Jews, did not merit the same respect as the northern barbarians. The Jews aroused this particularly violent reaction because they were Rome's ideological rivals; they, too, considered themselves a race predestined to govern the world.

According to a commonplace notion frequently found in Latin literature, the Britons were isolated and remote. At the time of Augustus, their subjugation to Rome was considered a most unlikely eventuality: "When the Britons and the troublesome Persians are annexed to the Empire," wrote Horace, "then Augustus will truly be a god."[18] Caesar was the first to cross the channel and land on the island, but in Rome, his enemies went around saying the strange country did not exist, that he had invented it.[19] In their reaction they unconsciously projected an ethnocentric mentality, the presupposition of the nonexistence of a country before its "discoverers" arrive. The conquest of the island was not completed until the reign of Claudius. Under Nero, however, bloody revolts broke out, and Agricola succeeded in quelling them only after long years of fighting.

According to Tacitus, the Britons were so proud of what the Romans thought of as remoteness that they transmuted an accident of geography into a moral quality. One Scottish chief boasted, "We, the noblest sons of Britain, stationed in its last recesses, far from the view of servile shores, have preserved even our eyes from the degrading sight of foreign conquerors: We, at the farthest limits both of land and liberty . . ." (*Agr.* 30.3).

Conquest was invariably followed by cultural assimilation,

forced upon the vanquished. Agricola accelerated the Romanization of Britain by opening schools and, quite likely, theaters. Archaeological remains and literary references confirm Tacitus's assertion that his father-in-law effectively developed a cultural life in that province. "They say," sneered Martial, "that now, even the Britons scan our verses."[20] Tacitus did not list that spiritual subjugation among his father-in-law's accomplishments. Along with Roman dress, eloquence, and laws, the Britons assimilated the victors' vices: "From their inexperience they termed civilization what in reality constituted a part of their enslavement" (*Agr.* 21.2).

Tacitus's somber, dramatic description of the Britons' revolt conjures up the despair of a people defending its own ethnic individuality and its sense of the sacred as well as its institutions, possessions, and the honor of its women. The Romans, in their landing devices, approached the island of Mona (Anglesey), the ancient seat of the Druids, and were paralyzed with fear by the sight that met their eyes: "On the beach stood the enemy array, a serried mass of men and arms, with women roaming between the ranks. In the style of Furies, in robes of deathly black, disheveled, brandishing torches, while a circle of Druids, lifting their arms to heaven, showered imprecations . . ." (*A.* 14.30).

The statue of victory, in the temple that Claudius had built, fell at about that time. "Women, possessed by prophetic visions, wailed that destruction was imminent and that alien voices had been heard in the invaders' senate house. The theater had resounded with shrieks and in the estuary of the Thames had been seen a vision of the ruined colony" (*A.* 32). These miracles and omens, unlike those that occurred in Judaea, were considered genuine. In that atmosphere of terror, the barbarians took the Roman garrison by surprise and killed soldiers and residents by the thousands. Tacitus gave his readers to understand that the violent reaction of the Britons was justified. The widowed Queen Boadicea, who had been de-throned and then flogged, rode through the countryside hold-ing the reins of a British chariot, of the type engraved on Caesar's coins. Her two daughters, who had been raped by Romans, accompanied their mother as she called to her peo-ple: "If the Britons consider in their own hearts the forces under arms and the motives of the war, on that field they must conquer or fall. Such was the settled purpose of a woman—the men might live and be slaves" (*A.* 35).

Tacitus also approved of the German and Batavian rebels. In his long, sorrowful meditation on liberty, he may have felt impelled to seek its vestiges beyond the capital, beyond Italy, far from civilized society, amid the people Rome had subju-gated and "bent to obey, but not yet to serve" (*Agr.* 13.1). Perhaps, moved by an inner desire for purity, he thought freedom might yet be found among those peoples who were still uncontaminated by wealth and ambition.

In his *Germania*, Tacitus accepts, from earlier authors, Caesar and Strabo[21] in particular, the descriptions of the tribes living on the other side of the Rhine. Posidonius and more recent historians, like Seneca and Pliny the Elder, sup-plied the details that enabled him most clearly to differentiate the barbarians from the Romans. He also learned from these writers about those characteristics of German social structure that survived well into the Middle Ages: the barbarians owned no private land; they had no cities founded in a mythi-cal past by a demigod, an eponymous hero, or a group of exiles; none of their cities exacted rigid ritual observances or consecrated space and men to supernatural powers, which had the inevitable result that walls and roads conformed to the cosmic order, and the very soul of the citizenry was narrowly circumscribed. In short, the urban plan of Roman cities re-flected a functional and social hierarchy. In contrast, the bar-barians lived in scattered settlements. Their gods were not represented in human form, nor did they believe in confining their deities within temple walls; they were unfamiliar, therefore, with images of idealized beauty. Their deliberations were held at night during meetings which all the men attended fully armed. Passionately loyal to their leader, they considered it a disgrace to survive him. However, they were unable to obey an abstract principle—be it represented by a dogma, a law, a statute, or a magistracy—an incapacity so firmly rooted that three hundred years later, Orosius could record that Ataulf, King of the Visigoths, recognized it as a sign of Germanic inferiority. The inability, or reluctance, of Ataulf's people to respect any code probably dissuaded him from an ambitious project: the substitution of a Gothic empire for the Roman one.[22] Even if the story is apocryphal, it is significant that the basic difference between the German character and Latin thought was thus pinpointed during the great barbarian wave.

Compared with barbarian customs, Roman ways appeared at their shoddiest. Usury was unknown among the barbarians. A master might kill a slave in a fit of anger, just as he might kill an enemy, but not as punishment. Newborn infants were never put to death; children were not abandoned to servants or nurses. The king or leader used persuasion rather than coercion to exact obedience from his followers. The absence of pornography, licentious spectacles, and frivolous pastimes protected their women from unchastity; they knew nothing of the vain pretensions of libertinism, which in Rome led even men of natural ability, such as Fabius Valens, "to seek a reputation by buffoonery" (*H*. 3.62). "No one there looks on vice with a smile or calls mutual seduction the way of the world" (*G*. 19.1). In those faraway lands the powerful forces that harass civilized men were unknown: they lived "without anxiety, hope or fear." No indulgence was shown to adulteresses.

From the barbarians living near the Empire's boundaries,

capable of observing a rudimentary discipline and strategy and spiritually akin to the true warriors of ancient Rome ("They consider fortune dubious and valor only certain" *G.* 30.2), Tacitus gradually passes on to tribes living farther inland, tribes that remained almost immune from contaminating contact with the Romans. His description proceeds in a crescendo of horror: The Arii's shields are black and their bodies painted. "They choose the darkest nights for an attack, like an army of ghosts . . ." (*G.* 43.4); the Fenni "live in a state of amazing savagery . . . their food is herbs, their clothing skin, their bed the ground." The historian's repeated use of the negative reinforces the contrast between Romans and barbarians: "They have no arms, no horses, no settled abodes." Another step into those dark forests, and accounts become intermixed with fancies—of men who were partially wild beasts: "These unauthenticated reports," the author adds with scientific scruple, "I will pass over" (*G.* 44.4).

Tacitus described countryside, climate, and somatic traits, stressing the differences that struck a Mediterranean observer: "Unexplored seas . . . a land rude in its surface, rigorous in climate, cheerless to the beholder . . ." (*G.* 2.1–3). Still, those men lived free from the competition, the calculations, the envy, and the useless torments that man created for himself with his bewitching mirages and foolish passions. They lived free from the tyranny of government and laws; from set rituals, social discrimination, the humiliation of poverty or anonymity, the insecurity of the morrow; they were untrammeled by the weight of a glorious past and the obsessive fear that glory and greatness were coming to an end. In order to escape all those real or imaginary anxieties it was essential that mankind retrace its footsteps and regress to that stage which Tacitus defined as "horrible want," thereby contradicting the myth that only simple, primitive men lived in a state of unspoiled happiness. The desolate northern landscape became a region of the spirit. There, liberty and justice were no longer incompatible but could be realized simultaneously. But this ideal fusion was possible only in lands remote from the contamination of civilization.

This nostalgia for the natural state, combined with respect for the barbarians, is manifested in the works of art produced under Trajan and Hadrian. Those majestic savages are the custodians of the pristine Roman values. The Arcadian romanticism inherent in the myth of the noble savage was gratifying to a tired, corrupt society. Although the behavior of these people was at times brutish, their excesses sprang from exuberance and vitality. Wild herbs always thrive in fertile soil. Seneca's judgment, some forty years before Tacitus's, was inspired by the same sympathy, but it also contained a note of foreboding: "These people know neither luxury nor wealth. Give them order and discipline, and you shall see. . . . All I can say is that we had better return to the ways of ancient Rome."[23] Their wretched way of life followed more closely the laws of nature than that of the Romans. "Regard the nations so far untouched by Roman civilization: those Germans and nomads in the Danube region. There they live in an eternal winter, oppressed by a dull sky; the arid soil barely produces enough to feed them; only roofs of thatch and branches protect them from the elements. And you think they are to be pitied. No man can be called wretched whose life follows the laws of nature."[24]

These were the only truly free men. "Liberty," wrote Lucan, "has retreated beyond the Tigris and the Rhine; it is the heritage of the Scythians and the Germans; it no longer even glances at Italy."[25] And Juvenal, Tacitus's contemporary, comments: "You may with impunity despise the cowardly inhabitants of Rhodes or the perfumed Corinthians . . . but beware of rugged Spain, the Gallic skies, the Illyrian shores. Don't provoke those harvesters who feed the City while she is intent only on circuses and theaters . . . beware of committing injustices against strong, ill-fated peoples. Even though you take away all their gold and silver, they will still have shields and swords, lances and helmets: a man stripped of all his possessions still keeps his weapon. . . ."[26]

Ignorant of intrigue, competition, adulation, and depravity, the barbarians created their own new, albeit brutish, golden age. From the time when Brennus and his Gauls invaded Greece, a stylized image of the fighting barbarian had come into being: half naked, long-haired, stalwart in battle, proud in defeat, arrogant in slavery. He had the virile traits of the Capitoline "Dying Gaul." Tacitus writes of his formal speeches about genuine grievances. No longer living free like a beast of the forest, he confronts a civilization that he rejects. Tacitus looks to the past for his ideals and mourns for bygone standards and customs. In the barbarian, he recognizes genuine *virtus* in its original purity, while in Rome "strength was corrupted by luxury in contrast to the ancient discipline and precepts of our fathers . . ." (*H.* 2.69).

While the fabled savages beyond the Rhine provided a mortifying example, the conquered, provincial ones were Tacitus's mouthpiece. They expressed his condemnation of Roman society, his interpretation of the causes of Rome's decline. The primary cause of provincial unrest was the poor government resulting from the gap between capital and dominions, Senate and military. The barbarians, "punished with harsh edicts or loss of territory" (*H.* 1.53), threw in their lot with the seditious border legions, which were made up of their compatriots. Tacitus insistently denounced the small proportion of Romans in the defense ranks. The soldiers of barbarian origin, aware of their numerical superiority, naturally sided with the provincial agitators: "Theirs were the hands that held the destinies of Rome, theirs the victories by which the Empire grew, theirs the names which Caesars assumed!" (*A.* 1.31).

Ever since Scipio recruited the Celtiberians against Hasdrubal, and Caesar launched first the Gauls against the Germans, then both Gauls and Germans against Pompey, the expediency of using "foreign" soldiers to fill depleted ranks, when the legions were far from home, had become an established practice. The barbarian auxiliaries, always placed in the front lines, fought in their own formations with their own weapons: the *spatha* (falchion) and *hasta* (lance), as opposed to the Roman *gladius* (sword) and *pilum* (javelin) (*A.* 12.35). Those mercenaries were soon to turn into national armies.

In the passage quoted above, Tacitus issued his first warning to the Romans. The barbarians were aware that they were the only barrier against the continual pressure from the tribes beyond the Empire's borders; that was why they condemned Roman indolence and the hateful administration of the provinces. Tacitus certainly had a premonition of what the outcome of this situation would be, even though he never expressly stated it. The barbarians' legitimate grievances implied their right to inherit power and their claim that they were protecting Rome not only from foreign invasion but, above all, from her own degeneration.

At the height of imperial power, under that Optimus Princeps, when Trajan had planned and achieved Rome's last territorial conquest—the annexation of Dacia—at a time when a new concept of Empire and a new interpretation of Rome's mission was expressed by the panegyrists and by contemporary iconographers, Tacitus foresaw decline and fall. He deemed that a nation unable to give proof of its moral superiority has no right to exercise power. Although some of Tacitus's statements may echo Livy and reflect the ancient moral code, he realized that these principles had become obsolete. He put them in the mouths of others. When Tiberius refused to have Arminius poisoned, he hypocritically affirmed that "it was not by treason nor in the dark but openly and in arms that the Roman people took vengeance on their enemies" (*A.* 2.88). Thrasea's* plea that the Senate "come to a decision consonant with Roman honor and firmness" (*A.* 15.20) proves his nostalgia for values of the past. These ethical norms were no longer valid in Tacitus's day. His entire work clearly demonstrates the incompatibility of historically superseded ethics and customs with the new demands of the times. It was impossible to reconcile the hegemonic postulate with the crimes committed by those in power—crimes that were such as to bring into disrepute the system of justice and threaten the very survival of the Empire.

From the very first riots in Gaul, recorded in the *Annals*, those that took place in A.D. 21, the leaders of the revolt exposed the roots of Roman baseness. "Just observe," they said, "the unwarlike city population, the feebleness of the armies, except for the leavening of foreigners" (*A.* 3.40). Sixty years later, the chieftain of the Britons harangued his countrymen in the same vein: "Rome's army is compounded of the most different nations, which success alone has kept together, and which misfortune will as certainly disperse. . . . In the very ranks of our enemy we shall find our own bands; the Britons will acknowledge their own cause; the Gauls will remember their former liberty; the Germans will desert . . ." (*Agr.* 32.3).

The same charge was repeated by the leader of the Batavians, Julius Civilis, who attempted to launch a huge German insurrection in A.D. 69: "Never has the Roman state sunk so low. Only old men and booty are in the winter camps. Lift your heads, Batavians, do not fear the empty name of legions. On our side are our strong infantry and cavalry, our kinsmen,

---

* A Stoic with republican sympathies and a senator who refused to participate in public affairs, he was condemned under Nero and forced to commit suicide (A.D. 66).

the Germans and Gauls animated by identical hopes" (*H.* 4.14). When inviting the Gauls to join the rebels, Civilis used the same arguments: "What forces are there left in Italy? It is by the blood of the provinces that provinces are won" (*H.* 4.17). The men fighting under the Roman banners were no longer Romans: "Most of them have either no home or a distant one" (*Agr.* 32.2). This denunciation pointed first to the Romans' ethnic and moral inadequacies and second to the demographic crisis, which was to culminate in the "tragic scarcity of men" that plagued all the emperors from the second century on. "Long live the Galatians, Syrians, Cappadocians, Gauls, Iberians, Armenians and Cilicians," wrote Lucan, "because after the civil wars, they will be the people of Rome!"[27]

Although still barbarians, these nations did not repudiate Rome; they denounced her unjust administration, her loathsome discrimination, but his history was also theirs. They even drew inspiration for their own legendary precursors from Roman sources: "[Claudius] Civilis, who was more cunning than the average barbarian, compared himself to a Sertorius or a Hannibal since, like them, he was squint-eyed . . ." (*H.* 4.13). Those barbarians without a past could not conceive of a future without Rome. Just as the "new men" from the Italic municipalities had flocked to Rome in the days of the Republic (Cato from Tusculum, Marius and Cicero from Arpinum, Sallust from Amiternum, Ventidius from Asculum), and in the Augustan era (Livy from Padua, Vergil from Mantua, Catullus from Sirmium), and had embraced the patrician moral code; so now the provincials, yesterday's barbarians, learned to expound the ancient principles: love for their native land, impartiality, and frugality. In this way Rome's cultural expansion had kept pace with her territorial conquests.

The men who defended their national autonomy were no

longer barbarians, but subject peoples who demanded an end to colonial exploitation. Their protest is so convincingly expressed that it implies Tacitus's unspoken assent: "Other nations, unacquainted with the dominion of Rome had neither felt her punishments nor known her exactions" (*A*. 1.59). "To ravage, to slaughter, to usurp under false title, they call Empire; and where they create a desert they call it peace" (*Agr*. 30.4).

The hatred and bitterness for Rome that prevailed in all the provinces was an old, recurring theme. Cicero wrote, "Between the seas, there is no place so remote or distant that it cannot be engulfed by the lust and iniquity of our men. . . ."[28] "These people," Pompeius Trogus wrote about the Romans, "have the soul of a wolf; insatiable for blood, greedy for power and money."[29] Lucan acknowledged that the more the subject populations came to know the Romans, the more they hated them.[30] There was nothing new in Tacitus's version of the rebels' accusations; but he brought to them a genuine understanding of their causes.

The increase in provincial protests was doubly significant during those years. The Empire was finding its ideological inspiration, which it had sought for more than a century, in Greek sources, and the idea of Rome was synthesized in the august person of the emperor. The original concept of the principate was fading into the past. The princeps—the first citizen—had been chosen because of evident personal merit and was entrusted with a temporary, revocable mission; he was a sentry to be relieved of duty when his strength began to fail—*statione relicta*[31] (a post relinquished)—the words are Augustus's. There were traces of the ancient magistracies in this conception of power, which, while remaining absolute, was nonetheless subject to constitutional forms and limitations, and repeatedly extended by the Senate as an extraordinary measure. The formula of names and qualifiers—emperor, Father of the Nation, proconsul, censor—became a fixed part of the power establishment under the Flavian dynasty. Throughout the entire first century, the monarchical idea progressed fitfully—with aberrant and at times theatrical features under Caligula and Nero, and with cautious, halting steps under the other emperors.

At the turn of the second century, it became evident that only a monarchy based on the Oriental model of totalitarianism could act as a breakwater against military anarchy and ethnic disintegration. The sovereign became the living incarnation of divine power. Trajan, by nature friendly and democratic, came in for his full share of providential attributes: invulnerable, farsighted, provider of food during famine, even in the most distant provinces. "Thus," wrote Pliny, "the [foreign] nations realize that it is more advantageous for them to obey one man than to abandon themselves to the liberty of dissension." The irresistible proof of the Emperor Nerva's divinity lay in his choice of a successor, for only divine inspiration could have guided him to designate Trajan, a man beyond compare.[32]

Symptoms of imperial apotheosis could be found not only in the eastern provinces, but also in Roman circles. The borderline between king and god had been blurred even in the case of the City's mythical ancestors: Evander, Saturn, Aeneas, Romulus. A variety of prodigies had cast a supernatural aura on the lives of many famous Romans. Scipio was believed to be mysteriously favored and boasted of secret communication with Jupiter. Sulla maintained that he was guided by the gods, who spoke to him in his sleep, and that he was assisted by Fortune. He consequently adopted the agnomen Felix, thereby putting greater emphasis on the partiality of the gods than on his personal merits. Marius posed as Bacchus and accepted offerings of first fruits.[33] Caesar declared himself a descendant of Venus, and had his statue placed in the door of her temple. Various provincial temples had been dedicated to Augustus.

Despite Tiberius's reluctance and Vespasian's good-natured irony, the title "Divus" became customary. The opposition from conservative Republicans notwithstanding, imperial deification made spectacular progress under Caligula and Nero, who considered themselves new Alexanders. The monarchy, although a typically Asiatic and Egyptian institution, and as such abhorrent to the Roman mind, responded to a deep-seated need in Rome's historical evolution. It was essential that whoever reigned over so many nations and unified them under his name be endowed with supernatural attributes. The rhetoricians of the Hellenistic world succeeded in becoming the theoreticians—if not the promoters—of an ideology that viewed the Empire as an earthly replica of divine order. They saw the sovereign as the solar light, the Supreme Power chosen by God to bring His justice to Earth. Among the Italics, only Pliny—the type of intellectual with an instinct for ethical adaptation who can be found in any age—took up this theme. He understood intuitively that by exalting Trajan he could transmute a down-to-earth, solid individual into a symbol, and thereby strengthen the Empire's spiritual cohesion.

Of those Greeks who had looked upon Roman power as merely a passing phenomenon, only a few now remained. While there grew up in obscurity those who would use as a basis for their doctrine the transitoriness of all human greatness, the rhetoricians formulated a cosmopolitan and providential conception of the Roman Empire. For centuries to come, the world would accept this concept as the historical rationale it perennially sought.

It was always hoped that the characteristics of the ideal monarch, which derived from Plato and other Greek sources, could be found in the first citizen. The Roman ethical scale of values fluctuated according to need. In the Republican era, there had been no distinction between private and political morality. In Tacitus's day, however, *virtus*, an attribute of the *vir* (man), was replaced by gifts bestowed by the gods rather than achieved through discipline and self-denial. These ensured *honos* (honor) and *gloria* (glory) not to the individual, but to the community as a whole. *Pietas* (devotion to the gods) assured divine benevolence to the ruler who practiced it and to his people. Once again the king assumed the magic functions of intermediary between his subjects and the celestial powers.

The abstract principles of Greek thought became political reality. Under Hadrian, the Stoic philosopher Epictetus wrote that "the universe is one single city-state."[34] This ecumenical and equalizing tendency found its doctrinal formulation in the second-century orations on the advantages of monarchy. Dio Chrysostom of Prusa and Aelius Aristides modeled their theories of the principate on the ideas of the Sophists and Plato, and made them fit the Empire. In sculpture and on coinage, the prince lost his individual traits and became stereotyped into a solemn hierarchic image. Realistic portraiture underwent crystallization and became an icon. The sovereign relinquished his proper name to become Augustus (the August One). During Tacitus's lifetime, imperial power found its justification at the cosmological level.

For Tacitus, however, this was a historical reality which he accepted for external reasons—order, defense, administrative uniformity—along with internal ones, primarily man's inability to live free. At Augustus's funeral, when evaluating the Emperor's achievements, Tacitus gives an abstract of a debate on power, aligning himself with those sensible men who opined that "the only remedy for a country torn by party strife was government by one man" (*A.* 1.9). Similarly, he has Nero's successor, Galba, propose a compromise solution—adoption—which Tacitus evidently approved. Like Tacitus,

Galba rejected the ideological temptation to reverse the current of history: "If the mighty structure of the Empire could retain its balance without a ruler, it would be proper that a Republic should begin with me" (*H*. 1.16). However, he very clearly wanted the designated heir to remember that he would be ruling over men "who did not know how to endure either complete slavery or complete freedom." Galba's appraisal contradicts a truism repeated by Cicero and Livy, according to which the Romans' distinguishing trait was that they were free men; but perhaps such an observation applies to all men.

During the crisis that rent the Empire in the interim between Nero's death and Vespasian's accession, men, for the last time, hoped that the Empire's dominion might end. The question of the best form of government was again foremost in speculative thought. At the time, concern centered on the stability and duration of nations rather than on economic justice. Galba's proposal to select the best—a principle followed by the Antonine emperors throughout the entire second century—gave the worthiest a chance. True, it was no longer the freedom of Republican times, but this form of monarchy was at least more democratic than a dynastic one. "Under Tiberius and Gaius and Claudius, we Romans were the heritage, so to speak, of one family; the fact that the emperors are now chosen will be for all a kind of liberty . . ." (*H*. 1.16).

Galba's wise decision and sagacious choice were followed by months of savagery and atrocities. Vespasian's accession marked a definite shift in Rome's policies. While respectful of the Senate because of his humble origins, the aged commander of Reate (modern Rieti) placed the stamp of monarchical absolutism on his power. He faced economic, juridical, and military problems on a world scale. In the months during which the entire expanse of the Empire had been ravaged by fire and sword as the contenders struggled for supremacy, a new hope must surely have arisen: for the return of peace on earth, either through a kingship dispensing divine justice, or through the restoration of the Republic.

An echo of this expectancy of change comes to us in an imaginary debate which had the neo-Pythagorean philosopher Apollonius of Tyana as protagonist. Encouraged by favorable omens and secure in the devotion of his soldiers, Vespasian, on the eve of his move against his rival Vitellius, is supposed to have summoned, in June of A.D. 69, some famous thinkers to Alexandria; his purpose was to consult them about the best form of government to be adopted once the present ruler was deposed and he himself had assumed power. Ancient historiography abounds in similar dialogues on this very theme. Various characters with antithetic points of view served as mouthpieces for the conflicting opinions, demands, and proposals of the day. Dio Cassius has Maecenas and Agrippa debate with Augustus; the Greek historians imagined similar debates between Persians or Athenians.[35]

Among the various thinkers consulted by Vespasian, the first encouraged him to restore the Republican system. The second argued that it was too late, since the habit of liberty had been lost. The third, Apollonius, favored monarchy because of contingent considerations symptomatic of the keen political intuition of the mystics. As a sage, he is not concerned with the type of constitution under which he happened to live, since "man's life is governed only by the gods." His one request of the future Emperor is care for the humble, a rule of justice and clemency; and let him be the first to respect not only the written laws but the moral laws as well.

A century after Tacitus, Philostratus wrote an account of this imaginary meeting. Undoubtedly he took his inspiration from the dialogues and other rhetorical compositions of the times, with which Tacitus must have been acquainted. Power was the central theme in the orations of Dio Chrysostom, a Greek sophist and rhetorician from Bithynia, who, after having been banished from Rome by Domitian, lived for a considerable length of time in barbarian territories. Dio returned to favor under Nerva and Trajan and in three orations pointed out to them what an intellectual brought up on Hellenistic culture expected from Roman rule. The first condition of good government was that the prince's moral superiority over his subjects be equal to his power over them. The prince should be vigilant, tireless, humane, and generous; he should prove himself worthy of the throne by virtue of his merits. His life should be at the service of the commonwealth.[36]

These ideas derived from Plato, the Sophists, and other sources. They had already been formulated by Seneca in his *De Clementia*, a work that the author had dedicated to Nero.[37] The hopes for a beneficent and superhuman prince merely cloaked, under doctrinary drapings, resignation to dictatorship.

While accepting some of the rhetoricians' principles, Tacitus was insensitive to the metaphysical undercurrents that agitated Roman political doctrine. His approach differs radically from the panegyrists'. They praised the prince's human qualities—moderation, courage, self-denial, valor—but emphasized the superhuman ones—his intrinsic "divinity," his surprising readiness to remember "that he, too, is a man," to consider himself "one of us."[38] At most, Tacitus was ready to respect the prince—provided he deserved this respect—as the lesser evil. Disenchanted and clear-sighted, he did not envisage a different world order. The will of the gods, fate, or ancient *virtus* had made the Romans the rulers of the world. It was their manifest destiny to exercise this power, but they would accomplish this only if their moral prestige was equal to their military might.

The Empire was a reality to which one had to submit. Even the proudest spirits bowed in mute acquiescence; they either suffered or accepted the principate. The barbarians had done the same. "You endure barren years, excessive rains, and all of nature's other scourges; in the same manner endure the extravagance or greed of your rulers. . . . For if the Romans are driven out—which Heaven forbid—then what would follow except universal war among all peoples?" (*H.* 4.74). Thus did Petilius Cerialis explain to the Gauls why they should submit to the Romans. In much the same words, Josephus Flavius, the Romanized Jewish historian, has King Agrippa, by then an ally of Titus, exhort the Israelites to lay down their arms. People much richer, stronger, and more numerous had done the same; they had resigned themselves. There was no resisting Rome's strength.

From the provinces, the intellectuals, the Senate, the philosophers, and the army, a consensus arose that, in a cosmopolitan and progressively egalitarian society, only absolute power guaranteed order and stability. A universal monarchy was the only dike against the barbarian threat. It was advisable to follow the example of the provincials who, after futile resistance, laid down their arms and resigned themselves to Rome's ineluctable domination. Tacitus, however, permitted himself the luxury of spiritual dissent. Until the end, he remained one of the few who considered servility shameful (*servire pudet*).[39]

> While the fate of the Empire is thus urgent . . .[40]
> —Tacitus *Germania* 33. 2

Tacitus accepted the deep-seated Roman belief that the Empire had been shaped by heavenly powers and that it was imperative to follow the road traced by Romulus. The defense and expansion of the Empire were the prince's primary duties. Thus Tacitus deplored Tiberius's passivity and Domitian's renunciations or hollow victories. In his *Germania* he may have hoped to call attention to the Rhine boundaries,

which, at that point, Trajan was ready to denude in prepara-
tion for his march on Dacia. The coins of the day bore the
inscription GERMANIA PACATA (Germany pacified), but Tacitus did not share this opinion. Two hundred years had passed
since Marius had turned back the Cimbri and the Teutons—
"So long has Germany withstood the arms of Rome . . . not
the Samnites, the Carthaginians, Spain, Gaul, or Parthia have
given us more frequent alarms; for the liberty of the Germans
is more vigorous than the monarchy of the Arsacids* . . ."
(G. 37.3). Cruelty, even to the point of genocide, was legitimate to guarantee the security of the Rhine border. Germanicus incited his soldiers to take advantage of the superiority of
their weapons and to massacre all the barbarians: ". . . only
the extermination of the race," he said, "would end the war
. . ." (A. 2.21).

Roman superiority over Israel was unequivocally asserted.
The Jews were the only conquered people to offer a spiritual
counteroffensive—more to be feared than military action.
The Jews never adopted the customs of the cities in which
they resided. They remained perennial aliens, aloof from the
rituals, the festivities, the calendar, the eating habits, and the
civil holidays of the host country. For them, Rome, Athens,
and Alexandria were simply transitory homes; their homeland
was Jerusalem. The gold of the emigrants flowed back to this
city; most of the malcontents took refuge there; directives
and the seeds of dissatisfaction that were to develop in other
cities originated there. In Jerusalem, dangerous intrigues with
the Parthians were plotted. "The Jews are extremely loyal
toward one another . . . but toward every other people they
feel only hate and enmity" (H. 5.5). And Juvenal wrote that
". . . they do not show you the way unless you are a core-
ligionary; they show the way only to the circumcised."[41]

Tacitus's feelings about the Jews were shared by other

---

* The royal dynasty of Parthia from c. 250 B.C. to A.D. 230, then a world
power reaching from the Euphrates to the Indus.

Latin writers—Cicero, Horace, Lucan, Pliny, Martial, and Juvenal. The Romans, themselves basically traditionalists, saw the negation of their own prestige in other nations' traditionalism. Tacitus lived at a time when Rome was beginning to formulate her own messianic concept of history, according to which the universal kingdom would be established by a man sent from the heavens. The thought that this might not be a Roman was unacceptable to Romans, who were unable to transfer the expectation of the kingdom to the metaphysical sphere; national sentiment regarded it as ambition for worldly dominion.

Those were years when feelings ran high. The ancient rivalry between the East and the West was still alive. People were sensitive to portents and prophecies. Tacitus is aware of these currents, records them in his concise prose; imperturbably he relates irrational occurrences and reports rumors that we also find in other sources: "Suddenly the doors of the shrine flew open and a superhuman voice cried: "The gods are departing . . .'" (H. 5.13). The historian Josephus Flavius noted: "From above, they heard terrible voices that cried out: We are departing!"[42] These phenomena, recorded as occurring on the eve of the fall of Jerusalem, appear also in the Apocrypha, where they accompany the death of Christ. The ancient prophets thundered from the clouds amid lightning flashes: "Let us forsake this place!" Precepts characteristic of Christian preaching ("He that loveth father or mother more than me is not worthy of me . . .")[43] filtered down to Tacitus: "Those who are converted . . . regard their parents, children and brothers of little account . . ." (H. 5.5). Those swift, dazzling flashes, those blurred disturbing images penetrated the Romans' consciousness, and made them intuit their subversive potential.

The fire that broke out in the Capitol during the struggle between Vespasian and Vitellius seemed to confirm these somber predictions. A nameless fear gripped men's souls. According to Tacitus, the fire was adjudged a bad omen. It had occurred at a time of peace throughout the Empire; Tacitus observes: "Rome had no foreign foe; the gods were ready to be propitious, had our characters allowed . . ." (*H.* 3.72).

If the Empire was to be considered the bulwark of world order, universal solidarity must perforce be appealed to and ethnic and religious differences wiped out in order to achieve harmony. It seemed almost as if a premonitory shudder were running through the Roman world and inducing its inhabitants to huddle close together within the safe, protected *limes* (boundaries) of the garrisons. Only Israel, persisting in her prejudices and her refusals, did not join in. As Tacitus wrote, "The Jews regard as profane all that we hold sacred; on the other hand they permit all that we abhor" (*H.* 5.4). The hatred the Roman writers bore the Jews gives a measure of the threat which that nation posed by virtue of its cohesion and intense spirituality. Rome might rout the zealots and, as Titus had done, crucify 5,000 Jews on the walls of Jerusalem, but she could not extinguish Israel's Messianism, her perennial expectation of a reign of justice, and her certainty that she alone would be called upon to establish it. Tacitus's harshness toward the Jews makes it clear that the Empire and the obligation to safeguard it were the basic tenets of his thought. This sense of the Roman mission increased in the face of the stiff-necked Jewish opposition, which not only sought to elude Roman dominion but also denied its validity.

It was difficult enough to carry on burdened by that bounden duty. At times, the historian's faith in the duration of the Empire falters. If it were no longer possible to reanimate Roman conscience and valor, he hoped for a weakening of the enemy strength: "May the nations retain and perpetuate, if not an affection for us, at least an animosity against each other; since while the fate of the Empire is thus urgent, fortune can offer us no higher benefit than the discord of our enemies . . ." (*G.* 33.2). At this point, it was fortune, not *virtus* as in the past, which could save Rome. This sentence, cryptic, like so many others, can only imply the historian's foreboding certainty that the Germans would attack the Empire in the future. It was a biting, ironic criticism of those Romans who, at least for the moment, enjoyed a safety that depended on discord among their enemies.

Tacitus borrowed the expression "while the fate of the Empire is thus urgent" from Livy, who had used it in connection with the imminent fall of Veii (6.22) and the Gauls' sack of Rome (6.36). The words convey more than anxiety; they ring out alarm. The amazement that Rome's world conquests had aroused—they were the fountainhead of Polybius's political inspiration, Vergil's metaphysical motivation, and Livy's ethical justification—had not yet died out. But the unsettling sensation that the Roman Empire might approach its end increased alarmingly. The pride of being Roman was not inseparable from an anxiety that led men to consider Rome's citizens either as Rome's potential defenders or as the agents of her greatness. Tacitus voices his sense of loss with regard to the territories abandoned under Domitian. He had hoped that, after Britain, even Ireland might become part of the Empire (*Agr.* 24.3; 41.3). Here he is not immune to imperialist sentiment; but he was firm in his skepticism: even if the Romans had superior military equipment for such undertakings, their spirits had flagged.

Tacitus has Germanicus represent the boundless imperialism of Rome. He was the son of Drusus, the child Livia was carrying when she married Augustus after her hasty divorce, and it is possible that the Emperor was Drusus's father. Augustus ordered Tiberius to adopt Germanicus, putting him ahead of Drusus the Younger, Tiberius's son, in the line of succession. When Germanicus died, many people thought that his uncle had poisoned him and thereby eliminated his own son's rival.

The figure of Germanicus looms with ambiguous brilliance. Facets of his character are in direct contradiction to the Republican concept of *virtus* and are even more antithetical to the values of Tiberius (and perhaps, as it has been naïvely conjectured, even those of Hadrian, the childless intellectual pacifist who ascended the throne precisely when Tacitus was writing those pages). Germanicus was spirited to the point of impetuosity, affable to the point of demagogy, reckless to the point of ostentatiousness: "Bareheaded, so he could be recognized, he incited his men to press on with the carnage" (*A.* 2.21). His sensitivity bordered on emotionality. When a storm in the North Sea had scattered the Roman ships, "Throughout all those days and nights, posted on some cliff or promontory, he continued to exclaim that he was guilty of the great disaster, and his friends with difficulty prevented him from finding a grave in the same waters" (*A.* 2.24). He gave the Germans no quarter, and penetrated into their territories to bury the Romans who, in the disastrous campaign of Varus, had fallen at Teutoburg. If Tiberius had not recalled him, he might conceivably have annihilated that race, to the greatest advantage of the Roman nation. This endeared him to Tacitus, who seems convinced that Germanicus would have been successful in subjugating the Germans had the Emperor not called him back to Rome "to celebrate his triumph . . . and the war, since he had been forbidden to complete it, was assumed to be complete . . ." (*A.* 2.41).

If Tacitus had been faithful to that Republican conservatism which is usually considered his most salient characteristic, he would not have been so effusive in his praise of the young prince. Being the son of the first Drusus, Germanicus's paternal grandmother was Livia, but he was descended from Mark Antony on his mother's side. His propensity for an Oriental-style monarchy, which Augustus had rejected in favor of a formally Republican principate, probably came to him from his maternal ancestor. Germanicus visited Egypt despite

Tiberius's orders to the contrary. He made demagogic grain distributions to the people. He went on a pilgrimage to Troy, and flaunted pro-Hellenic tastes. These affectations, adopted from Antony, placed him beyond the pale of that Augustan policy so scrupulously observed by Tiberius. Germanicus's behavior also justified the criticisms from the conservatives, headed by the patrician Piso. When the King of Arabia offered a massive golden crown to Germanicus and a lighter one to Piso, the latter "was heard to remark . . . that this banquet was given to the son, not of a Parthian King, but of a Roman prince" (*A.* 2.57). Tacitus provides no comment but leaves it to the reader to decide whether Piso's* resentment stemmed from an infraction of Republican customs or from pique because his crown was worth less than that given Germanicus.

Tacitus might not have spared Germanicus from criticism had he ascended the throne. After the young Prince's death, the historian poured out his frustrated hopes and his tormented love for Rome, mortified by the sad spectacle of his day. His regret for the young man who did not have a chance to prove his worth may well conceal his passionate love for his country. With Germanicus dead, no one else would suffice. As with Livy and the Augustan poets, it was still acceptable to greet with approval an emperor who stood for Rome's lofty destiny. Imperialism as a mission was the only valid ideal to compensate for the Senate's political impotency. That belief, however, must have seemed a shameful contradiction to a man who had observed Nero's and Domitian's rule and had heard from witnesses the details of Seneca's and Thrasea Paetus's suicides, and perhaps had been present when Helvidius Priscus† was condemned to death.

* Lucius Calpurnius Piso schemed, with Seneca and Lucan, to replace Nero as emperor and was executed in A.D. 70.
† Thrasea's son-in-law, an advocate of republicanism, who was executed under Vespasian (*c.* A.D. 75).

Had Germanicus in the Tacitean image lived, he would not have allowed such crimes to sully him; he came to combine all the gifts that the panegyrists envisaged, or hoped for, in rulers. He stood out among the fierce, surly members of the Claudian family. An exemplary father and husband, he was in sharp contrast to the court's corruption and Emperor Hadrian's particular passions. His boldness in war accentuated Tiberius's colorless cautiousness, Nero's folly, and Domitian's hollow victories. Germanicus was affable and modest. At least, this is how he was viewed in retrospect by the men who lived in an era when the Prince was beginning to don the solemn drapings of an immortal theocrat.

The contrast is most pronounced in comparison to Tiberius. The young Prince is all light, his uncle all shadow; the one outgoing and vibrant, the other withdrawn and sinister.

For Tacitus, imperialism was never an openly formulated conviction; inhibitions hampered him and made him express himself in hypotheses that never reached actuality. He seems to say that enthusiasm for Rome's greatness and firm faith in her matchless civilization would indeed be gratifying sentiments if the horrors and injustice of imperial rule were not abhorrent to decent men. Tacitus, therefore, could not, and did not, expound positive ideals. His true postulates can only be guessed at from a series of rejections, directed against cruel, vicious, inept emperors, servile, intriguing senators, greedy proconsuls—a hopeless situation he was powerless to change.

> There may be great men even under wicked rulers.[44]
> —Tacitus *Agricola* 42. 4

> In slavery of any kind, the door to liberty is always open.[45]
> —Seneca *De Ira* 3. 15

According to most scholars, Tacitus was the last Roman historian to convey irreducible nostalgia for a government by the *optimates*—the élite. Only men who embodied the Roman ideals of austerity, piety, and steadfastness would have been worthy of exercising supremacy in Roman society and of ruling the world. Unfortunately, however, the unworthiness of the ruling class emphasized the absurdity of this archaic ideal. The men whom Tacitus would have thought fit to govern had disappeared; some had perished in the civil wars, others had been corrupted by princes, and many had been swept away in heroically futile plots or by the fatal attraction of *taedium vitae* (boredom with life).[46] The occasional appearances of moderate sovereigns or honest functionaries could not suffice to attenuate Tacitus's pessimism. He deplored the transformation of protectorates into colonies, of the prince into a despot, of the national army into mercenary bands; he bemoaned the decline of private morality, the result of contact with foreigners. Rome, Lucan had written, was filled with the world's dregs.[47] The City was fanatically devoted to its actors, its gladiators, and its horses (*Dial.* 29.3). Its youth, "under the influence of foreign tastes, degenerated into votaries of the gymnasia, indulged in indolence, and in disgraceful love affairs—and this with the encouragement of the Emperor and the Senate . . ." (*A.* 14.20). "Once upon a time," Juvenal wrote with melancholy, "all the gold and silver men possessed shone on their weapons . . ."[48] Now luxury reigned everywhere, while vice and crime were rampant. A few residues of Rome's ancient virtue could still be found in remote municipalities which sent their most worthy men to the City, to introduce there the ancient, characteristically Italic habits of frugality (*A.* 3.55; 16.5). Such nostalgic praise of the provinces as the stronghold of archaic values links Tacitus to Juvenal, Sallust, Cicero, and Cato.

The spectacle of his times forced Tacitus, like so many others before him, to confront the alarming question of decadence. Unlike Polybius, he did not subscribe to the belief that political evolution followed an unchanging rhythm in every country and in every epoch, and that institutional forms succeeded one another in uniform cycles. The miraculous "mixed constitution" in which Polybius thought to recognize the origins of Rome's ascent and perhaps even the guarantee of the City's permanent survival, did not reassure Tacitus. "Every nation or city is governed by the people, or by the nobility, or by individuals; a constitution selected and blended from these types is easier commended than created . . ." (*A.* 4.33). In Rome, however, this ideal government had been brought into being, but it had not lasted long; its foundations had been undermined by wealth, greed, and ambition. According to Polybius, "the state is founded upon two principles: customs and laws . . ."[49] but Tacitus maintained that the laws are of little moment once the customs are weakened. The ancient customs of Rome were undermined "as the Empire became great and the ingrained greed for power . . . came to full growth and broke bounds" (*H.* 2.38).

Tacitus did not subscribe to the theory that power is transferred from one people to another through successive cycles, nor did he believe that states, like individuals, grow old and finally die. He invoked gods propitious or avenging, starting from the assumption that the Empire's greatness was divinely ordained. However, in his view it was divine wrath that gathered and rose like a whirlwind on the celestial summits rather than steadfast vigilance over Rome's destiny. "The gods care not for our safety but for our punishment . . ." (*H.* 1.3). If he looked to the past, it was only to try to understand why the Romans had sunk so low. Their spiritual decline could be traced to an excess of power, to graft, corruption, and lack of moral restraint. His inquiry starts in the past and moves slowly toward the City in spiraling circles. He examined the dangers that threatened Rome—in the *Germania*, the barbarians beyond the imperial borders; in the *Agricola* and the *Histories*, the gulf between Rome and the conquered nations;

again in the *Histories*, dynastic competition and civil wars. Finally, in the *Annals*, the fruit of the historian's maturity, his investigation proceeds backward from recent to remote times, and from the periphery to the center, from boundaries and provinces to the capital city, ending with Rome. The work opens with Tiberius's accession, since at that moment the principate seemed destined to endure; however, precisely at that point, its inherent vices became manifest. Here Tacitus probes the depths of man's soul, and finds that its authentic truth was revealed only at the moment of death.

"It was thus an altered world, and of the old unspoiled Roman character, not a trace lingered. Equality was an outworn creed, and all eyes looked for cues to the sovereign" (*A.* 1.4). These were Tacitus's comments on the Augustan era.

The degradation was immediate. Even the most skeptical were bitterly surprised as they realized how quickly men acquiesce. ". . . the nobility found a cheerful acceptance of slavery the smoothest road to wealth and office . . ." (*A.* 1.2). When it was rumored that Augustus lay dying, "a few voices began idly to discuss the blessings of freedom . . . the great majority merely exchanged gossip derogatory to their future masters" (*Ibid.*).

Of Tiberius, we catch only glimpses as he waits in the wings before entering the stage. Brief comments are followed by more explicit and numerous ones as time passed. This stern, scrupulous prince, evidently attached to a doctrine, is described according to tendentious sources, which favored Germanicus. Tacitus, however, has Augustus, who had made the young Tiberius part of his household, guess at his stepson's hidden perversity. "He had read the pride and cruelty of his heart, and had sought to heighten his own glory by the vilest of contrasts" (*A.* 1.10). Thus, even Augustus's motives for Tiberius's adoption were base.

Tiberius's character becomes clearer from the words of the

men who remember him or describe him to friends who lost sight of him after his voluntary exile to Rhodes. Tiberius was not immune to the traditional arrogance of the Claudian family. Ever since childhood, he had been accustomed to have first place. In Rhodes, he harbored his rancor, and kept his innate cruelty and lust a secret. When it became known for certain that he was Augustus's successor, "At Rome, consuls, senators and knights hastened to render him homage . . ." (*A.* 1.7).

In skillfully measured doses, Tacitus records the contrast between Tiberius, ambiguous and cautious to the point of irresoluteness, and the élite, who zealously prostrated themselves at his feet in a crescendo of adulation. Every line adds another touch, probes the characters. When the senator Valerius Messalla proposed that the oath of allegiance to the Emperor be repeated annually, Tiberius reacted brusquely ("Did I perhaps suggest such a thing to you?"), and Messalla hastened to answer that he had spoken of his own accord, "even at the risk of giving offense." "This," Tacitus comments, "was the only form of flattery still left" (*A.* 1.8).

With his habitual caution and false humility, Tiberius persisted in refusing the offices that the senators urged on him. They insistently begged him to accept, "their one dread being that they might seem to comprehend him" (*A.* 1.11). Step by step, they worked up to the extremes of supplication and tears. The most extraordinary proposals were made in the Senate to propitiate him. On one occasion it was suggested that the names of the tribunes should replace those of the consuls on public and private monuments, because Tiberius's son Drusus held that office, whereupon an elderly senator moved that the day's resolutions should be put up in letters of gold in the senate house. At this point a ripple of scorn ran through the assembly. The Senator was derided "as an old man who could reap nothing but infamy from his repulsive adulation" (*A.* 3.57).

Tiberius appeared unmoved by such abject flattery and requested that the stamp of Republican restoration, which Augustus had given the principate, be kept intact. He refused ovations, and the title Father of the Nation; he did not allow temples to be built in his honor. He scrupulously respected even the smallest details of legality, and kept the Senate informed even of trivia. He went to the length of wanting to bring the well-timed assassination of Agrippa Postumus, one of the potential competitors for imperial succession, to account before the Senate. However, a partner in the imperial secrets hastened to persuade him that such whims were dangerous. His mother, Livia, was warned to watch that Tiberius "did not weaken the power of the throne by referring everything to the Senate: 'It was a condition of sovereignty that the account balanced only if rendered by a single auditor' " (*A.* 1.6).

Tiberius, like Nero, is depicted by Tacitus as a typical tyrant: lustful, suspicious, cruel, hypocritical, the picture of a stage or rhetorical despot. But there is a blatant contradiction between the Emperor's psychological portrait and his actions. Tacitus never provides proof that this evil man did wrong. Tiberius respected the Senate, diligently attended its sessions; he was cautious, prudent in his conduct of war, free from the vices of vanity and demagogy, and scornful of adulation. He refused honors, wisely intervened in economic crises, found a solution to food shortages, organized transportation, and watched over the administration, currency circulation, and usury. On occasion he used the very words of the historian in describing the causes of evils both deplored. "Why was frugality once the rule? Because every man controlled himself; because we were all citizens of a single city . . ." (*A.* 3.54). While attempting to check the flow of gold from Italy for foreign luxuries, the Prince refrained from imposing his austerity measures in a demagogic fashion. He pointed to the peninsula's endemic evil. "By Hercules, does nobody care that the life of the Roman nation has been staked upon cargoboats and accidents of the sea?" (*A*. 12.43). Tiberius was the first to react with disgust at the degrading spectacle of the flatterers. "These men," he was heard to mutter as he left the Senate, "how ready they are for slavery!" (*A*. 3.65).

Tacitus's judgments are no doubt colored by a preconceived hatred. The Emperor Claudius is depicted as sleepy, grotesque, and cowardly, despite his strong dose of common sense, a few acts of generosity, and a sincerely egalitarian attitude toward the provincials. Nero is a violent man whose frenzies and passions knew no limits; he is pushed toward evil by his mother, by absolute power, and by an adulation that borders on idolatry. He is offered ovations, triumphal vestments, and even a statue in the Temple of Mars Ultor. The senators applaud him after he has poisoned his mother, and prepare triumphal festivities to celebrate his evil deed. Every crime he committed—from the murder of Britannicus to that of Octavia—is received with solemn thanksgiving.

Are the kings—according to a Republican prejudice—marked by a congenital baseness inescapably linked to the psychic deformation by power? Or were they pushed by others into arrogance and vice? Tacitus admits that, even in eras of moral decline, noble examples of dedication and sacrifice could still be found (*H*. 1.3). But he focused almost exclusively on examples of cowardice. Of the year 69, when Galba, Otho, and Vitellius contended for the throne, he writes: ". . . those who had opposed Galba approved with greater fervor; the indifferent—and they were the majority—with ready servility, for they had their private interests in mind and cared nothing for the state" (*H*. 1.19).

When Otho stepped forward to propose his own candidacy, he received little support. A few bodyguards acclaimed him, others waited "in silence, ready to take their cue from the results" (*H*. 1.27). The crowd thronged around the palace, and clamored for the conspirators' death "exactly as if they were calling for some show in the circus or the theater . . ." (*H*. 1.32). In the meanwhile, it was rumored that Otho had been killed. The undecided were quick to pronounce their support for Galba, though they were equally ready to betray him. They feigned anger that they had not personally executed his rival: "the more cowardly in time of danger, the bolder their words" (*H*. 1.35). Bloody incidents exploded, and nobody could arrest the violence. The soldiers, without regard for military custom or rank, seized weapons at random and started killing indiscriminately out of savage pleasure; "The chief incentive of the rascals was the grief of loyal men" (*H*. 1.38).

An all-pervasive confusion of values paralleled this chaotic violence. After Galba and Piso had been killed, their bodies were mutilated by men who had no reason to hate them. Their severed heads were hidden so that they could later be sold to the dead men's families. These and worse atrocities were committed during the struggles between Otho and Vitellius, and afterward between Vitellius and Vespasian. Cremona was burned to the ground, its citizens massacred, the young women and youths raped, and the old people dragged through the streets in mockery (*H*. 3.33). This is the harsh reality of history and of human propensities. The only light in this dark picture emanated from those few who knew how to die; thus, death had become the sole way of proving one's *virtus*. Vain, corrupt, frivolous, a man such as Otho fell back on the dignity of tradition when he ended his life by suicide (*H*. 2.49).

Tacitus dispassionately described the horrors committed by Vitellius's Germanic troops and by Vespasian's Oriental forces. From the two far ends of the Empire, killing, plundering, devastating, they converged on Rome. Answerable for all this violence was everyone—nobles and plebeians, rich and poor alike. Surveying the scene for men capable of rising above this wretched quagmire and redeeming Rome's true spirit, Tacitus found them among those who had withdrawn not only from government, from public life, from the promiscuous City, which swarmed with pimps and profiteers, but also from life, since it had become unbearable for them.

The Stoics were the doctrinary opponents. Though Tacitus dutifully recorded their memorable remarks and their heroic deaths, he reveals no sense of solidarity. He may have lacked the courage to denigrate them openly. Ever since the days of Octavian, after Caesar's death, a hagiographic literature had grown around the figures of Cato the Younger, Brutus, and Cassius, an idealization so solidly established that not even the court authors dared oppose it. Vergil contrasts Cato with Catiline—that is, respect for the constitution with conspiracy. Horace alluded to Cato's "noble death," and Velleius Paterculus mentions it with respect.[50] And yet we can deduce from some of Cicero's comments during Cato's lifetime to what extent the Stoics' narcissism and their ideal values shot through with utopian abstractness, clashed with the Romans' realistic view of life. "Cato does not always serve the Republic. He speaks in maxims as though he were living in Plato's Republic, not among Romulus's dregs." The Stoics' exemplary austerity appeared inhuman. "They are incapable of pity," observed the orator, "insensitive to entreaties and implacable . . . they have the key of all knowledge, they know no regrets, they never make a mistake, they never change their mind. . . ."[51] The men who slashed their wrists under Tiberius, Nero, and Domitian considered themselves Brutus's spiritual heirs, and the custodians of his message. This was enough to constitute a crime.

In the oppressive climate of denunciations and cruelty, an ideological current developed throughout the first century that drew inspiration from those illustrious names. As the senatorial tradition withered away, this trend changed from political to increasingly doctrinary overtones. Those exemplary heroes of the past became part of the national conscience. Seneca presented Cato as "the only man who rose up against the vices of a corrupt society, of a state that was sinking under its own weight. . . . Cato did not outlive liberty, and liberty did not outlive him."[52] Lucan made him the enemy of tyranny. Oratorical controversies centered on his name, and in accordance with a typically Roman custom, this debate was transferred from the realm of ethics to that of individual conduct. Was it fitting, it was asked, for intellectuals to take part in politics? "What are you looking for, Cato? Liberty is no longer the issue, because it has long since fallen into disuse. What matters is knowing whether Caesar or Pompey will be our master. What does their struggle matter to you?"[53]

The opposition was nurtured on the cult of such memories. Cremutius Cordus defended himself in vain before the Senate against the charge that he had praised Brutus and Cassius (*A.* 4.34). Despite his eloquent defense, he was condemned to death. In some Roman houses, libations were poured to commemorate the tyrannicides' birthdays.[54] The position, or, better still, the attitude, of the opponents was centered on a moral credo and the cult of tradition. It fed on a self-satisfaction that bordered on narcissism, and on the rancor typical of frustrated ambitions. In themselves these men did not constitute a threat to the Emperor but they were dangerous insofar as they aroused admiration and agreement, which, given the prominence of their families, they were all the more able to do. "The journal of the Roman people," charged the prosecution at the trial against Thrasea Paetus in the High Court, "is scanned throughout the provinces and the armies with double care for news of what Thrasea has not done." The prosecutor then proceeded to draw a contrast between Thrasea and Nero, reminiscent of the one between Cato and Caesar; he even openly defined the accused as "a rival of Brutus" (*A.* 16.22).

Cato's followers, the so-called descendants of liberty, did not aim at the restoration of the Republic. The Stoic philosophy not only admitted, but even hoped for a wise king. It did not propose innovative reforms, stricter conduct in the administration, greater controls on public spending, and, even less, guarantees for the lower classes. The Stoics represented Rome's conscience; they scrutinized both the Emperor and the Senate with the angry eyes of the long-lost Republicans. Abstention was their only form of action, and therefore the accusations against them met with the approval of many of their contemporaries, who nevertheless did not want to see them condemned. Thrasea had not set foot in the Senate for more than three years; he had refused to attend the ceremonies, to participate in the sacrifices for the Emperor's and the people's health, to take part in the City's civil and religious life: "For once let him actually fulfill his responsibilities as a senator . . . let him openly state what he would like to modify and to amend . . ." (*A.* 16.28).

The senators had become indolent, and as Nero had said without mentioning specific names, "they prefer to take care of their gardens . . ." (*A.* 16.27). This might appear an innocuous, almost joking remark, had it not been pronounced in a time when the Senate was completely surrounded by Praetorian Guards with unsheathed swords. "Let him show up in the Senate," repeated Eprius Marcellus, Thrasea's accuser; "it would have been easier for them [the senators] to hear his criticism than his silence, which is tantamount to total condemnation. . . ."

A cultured mind, a bent for meditation, do not in themselves constitute an impediment to public life. Like anyone else, a philosopher is a member of society, and, as such, cannot shun his civic duties. The Romans rejected pure thought unless translated into action; according to Pliny, action is "part of philosophy; actually, its most noble aspect is service to one's country." Quintilian stated that "the wise man I admire does not isolate himself in order to devote his life to theoretical dissertations, but demonstrates, on the basis of evidence, that he is part of society." In the *De Republica*, Cicero expounded this same principle in an imaginary dialogue held in Scipio's garden: "*Virtus* approaches the divine and secures an eternal place in heaven only when it is placed at the service of the fatherland."[55]

Devotion to theory, the disdainful smile, the scornful reserve of those aristocrats of the spirit were matched by their search for a theatrical death and for "famous last words," to be piously repeated by posterity. At the same time, the Stoics gave proof of a disconcerting passivity: "Even had I been narrating campaigns abroad and lives laid down for the Commonwealth, I should have lost appetite for the task. . . . The slavelike patience and the profusion of blood wasted at home weary the mind and oppress it with melancholy. The one concession I would ask from those who shall study these records is that they should permit me not to hate the men who died with so little spirit" (*A.* 16.16).

According to the Republican tradition, suicide was an act of dignity. Except for an occasional criticism that it was an act of desertion, suicide was generally viewed as an act of courage, exalted ever since Cato's example. Seneca proposed it as a liberation from the evil of life: "In slavery of any kind the door to liberty is always open: the bottom of a river, a well, or the sea." There is always an escape route; it can be found in a precipice, in a noose attached to a tree, in one's heart or throat, so easily pierced. "Do you wonder where to find liberty? In any vein in your body . . ."[56]

It was precisely in his veins that Seneca found his own liberation. He was at dinner with friends when he received Nero's order to take his life. He asked for tablets on which to record his will, but was refused. He apologized to his friends for his inability to reward their services, but he added that "he left them his sole but fairest possession—the image of his life." As the blood flowed from his veins, he called his secretaries and dictated his final thoughts. Unfortunately for posterity, Tacitus did not record his words, since they were known to his contemporaries in Seneca's own dictation (*A*. 15.62). The scene pictures the exemplary imperturbability but equally the typical self-satisfaction of Seneca and his friends. As he wrote to Lucilius, "I work for posterity, I write what can be of use to them. . . . I show others the right path. . . ." Though this was a strictly private activity, he considered it more useful than politics or rhetoric because "there are men who seemingly do nothing, but who, actually, perform more noble actions—they study things, both divine and human. . . ."[57]

Thrasea received notice of his death sentence at sunset, while he was with friends in his garden. He went on to discuss the immortality of the soul, just as Socrates had done in the past, and Julian Apostata would do in the future. This, too, formed part of the pagan hagiographic code. His last words are missing, since Tacitus's page is interrupted: "Turning his [that is, Thrasea's] glance toward Demetrius . . ."

A few lines above, however, Tacitus wrote that after Thrasea had cut his wrists, he let his blood sprinkle the earth, saying, "We are making a libation to Jupiter the Liberator. Look, young man! and may heaven, indeed, avert the omen, but you have been born into times when it is expedient to steel the mind with examples of fortitude . . ." (*A*. 16.35).

Taking inspiration from Socrates, Cato, and Brutus, the Stoics realized that their own examples would be venerated. Their conduct was a conscious effort to emulate Rome's ancient heroes. Thrasea walked out of the Senate because he refused to join his colleagues in the praise of Nero's matricide. For three long years, the proud Stoic did not set foot inside the Senate. As Tacitus pointed out, his conduct "created a threat for himself, but implanted no germ of independence in his colleagues . . ." (*A*. 14.12). Thrasea was denounced for neglect of obligations implicit in his title. He consulted with his friends whether or not he should defend himself before the Senate. Those who urged him to do so hoped that he would act his part in public until the end. "Let the nation see a man who could face his death; let the Senate listen to words inspired, it might be thought, by some deity, superior to human utterance. Even Nero might be moved by the sheer miracle . . ." (*A*. 16.25).

Thrasea chose to remain silent. His case was deferred to the High Court, and he was sentenced by default. He was charged with rejection of his senatorial duties, contempt for the gods and the Emperor, disregard for the laws and religion. His condemnation was based on his refusal to participate in the sacrifices for the Emperor's welfare, and to swear the customary oath invoking Jupiter, the penates (the old Latin guardian deities of the household and state stores), and the Emperor's genius. His was a case of spiritual desertion. As it would appear in Tertullian's *Apologeticum*, the same charges were later made against the Christians. The Romans' dislike of those stern, melancholy men brings to mind how bitterly Rutilius Namantianus* hated the monks. Thrasea was sentenced in A.D. 66. That same year, two obscure Jewish immigrants were executed—Peter was crucified, and Paul decapitated. Their condemnation was probably based on the very same charges as those preferred against Thrasea.

Though Tacitus admired those lay martyrs, he did not feel inspired to imitate them. Like his father-in-law, Agricola, the historian served under various emperors, but he never aligned

* The last Roman poet (fifth century A.D.) and a fervent pagan. He held official posts in Christian Rome and was bitterly opposed to Judaism and monasticism.

himself with the opposition of the aristocrats, all of whom were related by family ties. He did not share their assurance, nor did he join their method of opposition, which was proud to the point of being provocative, idealistic to the point of being abstract. Tacitus preferred men who worked for the good of the state. He lacked the opposition's haughty self-confidence, and he wondered whether "somewhere between scornful courage and repellent servility, there was a straight road clear of intrigues and of perils" (*A*. 4.20).

Tacitus knew that hope for a realization of his own ideals was unrealistic. "Do you think that Nero was the last tyrant? Those who survived Tiberius and Caligula thought the same. . . . The best day [for action] after a tyrant's death is the first" (*H*. 4.42). The historian applied to the citizens the same principles that Petilius Cerialis had expounded to the rebels: the acceptance of the lesser evil in the name of peace and the state, because they were more important than one's personal needs. "Let those men who are wont to praise illicit acts remember that there may be great men even under wicked rulers; that when submission and discretion are accompanied by a rigorous fulfillment of one's duties, man can achieve the same glory that others have attained through a flamboyant death, which is of no service to the state" (*Agr*. 42.4).

Perhaps this spirit of moderation, coupled with veiled disapproval of those members of the opposition incapable of providing constructive programs, was the result of Tacitus's prudence. Yet, in his preference for the hidden, humble virtues which served society, he was more Roman than the conservatives who claimed to be the guardians of traditional virtue, and also more forward-looking. The future would not need impassive men setting themselves apart in self-complacency, but, rather, men capable of self-doubt, painful self-interrogation, and humble self-sacrifice.

Tacitus slowly shifted his focus from the rebellious provinces and the Rhine, where the German barbarians were consolidating themselves, to Rome, the Senate, and the Caesars. Having recorded military actions, harangues, conspiracies, and national uprisings, he now approached the powerful, observed them at close range, and saw how they lived and died.

The theme of death pervades Tacitus's entire work. In the final moments of his characters and in their last words, he demonstrates his true talent—that of a great tragedian. The dramatic moments of his narration are of unforgettable impact: Agrippina's words to her handmaiden as she fled on hearing the approaching steps of the hired assassins: "Even you are deserting me?" (*A.* 14.8); the wretched end of Messalina, who wept "crouched at the feet of her mother, who was advising her not to await the slayer: 'Life was over and done; all that could be attempted was decency in death . . .' "; however, "the tribune stood over her in silence, while the freedman upbraided her with a stream of slavish insults" (*A.* 11.37); Britannicus seized by paralysis after having been poisoned at the table in sight of everybody, under the terrorized stare of Agrippina and Octavia (*A.* 13.16).

The scenes of mourning are just as pathetic and memorable; the lament that welcomed Germanicus's widow when she disembarked carrying the urn with his ashes in her arms. The resoluteness of Tiberius, who, after the death of his son, entrusted his grandchildren to the dismayed Senate; he did not burst into tears, but from time to time, only a "repressed groan" escaped from his breast (*A.* 4.8). Or the legionaries' pilgrimage to the site of the massacre at Teutoburg: "Survivors of the disaster told how here the legates fell, there the eagles were taken; where Varus received the first wound, and where he found death by his own luckless hand. They spoke of the tribunal from which Arminius had made his harangue . . . and the arrogance with which he insulted the standards and eagles. And so, six years after the defeat, a Roman army returned to the ground and buried the bones of the three legions; and no man knew whether he consigned to earth the remains of a stranger or a kinsman, but all thought of all as friends and members of one family, and, with anger rising against the enemy, mourned and hated at the same time" (*A.* 1.51–52).

These are solemn, noble passages, worthy of being anthologized; they reveal, among many of Tacitus's human qualities, the compassion and affection which elsewhere he so carefully tried to hide. Nowhere does he betray himself so fully as in the final words of Agricola, that simple, honest man on whom he must have looked as a second father. Agricola was dying, perhaps from poison, without a word of recrimination. Using the customary formula of funeral eulogies, Tacitus calls him fortunate, since by his death he escaped impending evil and was spared witnessing the excesses of tyranny. Aside from their grief, Tacitus as son-in-law and Agricola's daughter deeply regretted that they had not been able to minister to his last needs, to receive his last instructions. At the moment of his death, they were away from Rome. Still, they were tormented by the thought that "in the last light that your eyes beheld something was wanting . . ." (*Agr.* 45.5).

Tacitus was acutely sensitive to the problems of his times: defense, the provinces, the opposition, the principate. He noticed, in particular, the dangers that threatened the Empire in its full glory, as well as the insidious disintegration that was destroying men's souls. He observed the rampant decadence with lucidity, and felt chill fear in the face of the external and internal forces that patiently awaited the right moment to pounce on Rome. From his pages emanate a deep uneasiness and a tragic sense of history and life.

Decadence began with the Empire's rise: "The old greed for power . . . came to full growth and broke bounds as the

Empire became great" (*H*. 2.38). The struggles that bloodied the Empire before Augustus's and Vespasian's accession stemmed more from a race for power than from an ideological conflict. To expect, "in that most corrupt age," conciliation for the good of the fatherland was not to be hoped for (*H*. 2.37). The end of all moral principles was such a vast, overwhelming phenomenon that it transcended the historical dimension; more than an object of contingent research, it called for an investigation of human nature. As such it appears in Tacitus, rather than a study of decadence stemming from historical and economic factors.

Looking to the past and remembering the days before the civil wars was much the same as contemplating a burned-out planet, buried under its own ashes. Tacitus was not part of that past, which had been abolished forever. Rather, he belonged to a future still in formation, but to which he could not find the key. He is a stranger at the gates of spiritual mansions that remain closed to him.

He was fated to live in a period when all the values that give a sense of direction to life prove fallacious, while those of the future are not yet clearly delineated. He suffered from the lack of positive stimuli and was unable to restore that coherence between moral precepts and society which was perhaps the only feature of the past that he really missed. Though both senator and consul, he did not in any vital way participate in the society of his time. He refused to support the Empire, as Pliny did, or to oppose it after the fashion of Thrasea Paetus. As a consequence, his works are neither chronicles nor critical recordings of events; they are living matter in flux, following multiple currents, in which one must seek a coherent thread that often disappears underground, surfacing at some farther point. The thread and real purport of his work is the gradual growth of his awareness of human reality. It is a process of developing inner knowledge.

Every problem is viewed from within. Tacitus seeks a freedom of the spirit transcending that of the subject or citizen. Even with regard to God, Tacitus's posture is that of a man observing power—supreme power—and pondering the position he should assume, questioning whether man is only a passive object, whether it is possible for him to discover a norm in events which would make them acceptable to him, whether man's will and intelligence had any weight in the face of an "omnipotent Fortune and an inevitable Fate."[58]

In recording Tiberius's consultation of astrologers, Tacitus comments in a brief digression: "For myself, when I listen to this . . . my judgment wavers. Is the revolution in human things governed by fate and changeless necessity, or by accident? . . . Many hold to the firm belief that heaven does not concern itself . . . with mankind; others think that there is certainly a fate in harmony with events. . . . With most men, however, the faith is ineradicable that the future of an individual is preordained at birth" (*A.* 6.22).

In this passage, Tacitus examined the prevalent beliefs of his day—the Epicureans' complete negation of heavenly guidance, the Stoics' faith in superior causes, the astrologers' fatalism—but he did not take sides himself. "I am compelled to doubt," he wrote elsewhere, "whether . . . the sympathies or antipathies of princes are governed . . . by fate and the star of nativity, or whether our purposes count . . ." (*A.* 4.20). Perhaps this perplexity hid an embarrassment at his choice of a career, which cast a shadow of perennial uneasiness over his life. Though he worked his way through the hierarchy of honors under the various emperors, one discerns accents of keen remorse as he recognizes his personal responsibility in the death sentences of his day: As a senator, as a Roman, or simply as every man is responsible any time the authorities condemn a free man? "We dragged Helvidius to prison with our own hands . . ." (*Agr.* 45.1).

But Tacitus did not realize that the imprisonments and the slashed arteries were the irreversible results of a drive for dominion that had been the sole imperative and had crushed all other aspirations in the Roman world. The ultimate goal of every action and every thought was dominion; in its cause the dignity of individuals and the autonomy of nations had been trampled underfoot; *concordia* (harmony), *virtus* (virtue), and *libertas* (freedom) were dissolved in its name; oratory withered away, and Rome's spirit was extinguished. The logic of power demanded that the Empire's opponents be suppressed. The myth of Rome as the head of the world (*caput mundi*) left individuals and nations no choice but to submit to its inevitability or succumb to destruction.

A man of high culture and elevated social position could not help being conditioned by the bigoted deference that every Roman of his class felt for Rome. This veneration was the only sacred reality. Denying it meant aligning oneself with the enemy, joining in the chorus of ironic denigration of the Greeks and the curses of the seers. Tacitus still believed that Rome's greatness was providentially ordained. Like Vergil, he thought that the extermination of the Germans and the subjugation of the Batavians, Britons, and Jews was due, just and desirable, though cruel: "thus Jupiter's fierce will commands. . . ."[59]

Jupiter also commanded men to kill. The high price the Romans had to pay for their universal dominion was a rigid standard of behavior. Lately they had failed to live up to their divine obligations. Tacitus did not believe that the gods intervened in individual cases, but their justice would be visited on nations. The prodigies after Agrippina's death were not a sign of divine wrath because "Nero continued for years his dominion and his crimes" (*A*. 14.12). A friend of Soranus, one of the Stoics who were condemned to death, remained faithful to him. This generous gesture was requited by the confiscation of his property and exile, and was "proof of Heaven's impartiality toward good and evil" (*A*. 16.33).

And yet Tacitus feared the "wrath of the gods against the

state" (*A.* 4.1). He echoed and condensed some verses by
Lucan:[60] "Never was it more fully proved by awful disasters
of the Roman people or by indubitable signs that the gods
care not for our safety, but for our punishment" (*H.* 1.3).
The word *ultio* meant punishment as well as vengeance. This
double meaning gives the term a specific weight of gloom. It
evokes all the blood that had been uselessly spilled; it calls
forth all the dead who from Hades clamored for justice. It
was a word with stern, religious connotations. A contemporary Jewish prophet in Patmos had the martyrs cry to
heaven: "How long, O Lord, holy and true, dost Thou not
judge and avenge our blood on them that dwell on earth!"[61]

Tacitus is the historian of a failure: the Republican institutions had been proven inadequate for the administration and
the defense of the state. The men still formally representing
those institutions were the senators, whose only concern was a
lucrative office. For this, they were willing to pay the required price: obsequiousness, connivance, informing. The in-
dustrial and commercial initiative of the municipal bourgeoisie
had undermined the economy of the large estates. Only one
set of values prevailed—expediency and money. The opponents, in their haughty withdrawal, proposed suicide as the
only viable alternative to servile assent. The army revealed its
brutal, rapacious nature. The provinces, subjected to economic exploitation, political and cultural tyranny, and the corrupting influence of the proconsuls, had to choose between
submission or bloody, futile revolt. The princeps, elected
as necessity arose to support that flimsy structure, had
been pushed by power to the excesses of abject cruelty and
turpitude. Lastly, the plebeians—a promiscuous, fickle, super-
stitious multitude rather than a specific sociological class—did
not call for serious reforms; they were satisfied with the allot-
ment of parasitic offices, doles, and crude spectacles, which
often degenerated into atrocious exhibitions of torture. In

Tacitus's pages, the plebeians appear as an unstable, troubled presence, lacking cohesion and civic conscience. The protest that occasionally arose from those humiliated ranks against the ruling classes, the Empire, and its agents had not yet become articulate, overwhelmed as it was by the élitist intellectualism of cultured tradition.

Beneath the surface, however, ran currents of moral outrage, of intellectual and spiritual unrest. Only in this underground could offended spirits such as Tacitus and Juvenal have found an echo of their bitterness, a condemnation of the prevailing system as fervent as their own. But even if Tacitus had an intimation of the messianic ferment within the lower classes, he could not have approached them without losing caste. Songs of typically Oriental oracular inspiration, exalting hope and suffering, circulated among the people. The early Christian nuclei were concentrated in the Jewish ghettos, and as such, were influenced by their mentality and fiery, ecstatic language. Had Tacitus wanted to identify himself with those rebel outcasts, he would have been forced to deny his cultural and ethical tradition, renounce the creed most deeply rooted in his Roman consciousness: the power and duration of Rome.

The idea of Rome still dominated the national consciousness. In Tacitus's day, it had received new luster and confirmation from the Greeks. The physical and spiritual survival of the class to which Tacitus belonged was bound up with that idea which represented Tacitus's only political credo and his sole religion.

The balance Tacitus drew is a negative one, stated in grave yet understressed form shot through with ambiguities and inconsistencies, since it camouflaged the desolate impotency of a man who knew of no other dimensions and neither wished for them nor anticipated them. No intimation of spiraling metaphysical thought or of a different social order touched his mind; his eyes were never lifted above the spectacle of wickedness—wickedness forever unpunished, suffering unredeemed, bloodshed unavenged. The end was inevitable and perhaps near at hand.

Nothing brightened Tacitus's somber clear-sightedness. For that very reason, of all the great writers, he is closest to our time; he, also, no longer knew the meaning of hope.

NOTES

INTRODUCTION

1. *Si immortalem hanc civitatem esse vultis, si aeternum hoc imperium, si gloriam sempiternam manere, nobis a nostris cupiditatibus est cavendum.*
2. *Moribus antiquis res stat Romana virisque.*
3. Vergil *Aeneid* 8.315: a race of men born from trunks and from tough oaks.
4. Vergil *Georgics* 2.532–534: *Hanc olim vitam coluere Sabini / Hanc Remus et frater, sic fortis Etruria crevit / Scilicet et rerum facta est pulcherrima Roma.* (The Sabines once led this kind of life, as also Remus and his brother; in this fashion, indeed, did Etruria grow strong, and Rome become most beautiful in material objects.)
5. Livy 4.30: laws which prohibited these new cults were issued in 428 B.C.; 5.22: Camillus had the Juno of Veii transferred from Etruria to Rome and had a temple on the Aventine Hill dedicated to her in 396 B.C.; 29.11 and Ovid *Fasti* 4.305–407: In Rome they welcomed the Great Mother Cybele, the Trojan goddess (205 B.C.).
6. Livy 1.16.
7. For the prophecy referred to by Fabius Pictor, see Jacoby, frgm. G. H., Leyden, 1958, p. 864; Arnobius *Adversus Gentes* 6.7. The mission sent to Delphi brought back a Greek poem which was interpreted as follows: *"Lasciviam a vobis prohibetote"* ("Keep lust far away from yourselves") (Livy 22.11, 216 B.C.).
8. Livy 1.4.
9. For the theory of cycles see Polybius 6.9; Cicero *De Republica*

1.29.45; Seneca *Quaestiones Naturales* 3.29; Sallust *Bellum Catilinae* 2.1–4; Dion Chrysostomus *Oratio* 36.42.

10. Vergil *Eclogue* 4.7: *Nova progenies caelo demittitur alto.* See *Oracula Sibyllina* 3.608–617.

11. This naturalistic theory, previously presented in Plato's *Republic*, was followed by the Stoics and, generally, by classical historiography. See the authors listed in note 9 and Lucretius *De Rerum Natura* 2.1150–1152. Also see Vergil *Georgics* 1.198; Velleius Paterculus 2.11; Philo Judaeus *De Aeternitate Mundi* 6.27.

12. Livy 31.21.

13. Plutarch *De Pythiae Oraculis* 2.390 *c.*

14. Livy 31.1.

15. Livy 31.34.

16. Livy 33.7 and 36.17.

17. Livy 33.33, 197 B.C.

18. Daniel 2:31–45; 7:1–14. The final kingdom, the only lasting one, is Rome, for Dionysius of Halicarnassus, 1.2; for Appianus, *Preface* 9; for Velleius Paterculus, 1.6.

19. Suetonius *Nero* 57; Tacitus *Historiae* 1.2 and 2.8; *Oracula Sibyllina* 4.148.

20. Livy 1.7–8; Ovid *Fasti* 4.817; Plutarch *Numa Pompilius* 13.

21. Cicero, *Academica Priora* 2.37.119: *Fore aliquando ut omnis hic mundus ardore deflagret* (It will happen at some future time that all this world will burn with fire); *De Republica* 4.22: *Cum autem ad idem, unde semel profecta sunt, cuncta astra redierint . . . tum ille vertens annus appelari potest, in quo vi dicere audeo quam multa hominum saecula teneantur* (But when all the stars go back to the same spot whence they once came . . . then that year may be termed full in which I firmly dare to state how many human centuries may be contained); Ovid, *Metamorphoses* 15.183–185: *Tempora sic fugiunt pariter pariterque sequuntur / Et nova sunt semper; nam quod fuit ante, relictum est / Fitque quod haut fuerat, momentaque cuncta novantur* (The times thus elapse alike, and alike follow each other / And yet they are always new; for what previously existed is left behind / and what had not existed is now coming into being, and all moments are renewed); *ibid.*, 234–236: *Tempus edax rerum, tuque, invidiosa vetustas. / Omnia destruitis*

vitiataque dentibus aevi / Paulatim lenta consumitis omnia morte
(Time, swallower of things, and thou, envious old age, you destroy
everything, and what has been vitiated by the teeth of time you
consume, little by little, with a slow death).

22. Livy 7.3 (360 B.C.); C.I.L., n. 430, 4, for 263 B.C.; Valerius Maximus,
    3.4.5.

23. Cicero, see first quotation in note 21; Vergil *Eclogue* 4.4–6: *Ultima
    Cumaei venit jam carminis aetas / Magnus ab integro saeclorum
    nascitur ordo / Jam redit et virgo; redeunt Saturnia regna.* (Now
    the final age of the Cumaean song has come. The great order of
    centuries is born afresh; now returns the virgin; returns the reign
    of Saturn.)

24. Demosthenes *Oratio De Corona* 18.199; Saint Augustine, *Sermo De
    Urbe Excidio*, 6, 6; Possidius *Vita Augustini* 30.

25. Cicero *Philippicae Orationes* 11.24; Ovid *Fasti* 6.427: *Aeternam
    servate deam, servabitis Urbem!* (Keep the goddess safe forever,
    and you will save the City!).

26. Cicero *Catilinariae Orationes* 4.9.18: *ignem illum Vestae sempiter-
    num* (that everlasting fire of Vesta); Anneus Florus 1.2.3:
    Simulacrum caelestium siderum, custos imperii (Symbol of the
    heavenly stars, guardian of the empire).

27. Vergil *Aeneid* 9.448.

28. Cicero *De Legibus* 3.1.1: *difficillimam illam societatem gravitatis
    cum humanitate* (that society of seriousness, very difficult [to
    reconcile] with humanity).

29. Posidonius 2.112 (Jacoby, *loc. cit.*); Plutarch *Cato the Censor* 27.

30. Sallust *Bellum Catilinae* 10.1; *De Bello Jugurthino* 41; Velleius
    Paterculus 2.1; Livy *Epitome* 51.

31. Plato *Gorgias* 483d; Cicero *De Republica* 3.25.37; *De Officiis* 2.26;
    Tacitus *Historiae* 4.74; Saint Augustine, *De Civitate Dei*, 19, 21.

32. Polybius 30.25–29.

33. Livy 34.2.

34. Livy 32.26; 33.36.

35. Livy 31.19; 32.23.

36. Livy 31.7 (200 B.C.).

37. Plutarch *Tiberius Gracchus* 20; *Titus Quintius Flamininus* 21.

38. Plutarch *Tiberius Gracchus* 9.

39. Aemilius Paullus's speech at Perseus's surrender, Livy 45.8. Marcellus's tears, Livy 25.24. Scipio Aemilianus's tears when Carthage was in flames, Polybius 38.21; Appian *Punica* 132.
40. Valerius Maximus 4.1.10.
41. Herodotus 7.10.5.

SALLUST

1. *Ne, pueri, ne tanta animis adsuescite bella,*
   Neu patriae validas in viscera vertite vires.
2. Information on Sallust can be found in the following sources: Suetonius, *De Grammaticis et Rhetoribus;* Asconius Pedianus's comments on the oration *Pro Milone* by Cicero and in the pseudo-Acro's comments on Horace's *Satyra* 1.2. See also Dio Cassius 40.63 and 43.9. In the *Invective against Sallust,* attributed to Cicero, can be found mention of the wealth that Sallust accumulated in Africa (7.11) and in Aulus Gellius, 17.18, references to the adulterous relationship he was supposed to have had with Milo's wife, who was Sulla's daughter. Before 44 B.C., his literary production consisted of the two *Epistolae ad Caesarem senem* (the first supposedly written in 46 B.C. and the second in 50 B.C.), and an *Invective against Cicero,* but the authenticity of these documents is still under discussion. There are also remaining excerpts of orations and letters that were part of his *Historiae,* in which he planned to fill in the gap between the Jugurthine War (111–105 B.C.) and the Catilinian conspiracy (66–62 B.C.); in this way, he hoped to continue the volume by L. Sisenna, which went from 90 to 78 B.C. The only complete extant works by Sallust are his two monographs.
3. *Nulla est enim natio quam pertimescamus . . . domesticum bellum manet.*
4. Cicero *In toga candida, frgm., Orationum Latinarum,* ed. Müller, Leipzig, 1890.

5. . . . *alii intra moenia atque in sinu urbis sunt hostes.*
6. *Id est enim proprium et civitatis et urbis, ut sit libera et non sollicita suae rei cuiusque custodia.*
7. Suetonius *J. Caesar* 42; Dio Cassius 41.37.
8. Cicero *De Officiis* 2.22.78.
9. In the *Epistulae Ciceronis ad Atticum* 9.7. C.
10. Vergil *Aeneid* 6.835–836: *Tuque prior, tu parce, genus qui ducis Olympo, / Proiice tela manu, sanguis meus.*
11. *Sic est: acerba fata Romanos agunt / scelusque fraternae necis / ut inmerentis fluxit in terra Remi / sacer nepotibus cruor.*
12. Plutarch *Cato Minor* 3; Cicero *Catilinariae Orationes* 3.10.24.
13. The references to Sulla are numerous, both by his contemporaries and by later authors. See Cicero *Ad Atticum* 8.11.2 and 16.2; 9.10.6 and 7.3; 10.1; *De Officiis* 1.14.43, 109; 2.8.27 and 14.51; 3.22.87. One hundred years later, Lucan reconstructed the spirit of those days in his poem *De Bello Civili* (or *Pharsalia*), *passim*. See also Caesar *De Bello Civili* 1.14.
14. Aeschylus *Agamemnon* 520.
15. Plato *Republic* 8.545c-d.
16. Cicero *Epistulae ad Familiares* 5.15.3 and 4.13.2; Vergil *Georgics* 1.505–506: . . . *tot bella per orbem / Tam multae scelerum facies.* . . .
17. Cicero *Catilinariae* 1.13.32; *De Divinatione* 1.47.105; *De Haruspicum Responsis* 10.20 and 37.62.
18. See Zoroaster's myth in Dion Chrysostomus *Oratio* 36.39. In the second century, the oracle is cited by Justin (*Apologia* 20.44) and by Clemens Alexandrinus (*Stromata* 6.6.42); in the fourth century, by Lactantius (*Institutiones divinae* 7.15.19 and 18.2).
19. Vergil *Georgics* 1.466–468: *Ille etiam exstincto miseratus Caesare Romam / Quum caput obscura nitidum ferrugine texit / Impiaque aeternam timuerunt saecula noctem.* See Ovid *Metamorphoses* 15.782 ff.; Tibullus, 2.71 ff.; Suetonius *J. Caesar* 88.
20. *Oracula Sibyllina* 3.334–336.
21. Cicero *Philippicae* 1.2.5.
22. Horace *Epodon* 16.1–14.
23. *Audiet cives acuisse ferrum / quo graves Persae melius perirent.*
24. For Antony's campaigns, see Velleius Paterculus 1.82; Appianus *De Bello Civili* 5.7.75; Plutarch *Life of Antony* 34–36. For the

prophecies, see *Oracula Sibyllina* 8.190–342; Daniel 7:24; Isaiah 34:4; Cicero *Catilinariae* 3.8.18–20; 3.4.9 ff.

25. Cicero *Pro Flacco* 25.60; Appianus *Mithridatica* 10; Plutarch *Quaestiones Conviviales* 1.624.

26. Horace *Epodes* 7.9–10: *Sed ut secundum vota Parthorum sua / Urbs haec periret dextera?* Lucan *Pharsalia* 1.10–12: *Cumque superba foret Babylon spolianda trophaeis / Ausoniis umbraque erraret Crassus inulta, / Bella geri placuit nullos habitura triumphos?* See also 2.45–56 and 8.307–308.

27. *Con l'animo che vince ogni battaglia / se col suo grave corpo non s'accascia.*

28. Horace *Satyra* 2.2.77–79: . . . *corpus onustum / Externis vitiis animum quoque pergravat una / Atque adfigit humo divinae particulam aurae.*

29. *Concordia parvae res crescunt, discordia maxumae dilabuntur.*

30. Scipio's friendship for Jugurtha: Valerius Maximus 5.2.

31. Juvenal *Satyra* 8.272–275: *Et tamen, ut longe repetas longeque revolvas / Nomen, ab infami gente deducis asylum / Majorum primus, quisquis fuit ille, tuorum / Aut pastor fuit aut illud quod dicere nolo.* See Cicero *De Lege agraria* 2.1–2.1–5. *Catilinariae* 1.11.28.

32. *In tanta tamque corrupta civitate, Catilina* . .

33. Cicero *Ad Atticum* 8.11.2; 10.7.

34. Cicero *Pro Caelio* 6.13.

35. Cicero *Pro Murena* 24.49–51.

36. *Neque tamen exercitus populi Romani laetam aut incruentam victoriam adeptus erat.*

37. Cicero *Pro Caelio* 5.12.

38. J. Caesar *De Bello Civili* 1.7 and 22.

39. *Quisquis praesentem statum civitatis commutare non vult, et civis et vir bonus est.*

40. Cato *Origines*, fragments 163–164 (in Aulus Gellius, 6.3).

41. *Digest* 1.2.2.3.

42. *Ut civitas fundaretur legibus* (so that the commonwealth would be founded on laws).

43. Polybius 6.14; Cicero *De Republica* 2.31.54; *De Oratore* 2.48.199;

Livy 3.55–56; 2.8; 10.9. In 123 B.C., the *Lex Sempronia* had again confirmed that all death sentences must first be appealed to the people.

44. Cicero *Pro Sextio* 28.60; *Pro Murena* 38.83.
45. Appianus *De Bello Civili* 2.15.101.

LIVY

1. *Multa exempla majorum exolescentia . . . imitanda posteris tradidi.*
2. *Origini Romanae deos adfuisse et non defuturam virtutem.*
3. The so-called *Index rerum gestarum* (or the *Testamentum Ancyranum*) was found in a bilingual edition (Latin and Greek) at Ankara; fragments have been found in other cities. The text I used was edited by L. Malcovati for Paravia, Turin, 1962. For the description of Augustus's funeral, see Suetonius *Divus Augustus* 101 and Tiberius 23; Tacitus *Annales* 1.8 and 11; Dio Cassius 56. 32–34.
4. Valerius Maximus 4.1.10; Plutarch *Life of Numa* 16.
5. *Pacatumque reget patriis virtutibus orbem.*
6. C.I.L. 1².15: VIRTUTES GENERIS MIEIS / MORIBUS ACCUMULAVI / . . . / MAIORUM OPTENUI LAUDEM / UT SIBEI ME ESSE CREATUM / LAETEN-TUR. . . .
7. Vergil *Aeneid* 1.349: *Impius ante aras atque auri caecus amore;* 2.4: *Troianas ut opes et lamentabile regnum;* 2.503–504: *Quinquaginta illi thalami, spes tanta nepotum, / Barbarico postes auro spoliisque superbi / Procubuēre . . . / ;* 3.57–58: *Auri sacra fames.*
8. Vergil *Aeneid* 8.364–365: *Aude, hospes, contemnere opes et te quoque dignum / Finge Deo. . . .*
9. *Urbs in aeternum condita.*
10. Vergil *Aeneid* 1.278–279: *His ego nec metas rerum nec tempora pono / Imperium sine fine dedi. . . .*
11. Horace *Epistulae* 2.1.16–17: *Iurandasque tuum per numen ponimus aras / Nil oriturum alias, nil ortum tale fatentes.*
12. Tacitus *Annales* 4.44.

13. *Nostra autem respublica non unius esset ingenio sed multorum nec una hominum vita sed aliquot constituta saeculis et aetatibus.*
14. C.I.L. 5.2975.
15. Vergil *Aeneid* 6.682–683, 760–887; 8.626 ff. See Horace *Carmina* 1.12; Ovid *Fasti* 5.563–564.
16. Vergil *Aeneid* 12.435–436: *Disce, puer, virtutem ex me verumque laborem / Fortunam ex aliis.* . . .
17. Seneca *Epistula* 98.12.
18. Augustus *Index rerum gestarum* 26–27.
19. Cicero *De Republica* 6.16.16.
20. *Frangitur ipsa suis Roma superba bonis.*
21. Vergil *Georgics* 2.539–540: *Necdum etiam audierant inflari classica, necdum / Impositos duris crepitare incudibus enses.* See Lucretius *De rerum natura* 999–1000.
22. *Historia est proxima poëtis et quodam modo carmen solutum.*
23. Polybius 3.25; Dionysius of Halicarnassus 2.72; Cicero *De Officiis* 1.11.36; Plutarch *Numa Pompilius* 12.
24. Horace *Epistulae* 2.1.54: . . . *adeo sanctum est vetus omne poëma.*
25. Valerius Maximus 2.1.10.
26. Tacitus *Germania* 2.3; Cato, in Cicero *Brutus* 19.75; Cicero *Tusculanae Disputationes* 4.2.3. See Cato in Aulus Gellius *Noctes Atticae* 2.28.6. The opinion of Aulus Gellius is in *ibid.* 5.18.9.
27. Aristotle *Poetics* 14, 2, 1453b, 8.
28. *Ah, voilà les âmes qu'il fallait à la mienne!*
29. G. Leopardi, *Canzone all'Italia*, vv. 61–63: *O venturose e care e benedette / l'antiche età, che a morte / per la patria correan le genti a squadre.*
30. *Et facere et pati fortia Romanum est.*
31. Plutarch *Life of Pyrrhus* 20; Aulus Gellius 1.14.
32. Cicero *De Provinciis consularibus* 5.
33. *Malim unum Catonem quam trecentos Socrates.*
34. Plutarch *Cato the Censor* 12; Cicero *Epistulae ad Quintum Fratrem* 1.1.18.
35. *Libertas, dulce auditu nomen.*
36. For the temple on the Elbe, see Dio Cassius 55.10; at Narbonne, C.I.L. 12.4333; "the order of the priests of Augustus was instituted," Tacitus *Annales* 1.54.

37. Augustus *Index rerum gestarum*: the *Tribunicia potestas* for life, "by law" (10) *"nullum magistratum contra morem majorum delatum recepi"* (6). *"Dictaturam et apsenti et praesenti mihi delatam . . . non recepi. Consulatum quoque tum annuum et perpetuum mihi delatum non recepi . . ."* (5). *". Auctoritate omnibus praestiti, potestatis autem nihilo amplius habui quam ceteri qui mihi quoque in magistratu conlegae fuerunt"* (34).
38. *Sine lege nulla libertas.*
39. Cicero *Pro Cluentio* 146: *legum servi sumus ut liberi esse possimus.*
40. Cicero *Philippicae Orationes* 6.7.
41. Cicero *Paradoxa Stoicorum* 4.1.27.
42. Ovid *Fasti* 2.683–684: *Gentibus est aliis tellus data limite certo: / Romanae spatium est urbis et orbis idem.*
43. Suetonius *Divus Augustus* 31.
44. Plutarch *Life of Anthony* 24, 54, 56; Dio Cassius 48.39; Velleius Paterculus 2.82; *Oracula Sibyllina* 3.75–96; 8.190–212; 11.290 and 279.
45. Vergil *Eclogue* 4.18–22.
46. Saint Augustine, *Epistolae*, 138, 17; *De Civitate Dei*, 5, 13.

TACITUS

1. Tacitus was born about A.D. 55 of provincial, possibly Gallic origin. He pursued a regular political career under various emperors of the Flavian dynasty: Vespasian, Titus, Domitian (*H.* 1.1), and in his later years was honored with the *laticlavium* and the consulship. In A.D. 77, he married the daughter of the Consul Agricola. By that year, he was already a senator, under Domitian; in 97, he received the consulship under Nerva. A recently discovered marble inscription leads us to suppose that in A.D. 111 he may have been proconsul in Asia under Hadrian. Some of Pliny the Younger's letters prove that he was a good friend of Tacitus. We have no information about the date and place of his death.

The dating of Tacitus's works is still under discussion. Generally, the *Germania* and the *Agricola* are placed between A.D. 98 and 100, during the early years of Trajan's reign. Some scholars date the *Dialogus de Oratoribus*, which may or may not have been written by Tacitus, before 106, others in that year. The *Histories* are usually dated somewhere between 105 and 110, but only four books and part of the fifth have come down to us. The *Annals* begin with the advent of Tiberius (A.D. 14) and end in 66. We do not have the books from Part 7 or sections of Part 11, which described the decade 37 to 47—that is, the reign of Caligula and the first six years under Claudius. This work, however, belongs to the historian's maturity, and has been dated somewhere between 110 and 120, the years when Hadrian was ruling.

2. Lucan *Pharsalia* 1.670: *Cum domino pax ista venit.*

3. Caesar *De Bello Civili* 1.22.5: *vindicare libertatem a factione paucorum;* Augustus *Index Rerum Gestarum* 1: *rem publicam a dominatione factionis oppressam in libertatem vindicare.*

4. Seneca *De Beneficiis*, 2.20.2.

5. . . . *tuumque nomen, / Libertas, et inanem prosequar umbram.*

6. Seneca *Epistolae* 73.8; *De Providentia* 5.5–6.

7. Pliny *Panegyricus Traiano dictus* 55.9.

8. *Ibid.* 66.4.

9. Cicero *De Oratore* 2.9.36 and 15.62; *De Legibus* 1.2.

10. Sallust *B. C.*, 3.1.

11. C.I.L. 6.930; Suetonius *Vespasianus* 12; Dio Cassius 66.1.

12. Juvenal *Satyra* 1.170–171: . . . *Experiar quid concedatur in illis / Quorum Flaminia tegitur cinis atque Latina.*

13. Polybius 12.28, 1–5.

14. Pliny *Panegyricus Traiano dictus*, 1.3.

15. C.I.L. 13.1668.

16. Seneca *Epistolae* 114.1.

17. *Mes larmes aux vaincus et ma haîne aux vainqueurs.*

18. Horace *Odes* 3.5.3–4: *Augustus adiectis Britannis / imperio gravibusque Persis.* Propertius 2.27.5: *Seu pedibus Parthos sequimur seu classe Britannos.*

19. Plutarch *Julius Caesar* 23.

20. Martial 11.3.5: *Dicitur et nostros cantare Britannos versos.*

21. Caesar *De Bello Gallico* 21–22; Strabo 7.1–2.

22. Orosius *Adversus Paganos Libri Septem* 7.6.
23. Seneca *De Ira* 1.11.5; 2.15.2.
24. Seneca *De Providentia* 4.15.
25. Lucan *Pharsalia* 7.433–435: *Libertas ultra Rhenum Tigrimque recessit / Germanum Scythicumque bonum nec respicit ultra / Ausoniam.*
26. Juvenal *Satyra* 8.112–124: *Despicias tu / Forsitan imbellis Rhodios unctamque Corinthon / despicias merito . . . / Horrida vitanda est Hispania, Gallicus axis / Illyricumque latus; parce et messoribus illis / qui saturant Urbem circo scaenaeque vacantem. / . . . / Curandum in primis ne magna injuria fit / fortibus et miseris. Tollas licet omne quod usquam est / auri et argenti, acutum gladiumque relinquas / et jaculum et galeam: spoliatis arma supersunt.*
27. Lucan *Pharsalia* 7.540–543: *. . . vivant Galatae Syrique / Cappadoces Gallique extremique orbis Hiberi / Armeni, Cilicesque: nam post civilia bella / Hic populus Romanus erit. . . .*
28. Cicero *Verrinae Orationes* 2.3.89.207.
29. Pompeius Trogus-Justinus *Epitome*, 38.6.
30. Lucan *Pharsalia* 7.384–385: *Romanos odēre omnes dominosque gravantur / quod novēre magis. . . .*
31. Ovid *Tristia* 2.219; Tacitus *Dialogus* 17.3; Augustus *Epistolae* 22.10.
32. Pliny *Paneg. cit.* 23.4.
33. Livy 38.1–2; Aulus Gellius *Noctes Atticae* 6.1.6; Aurelius Victor *De viris illustribus* 3. For Sulla, see Plutarch *Sulla* 7, 12–43. For Marius, see Plutarch *Marius* 28.
34. Epictetus 2.10.3; 3.24.9.
35. Philostratus *Life of Apollonius of Tyana* 5.27–29. This imaginary debate recalls the one in Herodotus 3.80–83; Dion Cassius 52.19.
36. Dio of Prusa *De Monarchia* 1.12–21–23; 3.3.
37. Seneca *De Clementia* 1.13.4.
38. Pliny *Paneg. cit.* 2.4. (The panegyrist declares that he abstains from adulation, and that he would never compare the Emperor to a god; however, the qualities that he attributes to the Emperor are often superhuman.)
39. Lucan *Pharsalia* 7.444–445: *Ex populis qui regna ferunt sors ultima nostra est / quos servire pudet. . . .*

40. *Urgentibus imperii fatis.*
41. Juvenal *Satyra* 14.103–104: *non mostrare viam eadem nisi sacra colenti / quaesitum ad fontem solos deducere verpos.*
42. Josephus Flavius *The Judean War* 6.300.
43. Matthew 10:37; Luke 12:49–51.
44. *Posse etiam sub malis principibus magnos viros esse.*
45. *In omni servitute apertam libertati viam.*
46. This expression can be found in Aulus Gellius *Noctes Atticae* 7.18. 11. There were frequent suicides under Tiberius: Cocceius Nerva (*A.* 6.26), Sextus Papinius (*A.* 6.41), Arruntius (*A.* 6.47). For further references to the state of mind during those years when the world and morality seemed to be coming to an end, see Cicero *Ad Atticum* ep. 5.16, and Lucretius *De Rerum Natura* 3.79–81.
47. Lucan *Pharsalia* 7.405: *Romam . . . mundi faece replenam.*
48. Juvenal *Satyra* 11.109: *Argenti quod erat solis fulgebat in armis.*
49. Polybius 2.48.
50. Velleius Paterculus 2.35; Vergil *Aeneid* 8.670; Horace *Carmina* 1.12.35.
51. Cicero *Ad Atticum* ep. 2.1.8; *Pro Murena* 29.
52. Seneca *De Providentia* 2.9 and 3.4; *De Constantia sapientis* 2.2.3.
53. Seneca *Epistolae* 14.12.
54. Juvenal *Satyra* 5.36.
55. Pliny *Epistolae* 1, 10; Quintilian *Institutio Oratoria* 12.2.7.
56. Seneca *De Ira* 3.15.4.
57. Seneca *Epistolae* 8.
58. Seneca *De Providentia* 5.7; Vergil *Aeneid* 5.1.334: *Fortuna omnipotens et ineluctabile fatum.*
59. Vergil *Aeneid* 11.901: *Saeva Jovis sic numina poscunt.*
60. Lucan *Pharsalia* 4.807–809: *Felix Roma quidem civisque beatos / Si libertatis superis habitura tam cura placeret / Quam vindicta placet! . . .*
61. Apocalypse 6:10.

BIBLIOGRAPHY

ABBREVIATIONS

A.J.Ph.   *American Journal of Philology*
Ath.   *Athenaeum*
C.I.L.   *Corpus Inscriptionum Latinarum*
Cl.J.   *Classical Journal*
Cl.Ph.   *Classical Philology*
Cl.Q.   *Classical Quarterly*
Cl.W.   *Classical Weekly*
Har.St. in Cl.Ph.   *Harvard Studies in Classical Philology*
J.R.S.   *Journal of Roman Studies*
R.A.   *Revue Archéologique*
R.E.A.   *Revue des Etudes Anciennes*
R.E.L.   *Revue des Etudes Latines*
R.F.Cl.   *Rivista di Filologia Classica*
R.H.   *Revue Historique*
R.H.R.   *Revue de l'Histoire des Religions*
R.Ph.   *Revue de Philologie*
T.A.Ph.A.   *Transactions and Proceedings of the American Philological Association*
Vig.Chr.   *Vigiliae Christianae*
Y.Cl.St.   *Yale Classical Studies*

The following does not constitute a complete bibliography of the authors studied, but merely, among existing books, those from which I have derived information and ideas.

INTRODUCTION

A. E. Astin, *Scipio Aemilianus*, Oxford, 1967.

V. Basanoff, *Evocatio*, Paris, 1944.

J. Bidez et F. Cumont, *Les Mages Héllénisés*, Paris, 1930.

F. Boyanc, *La Religion de Virgile*, Paris, 1930.

R. M. Brown, *A Study of the Scipionic Circle*, Iowa City, Iowa, 1934.

W. Bruhl, "Le Souvenir d'Alexandre et les Romaines," in *Mélanges d'Arch. et d'Histoire*, 1930, pp. 202 ff.

J. Carcopino, *Virgile et le mystère de la IV Eclogue*, Paris, 1930.

F. Cumont, "La fin du monde selon les Mages occidentaux," in *R.H.R.*, 1931, p. 29.

J. Daniélou, "La Typologie millénariste de la semaine dans le christianisme primitif," in *Vig.Chr.*, 1940, pp. 1 ff.

M. Eliade, *Il mito dell'eterno ritorno*, Torino, 1968.

M. H. Fish, "Alexander and the Stoics," in *A.J.Ph.*, 1937, pp. 59 ff.

J. Gagé, "Hercules-Melquart, Alexandre et les Romains," in *R.E.A.*, 1940, pp. 425 ff.

L. Gernet et A. Boulanger, *Le Génie Grec dans la religion*, Paris, 1932.

A. Grenier, *La Religion Romaine*, Paris, 1948.

P. Grimal, *Le Cercle des Scipions*, Paris, 1955.

J. Heurgon, "La Datation de la prophétie de Vegoia," in *R.E.L.*, 1959, p. 40.

H. Hubeaux, *Les Grands Mythes de Rome*, Paris, 1945.

H. Jeanmaire, *Le Messianisme de Virgile*, Paris, 1930; *La Sibylle et le retour de l'âge d'or*, Paris, 1939.

C. Koch, "Roma aeterna," in *Gymnasium*, 1952, pp. 198 ff.

A. Lods, "Recherches sur le prophétisme israélite," in *R.H.R.*, 1931, pp. 270 ff.

R. MacMullen, *Enemies of the Roman Order*, Cambridge, Mass., 1967.

O. Nybakken, "Humanitas Romana," in *A.J.Ph.*, 1930, p. 396.

A. Peretti, *La Sibilla Babilonese*, Firenze, 1942.

J. Perret, "Pour une étude de l'idée de Rome," in *R.E.L.*, 1938, pp. 50 ff.; *Les Origines de la légende troyenne de Rome*, Paris, 1942 (many of this writer's ideas are considered erroneous by A. Momigliano, in *J.R.S.*, 1945, pp. 99 ff).

E. S. Ramage, "Early Roman Urbanity," in *A.J.Ph.*, 1960, pp. 65 ff.

S. E. Smeethurst, "The Growth of the Roman Legend," in *Phoenix*, 1949, pp. 1 ff.

H. Strasburger, "Poseidonius on Problems of the Roman Empire," in
J.R.S., 1965, pp. 40 ff.

J. Swain, "The Theory of the Four Kingdoms," in *Cl.Ph.*, 1940,
pp. 1 ff.

W. W. Tarn, *Alexander the Great and the Unity of Mankind*, London, 1933; *Alexander the Great*, Cambridge, 1948; "Alexander
Helios," in *J.R.S.*, 1932, pp. 135 ff.

K. von Fritz, *The Theory of the Mixed Constitution in Antiquity*,
New York, 1954.

H. Wagenvoort, *Studies in Roman Literature and Religion*, Leyden,
1956, p. 193: "The Origin of the Ludi Saeculares."

F. W. Walbanck, "Polybius and the Roman Constitution," in *Cl.Q.*,
1943, pp. 73 ff.; "Polybius and the Roman Eastern Politics," in
J.R.S., 1963, p. 1.

L. Zancan, "Dottrina delle costituzioni e decadenza politica in Polibio,"
in *Rendiconti dell'Istituto Lombardo*, 1938, pp. 499 ff.

SALLUST

A. Alföldi, "Der Neue Weltherrscher der IV Eklogue Vergils," in
Hermes, 1930, pp. 369 ff.

W. Allen, "Catullus and Sallust's B.C.," in *Cl.J.*, 1937, pp. 298 ff.; "The
Sources of Jugurtha's Influence in the Roman Senate," in *Cl.Ph.*,
1938, pp. 90 ff.; "In Defense of Catilina," in *Cl.J.*, 1938, pp. 70 ff.

E. Badian, *Roman Imperialism in the Late Republic*, Pretoria, 1967.

E. Bikerman, "La Lettre de Mithridate dans les Histoires de Salluste,"
in *R.E.L.*, 1946, pp. 150 ff.

E. Bolaffi, "I proemi delle monografie di Sallustio," in *Ath.*, 1938, pp.
128 ff.

T. R. S. Broughton, "Was Sallust Fair to Cicero?," in *A.J.Ph.*, 1936,
pp. 34 ff.

J. P. Chausseraie Laprée, "Les Structures chez les historiens Latins,"
in *R.E.L.*, 1963, pp. 281 ff.

M. Chouet, *Les Lettres de Salluste à César*, Paris, 1940.

G. De Sanctis, *Problemi di storia antica*, Bari, 1932, chap. VIII, pp.
187 ff.

D. C. Earl, *The Political Thought of Sallust*, Cambridge, 1961; *The Moral and Political Tradition of Rome*, London, 1967.

M. A. Ernout, *Pseudo-Sallust.*, Paris, 1962.

G. Ferrero, *Rerum Scriptor*, Trieste, 1962.

G. Funajoli, "La voce 'Sallustio,' " in *R. Encyclopedie Pauli Wissowa*, Stuttgart, 1920, p. 1913.

E. G. Hardy, *Roman Laws and Charters*, Oxford, 1912.

L. J. Hellegouach, *Le Vocabulaire Latin des relations et des partis politiques sous la République*, Paris, 1963.

P. Jal, "Concordia=Pax Civilis," in *R.E.L.*, 1961, pp. 210 ff.; *La Guerre civile à Rome*, Paris, 1963.

J. Jones, "Caesar, Crassus and Catilina," in *Cl.W.*, 1963, pp. 89 ff.

M. Laffranque, *Poseidonios d'Apamée*, Paris, 1964.

M. I. W. Laistner, *The Greater Roman Historians*, Berkeley, Calif., 1947.

I. Lana, "La libertà nel mondo antico," in *R.F.Cl.*, 1951, p. 1.

A. La Penna, *Sallustio e la rivoluzione romana*, Milano, 1968. (For the author's opinion concerning the authenticity of the *Epistolae*, see *Gnomon*, 1962, pp. 467 ff.).

H. Last, "On the Sallustian Suasoriae," in *Cl.Q.*, 1923, pp. 67 ff.

A. D. Leeman, "Le Genre et le style historique à Rome," in *R.E.L.*, 1955, p. 183.

M. A. Levi, *La lotta politica nel mondo antico*, Verona, 1963.

E. Manni, "L'utopia di Clodio," in *R.F.Cl.*, 1940, pp. 161 ff. (Concerning Clodius, see articles by Pocock, in *Cl. Q.*, 1924, pp. 9 ff. and Marsh, *ibid.*, 1927, pp. 30 ff.

S. Mazzarino, *Il pensiero storico classico*, Bari, 1966.

L. Mohler, "Sentina reipublicae," in *Cl.W.*, 1936, pp. 81 ff.

A. Momigliano, "Libertas as a Political Idea during the Late Republic and Early Principate," in *J.R.S.*, 1951, pp. 146 ff.

V. A. Oldfather, "Livy I.xxvi and the *Supplicium more majorum*," *T.A.Ph.A.*, 1949.

L. Olivieri Sangiacomo, *Sallustio*, Firenze, 1954.

V. Paladini, *Problemi Sallustiani*, Milano-Messina, 1948.

L. Pareti, *Storia di Roma*, Torino, 1953, vol. III, pp. 792 ff.

E. Pasoli, *Le "Historiae" e le opere minori di Sallustio*, Bologna, 1965.

P. Pecchiura, *La figura di Catone Uticense nella Letteratura Latina*, Torino, 1965.

P. Perrochat, *Les Modèles Grecs de Salluste*, Paris, 1949; "Les Digressions de Salluste," in *R.E.L.*, 1950, pp. 160 ff.

M. Rambaud, "Les Prologues de Salluste et la demonstration morale dans son oeuvre," in *R.E.L.*, 1946, pp. 115 ff.

L. Ross Taylor, *Party Politics in the Age of Caesar*, Berkeley, Calif., 1940.

A. Rostagni, *La letteratura di Roma*, Bologna, 1939, pp. 262 ff.

G. Schnayder, "De infenso alienigenarum animo," in *Eos*, XXX, 1927, pp. 113 ff.

R. Syme, *Roman Revolution*, Oxford, 1958; *Sallust*, Berkeley, Calif., 1964; "The Senator as Historian," *Entretiens de la Fondation Hardt*, T. IV, p. 187, Genève, 1956.

Tenney Franck, *An Economic Survey of Ancient Rome*, Baltimore, 1933, vol. I.

R. Ulmann, "Essai sur le Catilina de Salluste," *R.Ph.*, 1918, pp. 5 ff.

J. Vogt, *Homo novus*, Stuttgart, 1926.

W. H. Waddington, E. Babelon, Th. Reinach, *Recueil général des Monnaies Grecques d'Asie Mineure*, Paris, 1904–12.

H. Windisch, "Der Orakel von Hystaspes," in *Koninklijke Akademie*, Amsterdam, 1930.

Ch. Wirszbuzki, *Libertas*, Cambridge, 1950.

LIVY

S. Accame, "Il Senatus Consultum de Bacchanalibus," in *R.F.Cl.*, 1938, pp. 225 ff.

V. Arangio Ruiz, *Storia del diritto Romano*, Napoli, 1964.

J. Bayet, *La religione romana*, Torino, 1959.

E. J. Bikerman, "Origines gentium," in *Cl.Ph.*, 1952, pp. 65 ff.

R. Bloch, *Les Prodiges dans l'Antiquité*, Paris, 1963.

H. Bornecque, *Tite Live*, Paris, 1933.

F. Branchini, "Note su Fabius Pictor," in *Ath.*, 1961, pp. 358 ff.

J. P. Brisson, *Virgile, son temps et le nôtre*, Paris, 1966.

L. Bruno, "Libertas Plebis in Livy," in *Giorn. It. di Filol.*, 1966, pp. 107 ff.; " 'Crimen regni' e 'Superbia' in Tito Livio," *ibid.*, pp. 266 ff.

L. Catin, *En lisant Tite Live*, Paris, 1944.

L. Cerfaux - J. Tondriau, *Le Culte des souverains dans la civilisation Gréco-Romaine*, Louvain, 1956.

M. Charlesworth, "Some Fragments of the Propaganda of Anthony," in *Cl.Q.*, 1933, pp. 172 ff.

F. Christ, *Die Römische Weltherrschaft in der Antike Dichtung*, Berlin, 1938.

J. E. Crake, "The Annals of the Pontifex Maximus," in *Cl.Ph.*, 1940, pp. 375 ff.

F. M. Cramer, *Astrology in Roman Laws and Politics*, Philadelphia, 1954.

J. Declareuil, *Rome et l'organisation du droit*, Paris, 1924.

G. de Francisci, *Arcana Imperii*, Milano, 1948.

T. A. Dorey, *Latin Historians*, London, 1966.

E. Dutoit, "Le Thème de la force qui se détruit d'elle-même," in *R.E.L.*, 1936, pp. 365 ff.; "Quelques généralisations de portée psychologique et morale dans l'oeuvre de Tite Live," in *R.E.L.*, 1942, pp. 98 ff.; "Les Silences dans l'oeuvre de Tite Live," in *Mélanges Marouzeau*, Paris, 1948.

J. A. Foucault, "Tite Live traducteur de Polybe," in *R.E.L.*, 1968, pp. 218 ff.

P. Fraccaro, *Storia romana arcaica*, Milano, 1952.

A. Gagé, "Romulus-Augustus," in *Mélanges de l'École Française de Rome*, 1930, pp. 138 ff.

A. Garzetti, "Appio Claudio il Cieco," in *Ath.*, 1947, p. 175.

P. Grimal, *Le Siècle d'Auguste*, Paris, 1955; "A propos de la XVI Epode," in *Latomus*, 1961, pp. 721 ff.

L. Homo, *Auguste*, Paris, 1935; *Les Institutions politiques Romaines de la Cité à l'Etat*, Paris, 1950.

H. Jeanmaire, "La Politique religieuse d'Antoine et Cléopatre," in *R.A.*, 1924, pp. 241 ff.; *Le Messianisme de Virgile*, Paris, 1930; "Le Règne de la Femme des derniers jours et le rajeunissement du monde," in *Mélanges Cumont*, Bruxelles, 1936, IV, pp. 297 ff.; *La Sibylle et le retour de l'âge d'or*, Paris, 1939.

Kenneth Scott, "The Identification of Augustus with Romulus-Quirinus," in *T.A.Ph.A.*, 1925, pp. 82 ff.

A. Klotz, *Livius und seine Vorgänger*, Leipzig, 1942.

A. La Penna, *Orazio e l'ideologia del Principato*, Torino, 1963.

M. A. Last - R. M. Ogilvie, "Claudius and Livius," in *Latomus*, 1958, pp. 470 ff.

H. Levi-Bruhl, *Nouvelles Études sur le très ancien Droit Romain*, Paris, 1947.

M. A. Levi, "Tito Livio e gli ideali augustei," in *La parola del passato*, 1949, pp. 15 ff.; *Il tempo di Augusto*, Milano, 1951.

H. W. Lichtfield, *National Exempla Virtutis*, in *Har.St. in Cl.Ph.*, 1914, pp. 1 ff.

Q. H. McDonald, "The Livy Style," in *J.R.S.*, 1957, pp. 155 ff.

P. McGushin, "Vergil and the Spirit of Endurance," in *A.J.Ph.*, 1964, p. 225; "Aeneas Lasting City," in *Latomus*, 1965, p. 411.

N. Masckin, *Il principato di Augusto*, Roma, 1956, 2 vol.

Mason Hammond, "Hellenistic Influences on the Structure of the Augustean Principate," in *Memoirs of the Am. Academy in Rome*, 1940.

H. Mattingly, "Roman Virtues," in *Harvard Theological Review*, 1937, p. 103.

M. Mazza, *Storia e ideologia in Livio*, Firenze, 1966.

S. Mazzarino, *Il pensiero storico classico*, Bari, 1966.

A. Momigliano, "Livio, Plutarco e Giustino su Virtù e Fortuna dei Romani," in *Ath.*, 1934, pp. 45 ff.; "Perizonius, Niebuhr and the Character of Earlier Roman Tradition," in *J.R.S.*, 1957, pp. 102 ff.; "Linee per una valutazione di Fabius Pictor," in *Atti dell'Accademia dei Lincei*, VIII, xv, 1960, pp. 310 ff.

R. M. Ogilvie, "Livy, Licinius Macer and the Libri Lintei," in *J.R.S.*, 1958, pp. 45 ff.; *A Commentary on Livy's Books I-V*, Oxford, 1965.

E. Pianezzola, *Traduzione e ideologia, Livio interprete di Polibio*, Bologna, 1969.

A. Rostagni, *Da Livio a Virgilio*, Padova, 1942.

A. T. Rowell, "The Forum and the Funeral Imagines of A.," in *Memoirs of the Am. Academy in Rome*, 1940, pp. 131 ff.

E. M. Sanford, "Contrasting Views on the Roman Empire," in *A.J.Ph.*, 1937, pp. 437 ff.

J. Scott Ryberg, "Vergil's Golden Age," in *T.A.Ph.A.*, 1958, pp. 112 ff.

L. R. Taylor, *The Divinity of the Roman Emperor*, Middletown, Conn., 1931; "The Date of the Fasti Capitolini," in *Cl.Ph.*, 1946, pp. 1 ff.; "Indications of the Augustean Editing in the Capitoline Fasti," in *Cl.Ph.*, 1951, pp. 73 ff.

Tenney Frank, "Augustus, Vergil and the Augustan Elogia," in *A.J.Ph.*, 1938, pp. 91 ff.

F. Walbanck, "History and Tragedy," in *Historia*, 1960, pp. 216 ff. (from Aristotle, *Poetica* 14, 2, 1453 b. 8). (The author discusses the opinions expressed on this topic by K. von Fritz in *Entretiens de la Fondation Hardt*, Genève, 1958, pp. 85 ff.)

P. Walsh, "Livy and Stoïcism," in *A.J.Ph.*, 1958, pp. 355 ff.; *Livy, His Historical Aims and Methods*, Cambridge, 1961.

TACITUS

H. Bardon, "Dialogue des Orateurs et Institutiones Oratoriae," in *R.E.L.*, 1941, pp. 113 ff.

H. Benario, "Tacitus and the Principate," in *Cl.J.*, 1964–65, p. 97; "Tacitus and the Fall of the Roman Empire," in *Historia*, 1968, p. 37.

J. Beranger, "L'Hérédité du Principat," in *R.E.L.*, 1939, p. 171; *Recherches sur l'idéologie du Principat*, Basel, 1953.

K. L. Born, "The Perfect Prince According to the Latin Panegyrists," in *A.J.Ph.*, IV, 1934, p. 40.

A. R. Burn, *Agricola and Roman Britain*, London, 1953.

M. P. Charlesworth, *Five Men*, in Martin Classical Studies, 1936, chap. IV, pp. 73 ff.

J. Cousin, "Art et rhétorique dans l' 'Agricola,' " in *R.E.L.*, 1936, pp. 326 ff.

S. G. Daitz, "Tacitus' Technique of Character Portrayal," in *A.J.Ph.*, 1960, pp. 30 ff.

L. de Latte, *Les Traités de la royauté*, Paris-Liège, 1942.

D. R. Dudley, *The World of Tacitus*, London, 1960.

Ph. Fabia, *La Table claudienne de Lyon*, Lyon, 1929.

H. Fourneaux, *Vita Agricolae*, Oxford, 1898.

L. Ginzburg, *Rome et la Judée*, Paris, 1928.

E. R. Goodenough, "The Political Philosophy of Hellenistic Kingship," in *Y.Cl.St.*, 1928, pp. 53 ff.

P. Grenade, "Le Pseudo-épicuréisme de Tacite," in *R.E.L.*, 1953, p. 36.

F. Haverfield, *Roman Occupation of Britain*, Oxford, 1924.

J. Isaac, *Genèse de l'Antisémitisme*, Paris, 1950.

T. S. Jerome, "The Tacitean Tiberius," in *Cl.Ph.*, 1912, p. 3.

J. Juster, *Les Juifs dans l'Empire Romain*, Paris, 1914.

Kenneth Scott, "The Elder and Younger Pliny on Emperor Worship," in *T.A.Ph.A.*, 1932, pp. 56 ff.

I. Lana, *Lucio Anneo Seneca*, Torino, 1955; *Tacito*, Torino, 1967.

E. Loefstedt, "On the Style of Tacitus," in *J.R.S.*, 1948, pp. 11 ff.

H. P. L'orange, *Apotheosis and Ancient Portraiture*, Oslo, 1947; *Studies on the Iconography of Cosmic Kingship*, Oslo, 1953.

A. Magdelain, *Auctoritas Principis*, Paris, 1947.

D. McAlindon, "Senatorial Opposition to Claudius and Nero," in *A.J.Ph.*, 1960, pp. 19 ff.

Mason Hammond, "Pliny the Younger's Views on Government," *Har.St. in Cl.Ph.*, 1938, p. 115; "Libertas," in *Har.St. in Cl.Ph.*, 1963, pp. 92 ff.

A. Michel, "La Causalité historique chez Tacite," in *R.E.A.*, 1959, pp. 36 ff.; *Tacite et le destin de l'Empire*, Paris, 1966.

N. P. Miller, "Dramatic Speech in Tacitus," in *A.J.Ph.*, 1964, p. 277.

J. H. Oliver, *The Ruling Power*, Philadelphia, 1953.

E. Paratore, *Tacito*, Milano-Varese, 1951.

J. Perret, "La Formation du style en Tacite," in *R.E.A.*, 1954, p. 91.

C. Questa, "Il viaggio di Germanico in Oriente e Tacito," in *Maja*, 1957, p. 291; *Studi sulle fonti degli "Annali" di Tacito*, Roma, 1960. (The scientific investigation of the sources was posed by Mommsen in *Hermes*, 1870, pp. 295 ff.)

M. E. Reesor, *The Political Theory of the Old and Middle Stoà*, New York, 1932.

J. A. Richmond, *Romans and Natives in Great Britain*, London, 1958.

C. Saumagne, "La 'Passion' de Thrasea," in *R.E.L.*, 1955, pp. 241 ff.

A. Scramuzza, *The Emperor Claudius*, Cambridge, 1940.

Sherwin White, *Racial Prejudices in Imperial Rome*, Cambridge, 1966.

D. C. A. Shotter, "Tacitus and Germanicus," in *Historia*, 1968.

A. Sizoo, "Paetus Thrasea et le Stoïcisme," in *R.E.L.*, 1926, pp. 229 ff.

R. Syme, *Tacitus*, Oxford, 1963.

J. Van Ootheghem, "Germanicus et l'Egypte," in *Les Études Classiques*, 1950.

K. von Fritz, "Tacitus, Agricola, Domitianus and the Problem of Principatus," in *Cl.Ph.*, 1957, pp. 73 ff.

B. Walker, *The Annals of Tacitus*, Manchester, 1952.

A. G. Woodhead, "Tacitus and Agricola," in *Phoenix*, 1947–48, pp. 45 ff.

INDEX